THE CATHOLIC FAMILIES

THE
CATHOLIC FAMILIES

MARK BENCE-JONES

CONSTABLE · LONDON

First published in Great Britain 1992
by Constable and Company Limited
3 The Lanchesters, 162 Fulham Palace Road
London W6 9ER
Copyright © Mark Bence-Jones 1992
ISBN 0 09 470200 4
The right of Mark Bence-Jones to be
identified as the author of this work
has been asserted by him in accordance
with the Copyright, Designs and Patents Act 1988
Set in Monophoto Poliphilus 12pt by
Servis Filmsetting Limited, Manchester
Printed in Great Britain by
BAS Printers Ltd
Over Wallop, Hampshire

A CIP catalogue record for this book
is available from the British Library

TO CHARLES MOWBRAY

Contents

Illustrations

Preface

T H E Catholic families, most of them of ancient and illustrious lineage, form a distinctive group in the British aristocracy through having suffered for their faith during the centuries following the Reformation. And on account of their religion they tended to intermarry, so as to become almost like one extended family. This book is their story from 1778 down to the present day, a period not so long as to preclude detailed descriptions of individuals and everyday life. The year 1778 has been chosen as a starting point because it was the year of the first Catholic Relief Act which made things slightly easier for British Catholics while leaving them still shut off from the political and official life of the nation; it was also the year when the visit of King George III and Queen Charlotte to the Catholic Lord and Lady Petre set the seal on the allegiance of the Catholic families to the House of Hanover. Jacobitism, which a generation earlier had divided their loyalties, was not not just dead but well and truly buried.

The period of the book covers many landmarks in the history of the Catholic families. The second Catholic Relief Act of 1791 and its sequel, the granting of full Catholic Emancipation in 1829, which brought them back into the mainstream of national life – though they would continue to be something of a world apart for at least another century. The French Revolution, which even more than the Act of 1791, ensured that the children of the Catholic families would be educated in England rather than abroad, as had hitherto been the case; for it drove the expatriate English religious communities out of the Continent, so that they returned to their native land. The Napoleonic Wars, which gave some of the Catholics their first opportunity of fighting for King George as officers; the wars of later years, in which the Catholics took an increasingly active part. The nineteenth century conversions to Catholicism, associated with the Oxford Movement but in many instances due to other causes, which added to the number of aristocratic Cathlolic families. Most of these newcomers to the Catholic world married into the Catholic cousinhood, or their children did; making it easy for me to bring some of them into my narrative.

By continuing my narrative down to the present day I have been able to show how, despite their past tribulations, a remarkably high proportion of the Catholic families survive and still inhabit their ancestral seats. The number of present-day descendants who have helped me with this book is adequate proof that the Catholic families are alive and well. But while the names of these descendants may appear in the list of acknowledgements that follows, they cannot be held responsible for any opinions in this book, which are entirely my own.

To the many people who have so kindly given me access to papers and allowed me to quote from them, provided me with information and illustrations and helped me in other ways, I am extremely grateful; and would mention the following, not a few of whom have given me hospitality as well as help: Major-General The Duke of Norfolk, KG, GCVO, CB, CBE, MC; Countess Fitzwilliam; Anne Viscountess Norwich; Lord and Lady Mowbray and Stourton; Lord and Lady Camoys; Lady Herries; Lord Petre; Morag Lady Stafford; Lord Stafford; Lord Clifford of Chudleigh; Lord Talbot of Malahide, DL, and the late Lady Talbot of Malahide; Daphne, the Dowager Lady Acton; Lord Acton; the Dowager Lady Hesketh, OBE, DL; Lady Jean Bertie; Sir Joshua Rowley, Bt, HML and the Hon Lady Rowley; Sir Dermot de Trafford, Bt, VRD; Sir John Leslie, Bt, KCSG; Sir Joseph Weld, OBE, TD, DL, JP; Lady Grey; Hon Mrs Simon Fraser; Hon Andrew Fraser; Hon Dominic Petre; Hon James Stourton; Hon Mrs Douglas Woodruff; Mr Simon Towneley, HML, JP; Mr Peregrine and Lady Maureen Fellowes; Mr Peter Drummond-Murray of Mastrick, Slains Pursuivant, and the Hon Mrs Drummond-Murray; the Abbot and Community of Ampleforth; Mr Henry Bedingfeld, Rouge Croix Pursuivant of Arms, and Mrs Bedingfeld; Mr John Bridgeman; Mr and Mrs Michael Browne; Miss Maria Browne; Mr Paul Burns; Major and Mrs F.J. Charlton; Mr William Charlton; Mr George Chowdharay-Best; Mr Peter Constable Maxwell; Mr Kit Constable Maxwell; Mr Christopher Dalton; Mr and Mrs Michael Dormer; Mr and Mrs Gervase Elwes; Fra' Matthew Festing; Mr Nicholas Fitzherbert; Mr Arthur French; Mr and Mrs John Gaisford-St Lawrence; Mr John George, Kintyre Pursuivant, and Mrs George; M and Mme Krzysztof Gorski; Mr Antony Hornyold; Mrs T.H. Hornyold-Strickland; Mr John Hornyold-Strickland; Mr David Kingston; Mrs Lee Martin; Mrs Peter Maxwell-Stuart; Mr Michael Maxwell-Stuart; Mr Hugh Montgomery-Massingberd; the late Mr Edward More O'Ferrall; Mr and Mrs Terry Morriss; Rev Michael Napier; Mr William Plowden, JP; Mrs Cuthbert Rabagliati;

Professor William Ravenhill; Mr Desmond Seward; Mr John Somerville; Mr Henry Tempest, DL; Rev Henry Thorold; Mrs David Turville-Constable-Maxwell; Mr and Mrs Robert Turville-Constable-Maxwell; Mr and Mrs Patrick Vaughan; Mr Oliver Vaughan; Mrs Eileen Wallace.

A special word of thanks must go to Monsignor Alfred Gilbey for giving me the benefit of his unrivalled fund of anecdotes and social history as well as the freedom of his library; to Major David Trappes-Lomax, JP, for filling me in on many little-known points of English Catholic history on which he is such an authority, as well as giving me access to papers and lending me books; to Count de la Poer for giving me access to papers and to his nephew Mr Nigel de la Poer for reading part of my typescript and making helpful suggestions; to Mr John Martin Robinson, Arundel Pursuivant, for all the trouble he has taken over my illustrations and in giving me information, also for his masterly book *The Dukes of Norfolk* which I have found such a help as well as a pleasure; to Frances Dimond of the Photograph Collection, the Queen's Archives, to Mr Malcolm Hay, Curator of Works of Art in the Palace of Westminster, to Sarah Wimbush and Jane Cunningham of the Courtauld Institute, to Diana Lanham and Emma Lindsay of the National Trust Photographic Library, to Anne Woodward of the National Buildings Record, to Mrs Teresa Biggins of the National Library of Ireland and to Claire Stewart, Keeper of Art, Burnley Borough Council, to whose kind help I am indebted for many illustrations.

Finally I must put on record my gratitude to two people who are sadly no longer alive: to the late Rev and Hon Raleigh Addington for the wonderful letters of Frederick William Faber, which he edited and published as *Faber, Poet and Priest* and of which he generously presented me with a copy shortly before his tragic death; and to my late cousin Roly Price-Jones, who first aroused my interest in the subject of this book.

Since much of this book consists of narrative and glimpses of the life of individuals at various periods, I have taken the liberty of referring to people by Christian names or nicknames where this seems natural in the context; even at the risk of appearing unduly familiar. Also for stylistic reasons, I have dispensed with the title of Honourable when referring to the children or siblings of peers.

CHAPTER 1

Grandeur and frustration

WHEN in October 1778 King George III and Queen Charlotte visited Essex for a military review, they stayed with Lord and Lady Petre at Thorndon Hall, a vast newly-built Palladian house with a Corinthian portico facing towards the Thames estuary. Lord Petre had originally been given less than a fortnight's notice of the impending royal visit, and during that time his preparations had been frenzied; he had engaged painters, upholsterers, gilders, japanners and cabinet makers, about a hundred men and women all told, to redecorate and refurnish the rooms to be occupied by the King and Queen. Gold plate had been ordered specially; nine French cooks and a regiment of confectioners had come down from London with moulds and truffles to make Périgord pies. And then word had come that the royal guests, who had been expected on the fifth, would not be arriving until the nineteenth. The cooks had to be sent back to London, leaving their creations to be eaten up by fortunate army officers invited to Thorndon for the purpose, and returning two weeks later to start cooking all over again.

The mile-and-a-half-long avenue leading to the house was lined with troops and cheering crowds and the woods echoed with artillery salutes as the royal chaise came up at a gallop, accompanied by mounted attendants and horse guards and followed by horsemen collected from all over the countryside, with Lord Petre's steward and tenants at their head. The King and Queen were conducted into the house by Lord and Lady Petre and in the Great Drawing Room, newly hung with green Indian damask in their honour and henceforth to be known as the Presence Chamber, they seated themselves on chairs of state and gave them their hands to kiss. The forty-year-old King, with his bulging blue eyes and heavy affability, had long recovered from his first attack of insanity; the second was ten years in the future. The Queen was younger, closer in age to their host and hostess; a slight, stiff, almost childlike figure but with great dignity.

Thorndon Hall

After the ceremony of hand-kissing, the King and Queen dispensed with formality and asked to see the house, which meant that the servants were unable to lay the tables for dinner until the conducted tour was over. The King and Queen each dined alone, and in separate rooms; the King in the Great Hall, the Queen in the Parlour. They were waited on by their host and hostess respectively with other members of the company in attendance. At the end of dinner the King drank Lord Petre's health and Lord Petre, as he recorded in his journal, 'desired leave to do what I did every day of my life which was to drink His Majesty's Health'.[1] What with a discussion on military matters, a game of commerce and the royal supper, it was one in the morning when the Petres lighted the King and Queen to their rooms; and nearly three when they themselves finally got to bed, having had their own supper 'at ease'.[2]

The following day was mainly taken up with the review, which everybody agreed was 'perfect as a military exhibition'[3]; afterwards the colonels and peers who were in the camp dined with the King. Next morning, before they departed, the King and Queen appeared at a window to the people gathered to see them off; they were flanked by their host and hostess, the King holding the Petres' small daughter Anne in front of him. The King left a hundred guineas for the servants and some money for the local poor.

The two-day royal visit cost Lord Petre more than £1,000 in the money of the time. But he considered it money well spent, for the visit was of far greater importance to him than it would have been to other peers of his standing. 'I shall always hold it as the most flattering circumstance of my life', he wrote, 'that His Majesty gave me an opportunity of showing him in the ordinary course of life that respect, loyalty and affection which the laws of my country prevent me from doing on more important occurrences.'[4] The reason why the laws prevented Lord Petre from serving his Sovereign 'on more important occurrences' was that he was a Catholic, head of one of the most prominent among the surviving Catholic families of the aristocracy. It was this which set him apart from his fellow-magnates, just as Thorndon, while outwardly a very typical eighteenth century magnate's country house, differed from most other houses of its kind in that one of its two wings contained a large and richly-ornamented chapel, where Mass was celebrated for the family and its Catholic dependants and for the Catholics of the locality.

Lady Petre came from an even more illustrious Catholic family, for she was a Howard, a niece of the ninth Duke of Norfolk; but since her uncle's death, in 1777, his mantle as leader of the Catholics had descended on to her husband. The new Duke of Norfolk, a distant cousin, was a scholarly recluse, mainly interested in gardening and in writing learned books. The next senior Catholic peer, the fourteenth Earl of Shrewsbury, likewise played little part in public life so that Lord Petre, who, despite the double land tax and recusancy fines suffered by Catholics, was rich even by the standards of the Protestant territorial aristocracy with 20,000 acres in Essex and estates also in Lancashire, naturally assumed the role of leader. Some years later the Prince of Wales was to observe wittily that just as his father was head of the Protestant Church, so was Lord Petre head of the Catholic Church.

Lord Petre, the ninth baron, was chairman of the committee of Catholic laymen which had taken part in the negotiations leading to the Catholic Relief Act of June 1778. This first relaxation of the anti-Catholic penal laws enabled Catholics to buy and inherit land legally and made it no longer an offence punishable with life imprisonment to exercise the functions of a Catholic priest or to run a Catholic school. And since in bringing in this first measure of relief, Lord North's Government had the ulterior motive of getting Catholic Highlanders to enlist for the war against the American colonists and the French, Catholics were allowed to serve in the armed forces, but not as officers.

The Act made little material difference to the position of Catholics in Britain.

Robert Edward, ninth Lord Petre

There had been ways of getting round the disabilities regarding the ownership of land, and the laws against priests had seldom been enforced – though common informers from time to time attempted to bring prosecutions. As late as 1771 Bishop James Talbot, a brother of the Earl of Shrewsbury, had been brought to trial at the Old Bailey for 'exercising the functions of a Popish bishop' on the information of the notorious 'Protestant Carpenter' William Payne. The judge, Lord Mansfield, had acquitted him for want of evidence but the prosecution caused him a great deal of annoyance. His older contemporary Bishop John Hornyold, who came of an

Bishop John Hornyold, Vicar Apostolic of the
Midland District

ancient Worcestershire Catholic family, once had to put on a 'female cap' and throw
a woman's cloak over his vestments in order to escape arrest.

As well as ridding their clergy of a potential nuisance, the Relief Act represented a
great moral victory for the Catholics. In the words of a prominent Catholic lawyer of
the time, 'it struck the general prejudice against them to its centre, it disposed their
neighbours to think of them with kindness, it led the public to view the pretensions
to further relief with a favourable eye'.[5] Together with its sequel, the royal visit to
Thorndon, it established once and for all that Catholics were accepted by and
accepted Hanoverian Britain; that Jacobitism was not just dead but well and truly
buried.

Jacobitism among the Catholic nobility of Britain had died during the half
century following the collapse of the 'Fifteen'. Apart from a few Lancashire
gentlemen like Francis Towneley, who was executed after raising and commanding

Philip Howard, Earl of Arundel

the Manchester Regiment in support of Prince Charles Edward, and the two younger brothers of John Vaughan of Courtfield in Monmouthshire who fought for Prince Charles Edward at Culloden, the English and Welsh Catholic families stayed aloof from the 'Forty-Five', however much support it may have had among the Catholics of Scotland. Lord Petre's great-uncle Charles Radcliffe, who was captured at sea on his way to join the insurgents and was executed as his brother the Earl of Derwentwater was after the 'Fifteen', can hardly be counted; for though he was English, he had spent most of his life in exile. The change of heart that occurred among the English Catholics can be seen in the career of Lady Petre's uncle, the ninth Duke of Norfolk. As a young man in the 'Fifteen' he took up arms for the Pretender but by the time of his succession to the dukedom in 1732 he was fully reconciled to the House of Hanover. When, in 1737, Frederick Prince of Wales quarrelled with his father George II and was turned out of St James's Palace, the

Duke and Duchess of Norfolk had him and his wife to stay at Norfolk House, where their eldest son, the future George III, was born a year later.

So long as the Old Pretender, James III, had papal recognition as the rightful king of Great Britain, the British Catholics had – or were thought to have – some conflict of loyalties. But after the death of the Old Pretender in 1765 Pope Clement XIII ceased to support the claims of the exiled House of Stuart, having been released from the embarrassment of having to do so by Prince Charles Edward's conversion to Anglicanism – a move which alienated Catholics while arousing little or no enthusiasm among Anglicans. The erstwhile Bonnie Prince Charlie, now drink-sodden and pathetic, had no legitimate heir; his brother Henry, the Cardinal of York, was, of course, unable to marry being a Catholic bishop; so that the male line of the Stuart kings faced extinction. After the death of the Old Pretender, the Pope gave *de facto* recognition to George III, and the Vicars Apostolic – the Catholic bishops of the four districts of England and Wales – instructed their flock to pray for him at Mass, just as Catholics like Lord Petre drank his health. Lord Petre's Hanoverian loyalties were all the more striking in that he was a grandson of that most romantic of Jacobites, the young and chivalrous James Radcliffe, Earl of Derwentwater, venerated as a saint in his own county of Cumberland where the Aurora Borealis, which was seen at the time of his execution after the 'Fifteen', is known to this day as Lord Derwentwater's Lights.

Jacobitism was only the most recent of the tribulations suffered by the Catholic families in their adherence to the Old Faith. There were the sixteenth and seventeenth century persecutions which while varying in the extent to which they affected individual families, left their crop of martyrs. The Howards had Philip Howard, Earl of Arundel, who died in the Tower of London in 1595 after suffering many years of imprisonment on account of his Catholic beliefs. The Stonors of Stonor in Oxfordshire and the Turvilles of Bosworth in Leicestershire had Adrian Fortescue, a Knight of Malta executed by Henry VIII; the Yorkshire family of Anne had John Anne, a priest martyred in 1589. Sir Robert Constable, ancestor of the Constables of Everingham in Yorkshire who later became the Constable Maxwells, was not strictly speaking a martyr but he gave his life for the Catholic cause in Henry VIII's reign as a leader of the rising known as the Pilgrimage of Grace. The Elizabethan Sir Thomas Fitzherbert, who was imprisoned almost continuously for thirty years on account of his Faith and died, like Philip Howard, in the Tower, was venerated as a martyr by his collateral descendants, the Fitzherberts of Swynnerton in Staffordshire; his brother John Fitzherbert died in the Fleet having been thrown into prison and fined £10,000 after two priests were found in his house.

Coughton Court

Many families risked imprisonment by sheltering priests, as is testified by the priests' hiding places in old Catholic houses such as Oxburgh Hall in Norfolk, seat of the Bedingfelds, and Baddesley Clinton in Warwickshire, seat of the Ferrers family. Cecily Lady Stonor spent the last few years of her life in prison after allowing the Oxford scholar and Jesuit martyr Edmund Campion to run his secret printing press at Stonor in 1581; her daughter-in-law Elizabeth Lady Stonor was imprisoned under James I. Of the Catholics of standing who were imprisoned, some may have engaged in more obviously treasonable activities, such as Thomas Throckmorton of Coughton in Warwickshire who is believed to have been involved in the Babington Plot; just as his cousin Francis Throckmorton was involved in the conspiracy known as the Throckmorton Plot. Whether or not Thomas Throckmorton was guilty of treason, he certainly suffered for being a Catholic, not only from frequent imprisonments but also from heavy recusancy fines which reduced the family fortunes to a low ebb.

After some years of respite under Charles I, the Catholics suffered once again for being royalists, and therefore on the losing side, in the Civil War. Coughton was

Blanche Lady Arundell of Wardour

occupied, looted and set on fire by Roundhead troops, putting a further strain on the Throckmorton family fortunes which had recovered sufficiently before the war to enable Sir Robert Throckmorton to keep racehorses. Blanche Lady Arundell, whose husband, the second Lord Arundell of Wardour, subsequently died of wounds received in action, defended Wardour Castle in Wiltshire against the Roundheads in an epic siege; she eventually had to surrender, after which the castle was besieged by a royalist force under the command of her son, who agreed to the springing of a mine which left it in a state of ruin. The Cavalier general Sir Marmaduke Langdale, a Yorkshire Catholic, lost the then enormous sum of £160,000 in the service of the King, for which his only recompense, apart from the honour and glory, was to be made Lord Langdale by the exiled Charles II. William Stonor was killed in the defence of Basing House and his family's estates were much reduced through recusancy fines under the Commonwealth. During the

William Howard, Viscount Stafford

Commonwealth and Protectorate the Catholics suffered doubly as recusants and royalists.

With the Restoration, the position of Catholics at first improved. But the conversion to Catholicism of Charles II's brother and heir, James Duke of York, and rumours that the King was about to do likewise, brought the inevitable reaction. The first of the series of Test Acts, which eventually debarred Catholics from holding office under the Crown and from sitting in Parliament, was passed in 1672; and in 1678 there came the outbreak of anti-Catholic hysteria stirred up by Titus Oates with his allegations of a 'Popish Plot'. Among its victims was the Duke of Norfolk's uncle, William Howard, Viscount Stafford, who was convicted of high treason on perjured evidence and executed. Other Catholic peers were committed to the Tower of London, including the fourth Lord Petre who died there in 1683 after more than four years of confinement, and the third Lord Arundell of Wardour who having already suffered the misfortune of having to blow up his own castle during the Civil War was now imprisoned for five years.

The brief reign of the Catholic James II, when Lord Petre's Jesuit kinsman, the much-maligned Father Edward Petre, was the King's confessor and adviser, was followed by the Revolution of 1688. Coughton was once again damaged when a Protestant mob wrecked the chapel which a younger Sir Robert Throckmorton had recently made on one side of the courtyard. The medieval chapel at Hendred in Berkshire which George Eyston, similarly encouraged by the presence of a Catholic king on the throne, had done up in the previous year, was desecrated by stragglers from Dutch William's army; while in Scotland, Traquair House, seat of the Earl of Traquair, a Catholic Stuart, was sacked by a band of Protestants who carried off the plate and other devotional objects from the chapel, as well as the books, and burnt them at the Cross in the nearby town of Peebles. More serious than these scattered outrages in 1688 was the passing of the penal laws in the years that followed.

The position of the Catholic families for most of the eighteenth century was both better and worse than it had been in earlier times since the Reformation. Better in that they were no longer persecuted for their religious beliefs; the good sense and humanity of the authorities ensured that the penal laws were not too strictly enforced. They were able to maintain chaplains to say Mass for them and for the other Catholics of their neighbourhood; while acknowledging the fact that the Mass was still theoretically illegal by referring to it as Prayers and celebrating it behind locked doors. Nor, except in the abnormal circumstances of the two Jacobite risings, were they in any danger of being charged with treason. But while they were thus able to live unmolested on their estates and practise their own form of worship, their situation was worse than it had been in that the Test Acts cut them off from all public office, from holding commissions in the navy and the army, from politics and from the Bar. In earlier times they might have been accused of treason, but they could also enjoy royal favour; they were given peerages and baronetcies and had political influence. In the eighteenth century the whole great world of politics and patronage, with all its attractions and rewards, was closed to them.

There were those who found the frustrations of being a Catholic more than they could bear and so turned Anglican; causing a steady decline in the number of Catholic families throughout the eighteenth century. There was also a wastage through extinction; it is tempting to attribute this to the proverbial inbreeding of the Catholic families or to the fact that so many of their children became priests and nuns; but it seems more likely that it just happened, as with numerous Protestant families. What with defections to Anglicanism, extinctions, forfeitures for treason, real or alleged, and the effect of the recusancy fines, it is remarkable how many important Catholic landed families there still were in the England of 1778. As well as the Duke of Norfolk, the Earl of Shrewsbury and Lord Petre, the Catholic peers included Viscount Montagu, Lord Stourton, Lord Arundell of Wardour, Lord Dormer and Lord Clifford of Chudleigh. There was also James Radcliffe who had inherited the Scottish Earldom of Newburgh from his mother; he would also have been Earl of Derwentwater but for his uncle's attainder. One Catholic peerage had become extinct a year earlier with the death of the fifth and last Lord Langdale.

The Catholic peers were outnumbered by the Catholic baronets, whose titles all dated from the previous century. They included Bedingfeld and Jerningham in Norfolk, Mannock in Suffolk, Tichborne in Hampshire, Throckmorton in Warwickshire, Gerard and Stanley in Lancashire, Vavasour and Lawson in Yorkshire, Haggerston and Swinburne in Northumberland, Smythe in Shropshire, Mostyn in Flint. Apart from the richer Catholic peers and baronets, there were a number of untitled Catholic families in the magnate class such as the Welds of Lulworth in Dorset, the Constables of Burton Constable in Yorkshire and the Giffards of Chillington in Staffordshire. In fact, the Catholics were on the whole grander than the Protestant squirearchy; on the one hand it had naturally been the more substantial families that had survived, and on the other hand the fact that Catholics had ceased to be made peers and baronets after the departure of the Stuarts meant that there were numerous untitled families of an importance that would have qualified for peerages and baronetcies in the eighteenth century had they been Protestant. The exclusion of Catholics from the rewards of politics had another side to it in that they were spared the often crippling expenses of electioneering; it was this which made so many eighteenth century Catholic families surprisingly affluent, considering all they had been through.

The Catholic families were most numerous in the north of England. In Yorkshire there were, among others, Scropes, Vavasours, Tempests, Constables, Stapletons, Lawsons, Watertons, Annes and Langdales of the surviving untitled branch. In Lancashire, in addition to the Gerards and the Catholic Stanleys, the principal Catholics included the families of Towneley, Trafford, Blundell, Clifton and Scarisbrick. In Northumberland there were Charltons, Riddells and Erringtons, as well as the Haggerstons and Swinburnes. Away from the north, the Catholic families were fairly evenly distributed throughout England, with something like one, two or three to a county; though there were a few counties containing no notable Catholic families at all.

In Wales, the Catholic families were few; the Mostyns were perhaps the only Welsh Catholic family of consequence, apart from the Vaughans of Courtfield and the Joneses of Llanarth who being in Monmouthshire were not strictly speaking in Wales. In Scotland the Jacobite risings had taken their toll. The Jacobite Duke of

Melfort, of the great Drummond family, was in exile in France. The senior Catholic Drummonds, who were Jacobite Dukes of Perth, were by now extinct; though the redoubtable Jean Duchess of Perth, who was imprisoned in Edinburgh Castle for her support of the 'Forty-Five', had lived on in Scotland until her death at the age of about ninety in 1773. Her own family, the Gordons, had ceased to be Catholic after the death of her brother, the second Duke of Gordon, in 1728.

There was still a Catholic Earl of Traquair in Peeblesshire; he and his elder brother the fifth Earl had both been Jacobites in their day but had taken no part in the 'Forty-Five'. The fifth Earl had actually been in England at the time, which would seem to disprove the best-known of the different family traditions as to why the main gates of Traquair House are kept shut, namely that Prince Charles Edward visited the fifth Earl who after bidding him farewell at the gates vowed that they would never again be opened until he returned as king. Whatever the sympathies of the fifth and sixth Earls, the sixth Earl's son, Lord Linton, had joined with the Duke of Norfolk, Lord Petre and other leading Catholics in signing a loyal address to George III which had smoothed the way for the Relief Act. The mother of the fifth and sixth Earls of Traquair came of a great Catholic family in south-west Scotland, the Maxwells: she was the sister of the Earl of Nithsdale who had escaped from the Tower of London after the 'Fifteen' by changing clothes with his wife. The Maxwells of Nithsdale were now represented by his grand-daughter Lady Winifred Constable Maxwell, who was married to the heir of the Constables of Everingham in Yorkshire.

In addition to their Catholicism, almost all the Catholic families had one thing in common, namely their antiquity. The Duke of Norfolk was the Premier Duke of England, his dukedom dating from 1483; he also held the oldest existing English earldom, that of Arundel, which had been inherited by the Howards, along with Arundel Castle in Sussex, from the FitzAlans. The Earl of Shrewsbury, head of the great Norman house of Talbot, held the second oldest existing English earldom. Lord Arundell of Wardour had no connexion with the Earls of Arundel, but came of an ancient West Country family named Arundell, the name deriving from the French *hirondelle*, so that there were six swallows in the family arms as well as a white owl, a bird which traditionally appeared when the head of the family was dying. Lord Stourton's peerage dated from 1448 and was the oldest surviving English barony created by Letters Patent.

The Stourtons were one of many Catholic families with the proud distinction of being descended in the male line from a medieval ancestor who took his surname from his lands; though they no longer owned their ancestral estate of Stourton in Wiltshire which had been sold by the Jacobite thirteenth Lord Stourton in 1714.

But the Stonors were still of Stonor, the Tichbornes were still of Tichborne, the Towneleys were still of Towneley, the Traffords were still of Trafford, the Plowdens were still of Plowden in Shropshire, the Haggerstons were still of Haggerston, the Cliftons were still of Clifton though Lytham Hall was now their principal seat. The Stonors had been at Stonor and the Tichbornes at Tichborne almost certainly since before the Norman Conquest. The poor of the neighbourhood still received the annual Tichborne Dole of loaves made from corn grown on the land round which the dying Dame Mabella Tichborne crawled in the reign of Henry II, having made her husband promise to give the produce of as much land as she could move round to the poor.

The Cliffords, the Scropes, the Warwickshire family of Ferrers and the Berkeleys of Spetchley in Worcestershire were all descended in the male line from medieval peers. The Vaughans of Courtfield and another Monmouthshire Catholic family, the Joneses of Llanarth, were branches of the great Norman house of Herbert which had adopted Welsh patronymics. The Watertons of Walton in Yorkshire were collaterally descended from Sir Robert Waterton who is mentioned by Shakespeare in *Richard II*. Sir Thomas Strickland, ancestor of the Stricklands of Sizergh Castle in Westmorland, carried the banner of St George at Agincourt. The Nevills of Nevill Holt in Leicestershire were descended through the female line from the great medieval house of that name.

Without being Talbots, Cliffords or Stonors, the great majority of Catholic families were old by normal English squirearchical standards, having held lands and been of importance in their counties since medieval times. The two notable exceptions to this genealogical antiquity were the Welds and the Petres, two of the richest and most prominent of the Catholic families in the second half of the eighteenth century. The family fortunes of the Welds were founded by Sir Humphrey Weld, Lord Mayor of London in the reign of James I, though the family had been of some consequence since the end of the fourteenth century. The Petre family fortunes were founded by Sir William Petre, a rich tanner's son who became Secretary of State under the Tudors and obtained grants of monastery land. The Petres were not the only Catholic family enriched by the dissolution of the monasteries. Viscount Montagu's ancestor Sir Anthony Browne had been granted Battle Abbey by Henry VIII and cursed by a monk who had predicted that his line would perish by fire and water. The curse had not yet taken effect by the time of the 7th Viscount Montagu, who had succeeded in 1767; though his family had not been very fortunate in the preceding generations. His profligate grandfather, the fifth Viscount, had shot his confessor dead for refusing him absolution; his father had been obliged to sell Battle Abbey. He himself was having to sell more of the family estates, while managing to keep his ancestral home, the great medieval and Tudor mansion of Cowdray in Sussex.

Though acquiring monastery lands was not necessarily inconsistent with being a Catholic – there are plenty of examples in Ireland and on the Continent of families which did so while maintaining their Catholicism – Sir William Petre and his son, the first Lord Petre, seem to have conformed to the state religion, at any rate outwardly; it was not until the time of the second Lord Petre that the family became firmly Catholic once again. Other families were likewise indeterminate in their religious allegiance during the first hundred years after the Reformation. The Elizabethan fourth Duke of Norfolk was a Protestant, though he was executed for plotting to marry the Catholic Mary, Queen of Scots; his son was the Catholic martyr Philip Howard, Earl of Arundel; his grandson reverted to Protestantism but had a staunchly Catholic wife so that the succession to the dukedom remained Catholic. It could be said that the eighteenth century Catholic families had been consistently Catholic – apart from individual defections, such as that of the seventh Duke of Norfolk – since the reign of Charles I, which was when the Welds finally returned to the Old Faith. There were, however, two notable families whose Catholicism was more recent: the Cliffords, who owed it to the conversion of the first Lord Clifford of Chudleigh, a member of Charles II's Cabal, and the Actons of Aldenham in Shropshire who were actually eighteenth century converts.

In contrast to the Cliffords and the Actons, who had been Anglican for several generations, there were those families always professing Catholicism. Among them were the Stonors and the Throckmortons and most of the families in the north and in other more remote parts of the country. At Stonor, hidden away among the beechwoods of the Oxfordshire Chilterns, there was a medieval chapel attached to the house which had never known any form of worship but Catholic. This too was the case with the Eystons' chapel at Hendred and with the medieval chapel at Hazlewood Castle in Yorkshire, seat of the Vavasours.

It was a characteristic of the Catholic families to have lived in the same place for many generations. The Dukes of Norfolk were a notable exception having been somewhat peripatetic; over the years they had sold most of their original estates in East Anglia, they had more or less abandoned Arundel Castle in Sussex after it was reduced to a state of ruin in the Civil War. The favourite seat of the ninth Duke had been Worksop in Nottinghamshire, which had come into his family early in the seventeenth century, together with other northern estates and a major part of the industrial town of Sheffield, through marriage to an heiress of the Earls of Shrewsbury. After the burning of the Elizabethan Worksop Manor in 1761, the Duke, or more precisely the Duchess, had started building a palace larger than

The new Wardour Castle

almost any other English country house to replace it; but in 1767, when only about a third of the new Worksop had been built, all work on it had ceased owing to the death of the Duke's nephew and immediate heir, who was also the Duchess's nephew. The tenth Duke, a distant cousin, preferred to live at Greystoke Castle in Cumberland, which had been the seat of his own branch of the Howards before he succeeded to the dukedom, and at a comparatively modest country house in Surrey.

The architect of the unfinished Worksop, James Paine, also designed Lord Petre's great house at Thorndon, which was built at about the same time, and the new Wardour Castle in Wiltshire which the eighth Lord Arundell of Wardour started in 1770 and completed in 1776. After the destruction of the old Wardour Castle in the Civil War, Lord Arundell's forebears had lived either in its patched-up outbuildings or on their property in Hampshire, where the fourth Lord Arundell kept the earliest pack of foxhounds, the pack from which the Quorn is descended. But the eighth Lord Arundell, who had married an heiress and through his mother had inherited the Cornish estates of another branch of the Arundell family, could at last afford to build himself a house worthy of his rank. Like Lord Petre, who was his almost exact contemporary, he was still in his twenties when he commissioned his

The eighth Lord Arundell of Wardour

great house but his portrait by Reynolds, in which he proudly wears his peer's robes although debarred from sitting in the Lords, shows a look of determination in his boyish face; moreover he was said to be six foot six inches tall. He was a young nobleman who got what he wanted; a connoisseur who had formed a collection of pictures when he was in Italy on the Grand Tour; a perfectionist prepared to devote much time and trouble to getting things right.

As a result, Wardour, though of the same Palladian type as Thorndon, had a much greater refinement in its silvery-grey elevations, the severely plain north front,

The altar in the chapel of the new Wardour Castle

the Corinthian front facing south over the park towards the ruins of the old castle and the uplands of Cranborne Chase. Inside the house, a great circular staircase rose beneath a domed rotunda of Corinthian columns; and in the west wing there was a chapel on the scale of a church with more Corinthian columns and pilasters and an altar of inlaid marble by the Italian architect Giacomo Quarenghi. The altar had been commissioned for Lord Arundell by Father John Thorpe, a cultivated Lancashire Jesuit living in Rome who bought works of art for the English Catholic nobility; many of whom had been his pupils at the English Jesuit college at St Omers in the Low Countries. Lord Arundell, himself an old boy of St Omers, employed Father Thorpe as his agent in Rome for many years; not only for furnishing his chapel but also for adding to his picture collection.

The opening of the chapel, on All Saints Day 1776, was celebrated with a pomp in keeping with its splendour and all the more remarkable in that Catholic worship was still theoretically illegal. But while creating a more sumptuous setting for the Mass than existed anywhere else in England at that time, Lord Arundell had taken care not to overdo the ornament; as much in accordance with his own taste, one suspects, as in order not to provoke the authorities. As Father Thorpe put it, 'Angels holding candlesticks or crucifix may look pretty in a drawing, yet if executed on an altar will perhaps have too much of the Puppet show in England'.[6]

Another wealthy Catholic with a taste for building was William Constable of Burton Constable, a vast Elizabethan and Jacobean mansion facing towards the coast of the East Riding north of Hull. Starting in the 1750s, he had, over the years, remodelled and embellished the house; but instead of making it Classical, as most of his contemporaries would have done, he had preserved its original character as a testimony to his ancient lineage, of which he was inordinately proud. During those years he had gone on several Grand Tours and built up large and varied collections: copies of Old Masters, scagliola tables, books, fossils, minerals and shells. His interests were scientific as well as artistic and genealogical; he experimented with air pumps and electrostatic machines, he thirsted for the latest knowledge and dabbled in philosophy as well as science, absorbing the fashionable doctrines of Voltaire when living in France and corresponding with Rousseau. Not surprisingly, he ceased to be a practising Catholic and inclined towards deism; but since he had no children, the succession to Burton Constable remained Catholic.

William Constable was a Fellow of both the Royal Society and the Society of Antiquaries. More orthodox Catholics could also belong to these two learned bodies, which dominated the intellectual life of the capital. There was even a Catholic bishop among the Fellows of the Royal Society, the monk Charles Walmesley, Vicar Apostolic of the Western District; a scion of the Lancashire

Charles Towneley of Towneley and his friends in the gallery of his London house in Park Street, Westminster. From a painting by John Zoffany

Catholic gentry who was a mathematician of European standing. The scholarly tenth Duke of Norfolk was a Fellow of both Societies as were Lord Petre and Charles Towneley, the bachelor squire of Towneley in Lancashire, whose family fortunes had not been affected by his great-uncle's Jacobitism. Towneley had lived for seven years in Rome, building up a great collection of Classical sculpture and antiquities and distributing it between Towneley and the gallery of his London house in Park Street, Westminster. Here Zoffany painted him, with three of his friends from among the dilettanti. In this gathering, Towneley looks unmistakably the country gentleman; sitting solid and impassive, his dog at his feet.

It was through Towneley's inspiration – and with the help of the indispensable Father Thorpe – that Henry Blundell of Ince Blundell near Liverpool built up a similar collection. Blundell was a widower a few years older than Towneley to whom he was connected through his late wife; he was rich for the same reason that Lord Arundell and other Catholic magnates were rich, namely through having inherited additional estates from a kinsman. This had more than doubled the family income, which had already been large enough to enable his father to build a baroque mansion to take the place of the old Ince Blundell Hall. Henry Blundell himself was to admit that he did not count the cost when buying works of art. He bought pictures as well as Classical sculpture, including some very important works of the early Flemish and Italian schools.

Catholics like Towneley and Blundell were very much in the centre of the eighteenth century world of connoisseurship. So was the long-lived baronet Sir Robert Throckmorton, who having as a young man sat to Nicolas de Largillière, the court painter of Louis XIV, was to survive until after the outbreak of the French Revolution. In his middle age, Throckmorton had commissioned the fashionable Bath architects, the two John Woods, father and son, to build him an elegant Palladian villa at Buckland, an estate in Berkshire which had come to him through his mother and where he eventually lived in preference to his ancestral Coughton. Around the house he created an Arcadian landscape, complete with grotto and rotunda, winning the admiration of that much-derided Poet Laureate Henry Pye who sings of his having 'Clothed the declining slopes with pendant wood And o'er the sedge-grown meadows poured the flood'. Throckmorton's sons-in-law, the two Staffordshire neighbours Thomas Giffard of Chillington and Thomas Fitzherbert of Swynnerton, had also followed the fashion in making landscape parks; they were among the Catholic patrons of Capability Brown.

It was not necessary for a Catholic to be a wealthy collector or improver of landscapes to be accepted by the dilettanti and literati. Henry Swinburne, a younger brother of the Northumberland baronet and a man of only moderate means, was accepted because of his book *Travels through Spain*, a description of one of his many journeys on the Continent illustrated with his own elegant and accurate drawings of Roman and Moorish architecture. His travels are frequently mentioned by Edward Gibbon, and the writer and witty talker Hannah More, who met him in London society, described him as 'modest and agreeable, not wise and heavy like his books'.[7]

In fact, however much the Catholics may have been barred from the political and official life of eighteenth century England, fashionable society was open to them; they frequented the London season, they moved in the *beau monde* of Bath, York and Scarborough. In holding their own in cultivated society they may have had a positive advantage over Protestants through having been educated abroad. Since Catholic schools were illegal in England up to 1778, the sons of the Catholic families were mostly sent to be educated at the colleges run by the expatriate English religious communities on the Continent: by the secular clergy at Douai, by the Benedictines at Dieulouard, by the Jesuits who were at St Omers until 1762, at Bruges until 1773 and afterwards at Liége. The reason for these wanderings was the expulsion of the Jesuits from the territories of the King of France, in which St Omers was then situated, in 1762; and from Bruges by the Imperial authorities following Pope Clement XIV's suppression of the Society of Jesus in 1773. When, in 1773, an official came to the Bruges college in search of the mythical wealth of the Jesuits and ordered one of the boys to go and call the Rector, the boy, who happened to be the fourth Lord Clifford's son and heir Hugh Clifford, 'answered that he was not a servant to be sent upon his messages'.[8] Eventually the college was reopened in Liége under the protection of the Prince-Bishop, with some of the former Jesuits as masters. The education provided by these colleges was of a considerably higher standard than that obtained by many of the sons of the Protestant nobility from schools in England or from tutors; comparing favourably even with Oxford and Cambridge, which were then at a low ebb.

Not only were the sons of the Catholic families educated abroad, but also the daughters, who were sent to convent schools such as those of the Benedictine nuns at Cambrai and of the 'Blue Nuns' and the Augustinian Canonesses in Paris. This gave them the benefit of a formal education, something denied to most Protestant girls of their standing, as well as a fluency in French, an accomplishment much prized in the fashionable English society of the day. With the latter object in view, some parents preferred to have their daughters brought up by French nuns, such as the Paris Ursulines, rather than by English expatriates.

The cosmopolitanism of many of the Catholics, which commended them to the more sophisticated English Protestants, however much it may have aroused the suspicions of the John Bulls, was acquired not just through education. Cadets of

Sir Robert Throckmorton, fourth Baronet, by
Nicolas de Largillière

some of the Catholic families followed the example of the Irish 'Wild Geese' and
entered the service of Continental sovereigns; thus John Dormer, second son of the
seventh Lord Dormer, and Robert Swinburne, nephew of Henry Swinburne the
traveller, entered the Austrian service. Robert Clifford, a younger brother of the
schoolboy who snubbed the Imperial official at Bruges, was to enter the Dillon
Regiment, the famous regiment of Wild Geese in the army of the King of France;
Count Arthur Dillon, Colonel Proprietor of the regiment, being his first cousin.
Charles Jerningham, a younger brother of the Norfolk baronet, also entered the
French service. John Acton, cousin and heir of the Shropshire baronet Sir Richard
Acton of Aldenham, was in the service of the King of Naples, having previously
commanded the navy of the Grand Duke of Tuscany. The return of the Actons of
Aldenham to Catholicism was recent; John's father Edward Acton, who had

practised medicine in Besançon, had married a French Catholic bride and turned Catholic himself; while some years later his cousin in Shropshire Sir Richard Acton had also become a Catholic. Sir Richard's conversion appears to have been unconnected with that of Edward; nor did it bring him into English Catholic circles, from which he remained aloof.

Members of the Catholic families were in the habit of living on the Continent even when not making their careers there. William Constable and Charles Towneley were not alone among them in spending long periods abroad; it is likely that this custom originated in the exile of Jacobite forebears. The sixth Earl of Traquair, who in his younger days had lived, like Charles Towneley, in Rome, was himself a former Jacobite.

While in Rome, Traquair had become a Freemason. That was before Freemasonry had been condemned by two successive Popes, in 1738 and 1751; but even after those dates it was possible for Catholics to become Freemasons in England, where the Papal Bulls of condemnation could not be promulgated. At one time Freemasonry had been associated with Jacobitism; but the English Catholics who entered the Masonic Order later in the eighteenth century were staunch supporters of the House of Hanover; like Lord Petre, who was received into the Lodge of Friendship in London in 1771. A year later he became Grand Master of the English Freemasons; during his period of office the Masonic Hall in Great Queen Street was built.

That Catholics were admitted to the Masonic Order in England was a sign of how they had penetrated the traditionally Protestant world of commerce and the professions, which offered them ways of increasing their income and providing for their younger sons when politics and the services were closed to them. The ancient Lancashire Catholic family of Brockholes, a daughter of which had married the tenth Duke of Norfolk, founded Brockholes's Bank. Some of the Scropes were export merchants of Leghorn. The Yorkshire baronet Sir Henry Lawson's younger son was also in banking, having inherited a bank and coal mines from his mother's family; he proved himself to be a highly astute businessman and was to extend his interests as far as Jamaica. The younger sons of Stephen Tempest of Broughton, a cousin and county neighbour of the Lawsons, were less successful in business; they were apprenticed to a manufacturer of 'fustian checks and Manchester goods' which proved a disaster.[9]

Although unable to plead in court, Catholics could practise as solicitors and as barristers working in chambers; their speciality was conveyancing. The fifteenth Lord Stourton, who married Lord Petre's grandmother, the widow of the seventh Lord Petre, had been admitted to Gray's Inn before succeeding to the peerage and had followed a legal career. The sons of other Catholic families practised medicine; among them Charles Throckmorton, a younger grandson of Sir Robert.

For Catholics who regarded business and the professions as beneath their dignity, but who did not wish to enter the service of foreign kings, there was another option: they could become officers in the Hanoverian army. In this way they were able to serve King George in his capacity as Elector of Hanover, a country in which there had been no Test Acts. English Catholics in the Hanoverian army included Charles Langdale, John Jones of Llanarth and Thomas Sheldon, a younger son of a Warwickshire family.

In spite of being to all intents and purposes an officer of King George, Sheldon felt the sense of frustration suffered by so many Catholics in eighteenth century England. He expressed it forcibly in a letter to his mother, in which he said that being born a Catholic was something he would not wish on his worst enemy.[10] Even after the 1778 Relief act, the defections to Anglicanism continued; 1780 saw that of the heir to the leading Catholic family of all: Charles, Earl of Surrey, thirty-four-year-old son of the tenth Duke of Norfolk. This was less of a blow to the Catholics than it might have been, in that he had no legitimate offspring, though he had been married twice. His second wife had gone mad and was shut up; so long as she lived, he could not remarry, which made it likely that the dukedom and estates would eventually pass to a Catholic cousin.

Surrey was coarse in his appearance and manners, so that he was likened to a 'grazier and butcher'[11]; he was raffish, aggressive and dressed shabbily. The ninth Duke of Norfolk and his Duchess had invited him to meet them after their nephew's death had made him the eventual heir; the contrast between him and the lamented nephew had been so distressing to the poor Duchess that she had burst into tears and walked out of dinner. On the other hand he was affable, generous and endowed with political common sense; he got on well in aristocratic Whig circles where his fellow-Catholics had hoped he would wield influence on their behalf. It was his taste for politics which caused him to turn Anglican, in order to contest an election at Carlisle. He changed his religion quietly, 'that I might give as little mortification as possible to a set of men who are labouring under persecution'.[12] In his more convivial moments he would give as his reason for changing, 'I cannot be a good Catholic, I cannot go to Heaven, and if a man is to go to the devil he may as well go thither from the House of Lords as from any other place on Earth.'[13]

CHAPTER 2

'Mrs Fitzherbert makes a great deal of talk'

THE year 1780 saw a worse set-back to the Catholic cause than Surrey's apostasy. The Relief Act had brought the inevitable reaction; there were anti-Catholic riots in Edinburgh, and in England a Protestant Association was formed. Its president was Lord George Gordon, an earnest and rather crazy young MP whose father, the third Duke of Gordon, had started life as a Catholic and whose great-aunt, the Duchess of Perth, had been a mainstay of Scottish Catholicism. In June 1780 a mob of more than 100,000, consisting of the Association and its supporters and led by Gordon with his solemn face and long red hair, marched on Parliament to present a petition for the repeal of the Relief Act; then, after the debate on the petition was adjourned, the mob started burning Catholic chapels and houses belonging to Catholics or to Protestants known to be sympathetic to the Catholic cause. The rioters threatened to attack the house of Charles Towneley the collector, who had his favourite bust of Clytie, which he used to call his wife, put into his carriage for safety; but the threat never materialized.

There were riots at the same time in Hull and in Bath, where the mob burnt the Catholic chapel and the house of the mathematician Bishop Walmesley, who lost his library and his manuscripts. Charles Stonor of Stonor, who spent much time in Bath, his uncle John Stonor being a permanent resident, was here with his family at the time of the riots. They made a deep impression on his six-year-old son Henry, who long afterwards recalled, 'In the dead of night I was obliged to get up hastily and was led by my father to York House, where we all passed the remainder of the night, and early next morning we set off for Stonor, leaving the Catholic chapel in flames.'[1]

The rest of the country remained virtually undisturbed. At Wardour, there was a false alarm – a mob was about to invade Lord Arundell's newly-completed house and chapel – and a regiment of dragoons was sent to guard the place. In the nearby

The Gordon Riots. From a contemporary print

county of Dorset, Thomas Weld made plans for his pregnant wife Mary and their children to be taken in by Protestant neighbours in the event of Lulworth being attacked; but this, too, proved unnecessary.

Having lasted a week, the riots were quelled by the military. They served as a grim reminder to the Catholics that popular outbursts against them could still occur. On the other hand, it was reassuring that the Government did not allow itself to be intimidated into repealing the Relief Act.

Thomas Weld was known as 'the handsomest small man in England'. He was a considerable figure in Society, being one of the richest Catholics, with estates not only in Dorset but in Lancashire and elsewhere. Lulworth, his family seat near the Dorset coast, a tall Elizabethan fantasy castle of grey stone with round corner towers and battlements built not for defence but for show, had been bought by the Welds from a branch of the Howards in 1641. After succeeding his elder brother in 1775, Thomas had remodelled the interior of the castle so that the principal rooms, including the chapel, were in the most elegant contemporary taste. He and Mary lived well here; lobsters and apricots were often on their table, oranges were bought all through the winter. Thomas was as generous to the Church as he was with his household expenses; maintaining chaplains not only at Lulworth but also at

Maria Fitzherbert. From the portrait by John Hoppner

Stonyhurst in Lancashire, where he had inherited the great house and estate of the extinct family of Shireburn, and in Berkshire and Staffordshire where he had yet more property.

Thomas's elder brother Edward had married Mary Anne Smythe, whose father was a brother of the Shropshire Catholic baronet Sir John Smythe of Acton Burnell and whose mother was an Errington from Northumberland. Maria, as she was known, was not exactly a beauty, having too aquiline a nose and too determined a chin but her pink-and-white complexion was unusually smooth and set off by luxuriant fair hair and her hazel eyes had an expression both animated and kind. Hers was the sort of bosom on which every man would wish to lay his head. Moreover she was, as the plain-spoken Lady Hester Stanhope remembered her, one of those people 'who are sweet by nature and who even if they are not washed for a fortnight are free from odour'. Though she had grown up in comparatively modest circumstances in Hampshire as one of the six children of a younger son, she had

Lulworth Castle

acquired perfect French and a cosmopolitan polish through being educated by the Ursulines in Paris.

It is not surprising that, at the age of eighteen, she should have attracted the attention of Edward Weld, a widower but still young and gay at thirty-four and the greatest English Catholic *parti* of the time. And that after Edward's death, caused by a fall from a horse within a few months of their marriage, she should have married in 1778 another highly eligible Catholic, Thomas Fitzherbert, the thirty-one-year-old son and heir of Thomas Fitzherbert of Swynnerton and a grandson of old Sir Robert Throckmorton. Maria's second husband, a tall, powerful man inclined to run to fat to counteract which he ate sparingly and took violent exercise, had taken part in the negotiations leading to the passing of the Relief Act in the year of their marriage. In the autumn of that same year his father had died and he had inherited Swynnerton in Staffordshire, an early eighteenth century mansion with a centre of pilasters and a skyline of urns, facing over the park which Capability Brown had improved.

A couple of years after their marriage, the Fitzherberts were driving in Park Lane, close to their London house in Park Street, when Thomas turned round and said,

Swynnerton

'Look. There is the Prince.' Maria saw for the first time the eighteen-year-old heir to the throne, George, Prince of Wales. She saw him again a few days later when she and her husband were on their way to a party given by one of the Towneleys; this time she realized that he had followed her and had stopped to look at her.

Maria Fitzherbert had acquired perfect French and a cosmopolitan polish through being educated by the Ursulines in Paris. In 1784 the Norfolk baronet Sir William Jerningham and his wife Frances travelled to Paris to put their fourteen-year-old daughter Charlotte to school at the Ursulines. 'How does my poor dear little girl do today?' Frances wrote to Charlotte after they had left her. 'I have been awake all night thinking of you, and regretting you . . . I have told Simon to carry you a *brioche* and a pot of sweetmeats.'[2] From each stop on their somewhat circuitous journey home she wrote to her 'poor dear little girl' giving her their news. In Lille, Frances had gone to the play, 'a tolerable theatre, but as empty of company as the Norwich playhouse is of a common night'.[3] At St Omers they had entertained 'an assembly of Cats' – her abbreviation for Catholics – including the Duke of Norfolk's elderly clerical cousin Dr Charles Howard, a former President of the English Seminary in Paris.

Frances, Lady Jerningham

Dr Howard had two nieces in Paris, at the Blue Nuns' convent where one of the nuns was his and Sir William Jerningham's mutual cousin Lady Anastasia Stafford-Howard, a great-grand-daughter of the unfortunate Viscount Stafford who was executed at the time of the Popish Plot. Frances arranged with Lady Anastasia for Charlotte to spend the Feast of the Holy Innocents, which was a holiday, with her. For a homesick girl, the Blue Nuns would have been like a bit of England after the French atmosphere of the Ursulines.

The Jerninghams lived at Cossey Hall, sometimes spelt Costessey, near Norwich, a gabled sixteenth-century house built by Sir Henry Jerningham, the first among the knights of Norfolk and Suffolk to declare openly for the Catholic Queen Mary Tudor, who had rewarded him by granting him Cossey and other manors. Sir Henry's descendants had mostly married outside the somewhat restricted world of the East Anglian Catholic gentry: thus Sir William's mother was a Shropshire

Plowden, and a grand-daughter of the unfortunate Lord Stafford, while his wife Frances was a Dillon and therefore Irish. Her eldest brother, the future twelfth Viscount Dillon, had turned Anglican but her two younger brothers remained staunch to the Catholic and Wild Geese traditions of the family and were both generals in the French service; one of them, Count Arthur Dillon, was Colonel Proprietor of the Dillon Regiment. Sir William also had a brother who was a general in the service of the King of France. This was Charles Jerningham, known in the family as the Chevalier. He was then living in Paris and Frances told Charlotte to enlist his help if there was anything she disliked about her convent; he was in a good position to speak to the nuns being not only a French general but also a Knight of Malta and therefore himself a religious of the Catholic Church.

Sir William's other brother Edward Jerningham was in complete contrast to Charles, the military monk; except that, like the Chevalier, he was single. He had conformed to Anglicanism after witnessing its splendours at the Coronation of George III and was well-known in Society; an amiable pussy-cat described by Fanny Burney as 'a mighty delicate gentleman, all daintification in manner, speech and dress'.[4] He was a friend of Horace Walpole and of the Lord Chesterfield of the letters; he himself had literary pretensions and was the author of a tragedy which ran for five nights at Covent Garden as well as being a minor poet. He sings the praises of breast-feeding – a somewhat unlikely subject to inspire a 'daintified' bachelor – in twenty-three stanzas entitled, with Italianate delicacy, Il Latte:

> Unsway'd by Fashion's dull unseemly jest,
> Still to the bosom let your infant cling,
> There banquet oft, an ever-welcome guest,
> Unblam'd inebriate at that healthful spring.

By coincidence, the other Norfolk Catholic baronet, Sir Richard Bedingfeld, also had a younger brother who was a poet. He was an almost exact contemporary of Edward Jerningham and also called Edward. But Edward Bedingfeld, though a friend of the unbeliever Thomas Gray, remained a Catholic and, unlike the other Edward, he was married; his wife being Mary, daughter of Sir John Swinburne.

During Charlotte Jerningham's three years at the Ursulines, her mother continued to write her long and entertaining letters, expressing satisfaction at the letters which she received in return. 'Dear little girl, I cannot enough praise you for it, the style is as good as the sentiments for me are delightful.' She considered that the £200 a year which their daughter's education was costing them – almost as much as a public school education costs at the present time, allowing for the difference in the

Charlotte Jerningham, a self-portrait

value of money – was 'money excellently well laid out'. But since they were 'not very affluent', she was 'a little uneasy' about the extra expense of an Italian master and 'additional geography'; moreover she feared that 'such a number of different lessons' might 'defeat the wished-for purpose of general information'. But when she had told Sir William that Charlotte had no pocket money left for the rest of the month, he had said, 'Poor girl, that's hard upon her' and 'the guinea was immediately agreed to'. One can understand how the Jerninghams were 'not yet very affluent' since they also had three sons to educate, two of whom were already at school abroad.

As well as writing stylish letters, Charlotte was a talented artist. A self-portrait shows that she was growing into beauty, with large, expressive eyes. She also did a

At the Convent of the Dames Ursulines at Paris where my Mother went for three years, at the age of 14 - in the year 1784 -

/Mcarry/

Her own portrait is probably the Scholar in black - as Hedellers, mention having going into mourning for her Grand Mother Lady Jerni

A scene at the Ursuline Convent in Paris, by Charlotte Jerningham, who is believed to be the girl in black sitting at the far side of the table

lively group of herself and other girls engaged in various pursuits, a nun presiding primly at the head of the table.

Frances Jerningham kept her daughter well supplied with home news and gossip. 'I see in the papers that Dr Johnson is dead'. She and Sir William had gone to see Mrs Siddons in *The Fatal Marriage*. She thought the great Sarah – who was, incidentally, like her brother John Philip Kemble and other leading theatrical figures of the day, a lapsed Catholic – 'a very handsome woman' who acted 'with a great deal of feeling'. However, as she told her daughter, 'Mr Pitt, the Prime Minister, was in our box, which was a greater treat to my curiosity than the actress.'[5]

They had given a small dance at Cossey, for the three nieces of the Bishop of Norwich, whose wife had lamented to Sir William that 'it was impossible to give a ball at the Palace', while owning 'that she was herself passionately fond of dancing'. It is a sign of how little sectarianism there was in the grander county society of the time that the local Catholic baronet and his wife should have given a dance for the nieces of the Anglican bishop. They danced in the parlour, 'now very neat, new painted and the white paper in it with a green border'; the hall was used for supper, the library for cards. The Catholic world was not much in evidence among the guests, who were mostly Norfolk neighbours. Frances herself did not dance, but Sir William did and so did her brother Count Henry Dillon. The Bishop's daughter 'danced like a fury'; Miss Wodehouse danced well but was 'as ugly as sin' and wore 'the most frightfully shabby chip-hat'. She professed 'an *immense* regard for Charlotte and had written to her more than once; Frances urged her daughter to 'answer a few lines . . . she has enough to be mortified about in her face!'

A more favoured girl of Charlotte's acquaintance was Eleanora Arundell, the twenty-year-old daughter of Lord Arundell of Wardour. She was about to marry Frances's cousin Charles Clifford, a brother of Hugh, now the fifth Lord Clifford of Chudleigh, who as a schoolboy had snubbed the Imperial official at Bruges, and of Robert in the Dillon Regiment. Charles came next to Hugh in age; and as Frances told Charlotte, 'He or his children will most likely have the Clifford estate and title, as his elder brother has now been married seven or eight years and never had a child.'[6]

Among the pieces of gossip which Frances Jerningham retailed to her daughter in 1786, the most sensational, from the point of view of the English Catholic world, concerned Maria Fitzherbert.

She has taken a box to herself at the Opera, a thing which no lady but the Duchess of Cumberland ever did – a hundred guineas a year! The Prince is very assiduous in attending her in all public places, but she lives at her own house and he at his.[7]

Maria had been widowed a second time in 1781; Thomas Fitzherbert having gone into a decline variously attributed to his keep-fit exercises and to his having bathed when overheated after his exertions during the Gordon Riots. Since their only child had died in infancy, Swynnerton passed to Thomas's brother Basil; but Maria was comfortably provided for with £2,000 a year and the house in Park Street. She lived quietly for the first couple of years of her widowhood but then in 1784 the Earl and Countess of Sefton persuaded her to enjoy a London season under their wing. Lord Sefton, formerly Viscount Molyneux, was a connection of Maria's mother; he came of a Lancashire Catholic family, but had conformed at the time of his marriage to a daughter of the Earl of Harrington and had been advanced to an Irish earldom three years later – as Frances Jerningham put it, 'he was hardly twenty when Lady Harrington got possession of him, made him conform and made him Earl of Sefton'.[8]

Since the Seftons were in the centre of fashionable Whig society, it was to be expected that Maria should have met George, Prince of Wales, who then adhered to the Whigs. The Prince at once fell desperately in love with her. That someone as spoilt as he was with regard to the favours of the fair sex should have become so attracted by a woman six years his senior whose looks were pleasant but by no means outstanding would suggest that he saw in her some special quality; very likely it was her sheer goodness of character, in contrast to the worldly cynicism of the nymphs who gave themselves to him so readily. He lost no time in pressing his suit, bombarding Maria with invitations to parties at Carlton House, the delightful little palace which he had built for himself; her failure to attend one of them brought him knocking on her door in Park Street.

The Prince's infatuation with this virtuous widow became the sensation of that season. As well as her house in Park Street, Maria had a villa on Richmond Hill; so people sang the old ballad *The Lass of Richmond Hill* with her in mind – 'I'd crowns resign To call thee mine. . .' It had been sung a quarter of a century earlier of Lady Sarah Lennox, daughter of the Duke of Richmond, when the Prince's father, the youthful George III, had been in love with her, but it fitted Maria even better.

Maria naturally began by feeling flattered at the Prince's attentions. He was, after all, heir to the throne; he could be extremely charming and at twenty-two, even after four years of dissipation, he was still handsome – if no longer quite the Prince Florizel he had been at eighteen. On the other hand, the inevitable publicity embarrassed her and she knew that his infatuation for her could only lead to trouble. Not only was he prevented by the Royal Marriage Act from marrying without the permission of his father, who would have insisted on his marrying a royal princess, but he would have been excluded by the Act of Settlement from the succession to the throne had he married a Catholic. Only if his father died and Maria turned Protestant could he hope to marry her legally and keep his throne; and while the former contingency was always possible, given George III's porphyria and the doctors of the time, Maria would never have agreed to changing her religion. Nor would she for one moment have considered becoming the Prince's mistress. The Prince, to his credit, realized that he could never possess her without making her his wife and indeed he soon genuinely wanted to make her his wife, so much was he in love with her. Being who he was, he could not forbear from blurting out his intention of marrying her to friends of his such as the brilliant young Georgiana Duchess of Devonshire, distressing them by threatening to kill himself when they remonstrated with him.

One night in July 1784 three of the Prince's men friends with a surgeon in tow arrived at Park Street 'in the utmost consternation' and told Maria that he had stabbed himself and that 'only *her* immediate presence would save him'.[9] At first she suspected 'some stratagem derogatory to her reputation' and 'resisted, in the most peremptory manner, all their importunities, saying that nothing should induce her to enter Carlton House'.[10] But they managed to convince her that the Prince really was in danger and so she agreed to go to him, on condition that they took 'some lady of high character' with them. They decided to take the Duchess of Devonshire, and called for her on their way to Carlton House, where Maria found the Prince 'pale, and covered with blood'. She almost fainted at the sight; she was convinced that the wound was genuine and not just a trick; indeed, she afterwards saw the scar on his breast. When he told her 'that nothing would induce him to live unless she promised to be his wife',[11] she let him put a ring, borrowed from the Duchess, on her finger. She and the Duchess then went back to Devonshire House, where they drew up and signed a deposition stating that they regarded 'promises obtained in such a manner' as 'entirely void'.

Next day Maria left for the Continent. She was abroad for more than a year, travelling in France, Holland, Germany and Switzerland. In Holland she was befriended by the Stadtholder and his family, including his daughter the Princess of Orange, who was at that very time being considered by the British Royal Family as a bride for the Prince of Wales. Meanwhile the Prince of Wales was writing eighteen-page screeds to Maria and signing himself 'tenderest of husbands'. Letters from him were brought to her by a stream of couriers, who came so fast and so frequently that the French authorities suspected them of espionage and clapped three of them into prison. Often during those months the Prince threatened to commit suicide; he planned to follow Maria abroad and he told Maria's mother and her uncle Henry Errington of his determination to marry her; embarrassing the Smythe family by calling on them for consolation and advice; his visits are said to have given Maria's invalid father heart attacks. By the beginning of 1785 Maria was sufficiently moved by his entreaties to promise him that she would never marry anybody else. And then, towards the end of that year, she suddenly gave way and agreed to return to England and become his wife. It may have been homesickness or fear for his safety; it may also have been that she had fallen in love with him.

On 15 December, a few days after her arrival in England, she and the Prince were married by an Anglican clergyman; the ceremony took place in the drawing room at Park Street. The only others present were the two witnesses, her brother Jack Smythe and her uncle Henry Errington, both of them Catholics. The marriage was illegal and the clergyman and witnesses were technically guilty of a felony; but it was valid according to the laws of the Catholic Church, which then did not require the marriages of Catholics in England to be solemnized by a Catholic priest. Maria regarded the Prince as her lawful husband in the eyes of God and the Prince, despite his treatment of her in later years, never seems to have ceased to regard her as his lawful wife.

It was agreed between them that their marriage should be kept secret; Maria never spoke of it, or showed the marriage certificate to anybody, as long as she lived. The Prince, however, treated her publicly as his wife, insisting on her being given the place of honour on all occasions. They still ostensibly lived apart, he at Carlton House, she in a house nearby in Pall Mall; but her house was now his real home.

Rumours that they were married quickly started to circulate. Maria and her Prince continued to be a prime subject for gossip, particularly among the Catholics. Mrs Charles Talbot mentioned Maria when writing to her son-in-law Francis Fortescue Turville, who was abroad at the time:

> Mrs Fitzherbert makes a great deal of talk. I make no doubt but she is married to the Prince of Wales, he goes by my door every day at the same hour and seems very constant to her at present; it is said she is with child. After a while she will be a most unhappy woman.[12]

The rumours of her being with child never seem to have been anything more than rumours; while the report that she had been made Duchess of Cornwall, which was retailed to Francis Fortescue Turville by his mother-in-law, was entirely false.

Turville, who was then living in Nancy, also received news of the Maria Fitzherbert affair from Thomas Potts, the chaplain at Bosworth Hall, his family home in Leicestershire. Potts told him that whereas all the Anglican clergymen with whom he had discussed the matter considered the marriage to be valid, in his own opinion and in that of some other Catholic priests of his acquaintance it was 'null to all intents and purposes'.[13] They probably thought the marriage was clandestine, which would have made it invalid according to Catholic teaching; but in fact it fulfilled the requirements of the Catholic Church by taking place before witnesses.

Potts not only ministered to the Catholics of the neighbourhood but during Turville's absence abroad he looked after the house and estate at Bosworth; his letters are full of tree planting and the state of the fishponds as well as of politics, gossip and local affairs. Turville, who came of an ancient Leicestershire Catholic family, had inherited Bosworth from the Fortescues, from whom he was descended in the female line; Adrian Fortescue, the Knight of Malta martyred under Henry VIII, was his collateral ancestor. His own illustrious Catholic lineage was, however, surpassed by that of his wife Barbara whom he had married in 1780 when he was twenty-eight. She was a Talbot, niece of the fourteenth Earl of Shrewsbury and sister of his heir;

Francis Fortescue Turville in later life

her mother was a daughter of the Welsh Catholic baronet Sir George Mostyn of Talacre and her grandmother was a Towneley. Turville's marriage had also linked him closely with the Dormers; Barbara's uncle Lord Shrewsbury and her aunt Mary Talbot having married the seventh Lord Dormer's daughter and son. Turville probably met Barbara through his friendship with her cousin Charles Dormer, who shared his passion for foxhunting though not to the same extent. Dormer had chided Turville before his marriage for staying on in the country in March, to get more hunting, instead of joining him in London where he was having a good time. 'Consider what havoc you must make among the poor foxes . . . the honest farmer has already begun to sow his grain, is already busy in repairing his mounds and fences, but you cruel foxhunter render all his labour as vain as was that which Penelope bestowed on her web.'[14]

With his ample, cheerful countenance, Turville looks the typical foxhunting squire of Georgian England; he was over six foot with a loud and carrying voice and a tremendous sneeze. It must have been a wrench for him when in 1783 he and Barbara and their infant son George went off to live in France. Their reason for going seems to have been the usual one of economy. 'You may easily live in the *country* here for about £600 sterling a year, and certainly if you like it, for less' Barbara's cousin Charles Browne Mostyn, who had himself settled in Lyons, told them. 'The advantage of living abroad is that a man may live as he likes and as his circumstances demand without being taken notice of.'[15]

The Turvilles at first followed Browne Mostyn's example and settled in Lyons, then in 1785 they moved to Nancy. In Lyons they had the excitement of watching the ascent of a hot air balloon carrying seven passengers. Barbara's brother George Talbot wished he could have made a balloon of his own of Lyons silk and brought it to England; reckoning that it would have cost him no more than £600 and that he could have sold it in London for £10,000.

While George was thinking about balloons, a match was being planned for his unmarried sister Elizabeth by their uncle Bishop James Talbot, Vicar Apostolic of the London District. James was one of two brothers of Lord Shrewsbury in the Catholic episcopate, the other being Bishop Thomas Talbot, Vicar Apostolic of the Midland District. Bishop James's choice for his niece was Charles Mawhood, son of the prosperous London woollen draper William Mawhood; a sign of how marrying into 'trade' – provided it was to a Catholic, like young Mawhood – was more readily accepted at this time among the Catholic nobility than it was by Protestants of similar standing.

It was the Bishop who took the initiative and 'made an offer of his niece',[16] telling the young man's father that she would have a fortune of £3,000 and asking him what he would be prepared to settle. William Mawhood assured the Bishop that his settlement would be adequate, without naming a sum; the Bishop suggested that the young people 'might choose to live without trade',[17] but did not seem to mind when Mawhood told him that this was not his intention.

Mawhood consulted a friend, who advised against the Bishop's proposal, 'as nobility seldom suits a tradesman', and told him that if he did accept it, he should keep control of the business and make the young people an allowance of £300 a year.[18] Nevertheless, he passed on the offer to his son, who found it attractive. Elizabeth's fortune was raised to £3,500, but William Mawhood declared that this would not be enough to buy Charles a share in the business and that he would have to carry on working for a few years on an annual allowance of £300. Elizabeth then demanded a settlement larger than her fortune and Charles accused his father of going back on a promise to give him a share in the business after three years.

The matter ended when Elizabeth suddenly announced that her 'affections were fixed on some other person'; much to the annoyance of her uncle, who feared she would 'throw herself away'; though in the event she never married. Meanwhile Charles, who does not appear to have been a very satisfactory young man, was consoling himself with the maidservant. When his father spoke to him about it, he 'denied that he had any carnal knowledge of her'.[19]

In 1787, two years after Elizabeth Talbot jilted Charles Mawhood, her uncle Lord Shrewsbury died, leaving no children. Since no will of his more recent than forty years old could be found, his widow got half his personal fortune and the other half was divided among ten heirs-general. Elizabeth's eldest brother Charles, who was then thirty-four and unmarried, became the fifteenth Earl of Shrewsbury, holder of an earldom conferred in 1442 on his ancestor 'Le Grand Talbot' – Shakespeare's 'Great Alcides of the Field' – who won forty battles against the French before being defeated by Joan of Arc. His inheritance was not too badly affected by the problem of his uncle's will, for the settled estates passed to him automatically, including the principal family seat, Heythrop in Oxfordshire, a baroque palace with a front of Corinthian columns built at the beginning of the eighteenth century by the Duke of Shrewsbury, who having turned Protestant and supported the Revolution of 1688 was rewarded by William III with a dukedom which died with him. There was also Alton, the family seat in Staffordshire, where the Shrewsburys owned a great deal of land. It was a goodly patrimony, though it no longer included the valuable northern estates which had passed, by way of a seventeenth century heiress, to the Dukes of Norfolk.

Soon after inheriting, the new Lord Shrewsbury sold one of his Staffordshire estates. 'I have no patience with him for parting with old landed properties in order to buy villas' his cousin Charles Dormer wrote disapprovingly.[20] Buying a villa was not his only expenditure; he was enlarging his London house and carrying out great alterations at Heythrop, where, among other improvements, he put in hot and cold baths. The cold bath was large enough to swim in, according to his brother George Talbot, 'You may judge of its size and beauty by the price, which will be fourteen hundred pounds'.[21] George was given a large billiard table from the house which Shrewsbury did not want.

The new Lord Shrewsbury, whose chief interests were music and mechanics, had little taste for public life. This was unfortunate, for he was the premier Catholic peer, there being now no longer a Catholic Duke of Norfolk; the tenth Duke having died in 1786 and been succeeded by the apostate Surrey. While the loss to Catholicism of the Norfolk dukedom seemed likely to be only temporary, for the new Duke had no legitimate offspring and his heir was a Catholic, the year 1786 also saw the defection to Anglicanism of Viscount Montagu, whose wife had turned

Methodist and whose young son and heir was being brought up a Protestant. Lord Montagu made a deathbed repentance in Brussels a year later; but this did not bring his son back to the Catholic fold.

In 1788 the Catholic world was disturbed to hear of the marriage of Thomas Giffard, the wealthy young squire of Chillington in Staffordshire, to a Protestant, a daughter of Viscount Courtenay. He was said to have 'made her a very extraordinary compliment, on marrying her, of his religion'.[22] This was then denied and it was reported that Giffard, having handed his wife to her pew in the local Protestant church, 'immediately left the church *en bon catholique* and rode away to the chapel'.[23] But a few months later it was heard that Giffard had apostatized, along with Henry Howard, a younger brother of the Duke of Norfolk's heir. 'Their aim is to get into the next Parliament' Charles Browne Mostyn told Francis Fortescue Turville, who was still abroad. 'I most sincerely wish they may fail in it.'[24]

Mostyn's wish was granted, in that neither succeeded in obtaining a Parliamentary seat. But in that same year the young Northumberland baronet Sir John Swinburne, who had conformed a few months earlier on his marriage to the Duchess of Northumberland's niece, got into Parliament as member for one of the Duke of Northumberland's pocket boroughs. Young Sir John's father, Sir Edward Swinburne, a brother of Henry Swinburne the traveller, had quarrelled with his chaplain at Capheaton Hall, the family seat, shortly before his death in 1786, which may have had something to do with his son's apostasy. On turning Protestant, Sir John dismissed the chaplain and pulled down the chapel, showing himself to be less broadminded than the new Duke of Norfolk who continued to maintain Catholic chaplaincies at Arundel Castle and at Greystoke Castle in Cumberland.

At about the same time as Lord Montagu, Thomas Giffard and Sir John Swinburne ceased to be Catholic, the ancient Suffolk Catholic family of Mannock became extinct. Sir George Mannock, a Jesuit, was the last of his line; he had succeeded to the family baronetcy owing to the death of his schoolboy nephew in 1776. He decided to travel to Rome to seek permission to marry, in the hope of producing an heir; he set off on the Dover Mail Coach in the summer of 1787 but the coach overturned and he was killed.

Lady Mannock, the sister-in-law of the ill-fated Jesuit baronet, was formerly Elizabeth Stonor, sister of Charles Stonor of Stonor who had died in Normandy in 1781 aged only forty-three. As well as looking after Giffords Hall, the medieval and Tudor seat of the Mannocks in Suffolk, she kept an eye on the welfare of her Stonor nephews and nieces. Their mother, who came of a Berkshire Catholic family, the Blounts of Mapledurham, was a hard and selfish woman. Soon after Charles Stonor's death she had married again and sold all the furniture out of Stonor to pay

Thomas Giffard of Chillington, painted by Pompeo Batoni when he was in Rome on the Grand Tour

Stonor

the debts of her second husband.

So when in 1787 the eldest son Thomas came of age, his rambling ancestral home among the beechwoods of the Oxfordshire Chilterns, with its Tudor and eighteenth century front of brick and flint and its chapel and inner courts dating from medieval times, was more or less empty. It was looked after by the family chaplain Dr Joseph Strickland, one of the Stricklands of Sizergh Castle in Westmorland. This excellent old priest was in fact the childrens' great-uncle on their mother's side and acted as a father to them, particularly to the two youngest, Henry, on whom the Gordon Riots had made such a deep impression, and Fanny. Henry and Fanny had been left at Stonor in the care of Dr Strickland when the three elder boys were away at school at Douai and the elder girl, Mary, in Paris; Henry had gone to a small secret Catholic school at Edgbaston near Birmingham until he was old enough to join his brothers at Douai, where he was unhappy. In 1787 at the age of thirteen he tried to run away, stuffing his pockets with bread for the journey, but he was caught at an inn and brought back.

Meanwhile his eldest brother Thomas was enjoying the Grand Tour. Dr

Strickland, who knew Italy well and also Vienna, arranged introductions for him to various British diplomats and consular representatives; and he wrote to him giving him hints on correct behaviour, such as how to write thank-you letters. 'When you direct a letter to a peer, before the word "Lord" you must always put 'The Right Honble".'[25]

While Thomas was touring Europe, his elder sister Mary was back at Stonor having completed her education, a tall and attractive girl of nineteen. She went up to London for a party and sent a messenger to ask Dr Strickland to look for a bodkin which she had left behind. 'The bodkin was found in Miss Mary's room, which on account of the quantity of grease and powder that besmears the floor and all the furniture looks more like a barber's shop than a young lady's bedchamber', Dr Strickland reported in a letter.

I am at a loss to know how they manage in great homes, where the furniture is for the most part very valuable, for certainly no furniture whatever can stand the modern method of ladies making so much use of powder and pomature. This, however, is not meant as the least reflection upon Miss Mary, who must do and dress like other people. It only says that she has the misfortune to be born in a very flashy and dirty age.[26]

CHAPTER 3

Relief and revolution

IN 1787 a committee of prominent Catholic laymen, which had been originally formed to work for the passing of the 1778 Relief Act and then refounded in 1782, was formed yet again to obtain further relief from the penal laws. The Committee included three peers, Petre, Stourton and Clifford, and three baronets, Sir William Jerningham, Sir Henry Englefield from Berkshire and Sir John Lawson from Yorkshire. There were also the heir to a baronetcy, John Throckmorton, grandson of the aged Sir Robert, John Towneley, uncle of the collector Charles and Towneley's brother-in-law, the Worcestershire landowner Thomas Hornyold of Blackmore.

The fact that the Committee, like its predecessor, set out to represent the episcopal districts without including any clergy in its membership offended some of the English Catholic bishops, who also mistrusted the ruling triumvirate of Petre, Englefield and Throckmorton – 'a closed corporation of the polite unenthusiastic Catholicism of the Thames Valley', as a recent historian has described them.[1] As an example of Lord Petre's lack of religious enthusiasm, when the woollen draper William Mawhood met him before a meeting of the 1782 committee and told him that, having an hour to spare, he had attended Mass to pray for the success of the meeting, 'His Lordship made much ridicule'.[2] Lord Petre was, moreover, a Freemason; and while Freemasonry was still permissible for Catholics in England, it had already been condemned by the Pope.

Englefield and Throckmorton, who were cousins, both belonged as much as did Petre to the civilized world of Georgian England. Throckmorton lived at Weston Underwood in Buckinghamshire, a lesser house of his family, but had a footing in the Thames Valley since the Throckmortons owned Buckland Park in Berkshire as well as Coughton, their ancestral seat in Warwickshire. At Weston he had as a neighbour the poet Cowper, who was befriended by his wife Maria, a sister of the

Hugh, fifth Lord Clifford of Chudleigh

apostate Thomas Giffard of Chillington. Cowper would write to her affectionately as 'my dear Mrs Frog'; he also wrote verses 'On the death of Mrs Throckmorton's Bullfinch'.

The attitude to the Catholic Church of men like Petre, Englefield and Throckmorton came to be known as Cisalpine; a term which, meaning as it does 'on this side of the Alps', denotes something different north of the Alpine range to what it does in Italy. In England Cisalpine Catholics emphasized their moral obligations to the state and were opposed to papal influences except in the matter of Catholic dogma. They believed, for example, that the English Catholic bishops should be elected in England rather than appointed directly by Rome and that their appointment should be subject to a government veto.

Among the English Catholic aristocracy of those days, the Cisalpine spirit was prevalent though by no means universal. Even within the Committee, Sir John Lawson was unsympathetic to the attitude of Petre and Throckmorton and so was Hugh, Lord Clifford of Chudleigh. This thirty-year-old peer, a man of

Francis Plowden

'extraordinary beauty of person and fascinating urbanity of manners',[3] lived in Devon at Ugbrooke, an old house with a courtyard, given regular façades and an Adam interior by his father, surrounded by a romantic hilly park. His health was poor so that he and his pretty wife Apollonia, a daughter of the last Lord Langdale, spent much of their time wandering in Italy and Germany which prevented him from playing much part in the affairs of the Committee.

The most formidable opponent of Cisalpinism among the laity was Thomas Weld, who was asked to join the Committee on four different occasions and each time refused. His views were shared, though to a lesser degree, by his friend Lord Arundell of Wardour. Weld, Arundell and Clifford were all three of them old pupils of the Jesuits to whom the Cisalpine idea of a national church with a minimum of papal influence was repugnant. And Weld had as his chaplain at

Lulworth the distinguished Jesuit scholar, writer and controversialist Father Charles Plowden, who was to be a thorn in the side of the Committee throughout its activities. Father Charles was the seventh son of William Plowden of Plowden Hall in Shropshire, a modest half-timbered house which did little to reflect the standing of the Plowdens who as well as having the distinction of taking their name from their lands, were related to the Dormers and the Jerninghams and other influential families.

Of Father Charles's brothers, Robert was also a Jesuit; and of his sisters, two were nuns at Bruges. The youngest brother Francis had at first followed Charles and Robert into the Society of Jesus but having not yet been ordained priest by the time of the Society's suppression in 1773 was released from his simple vows and returned to a secular life. He had married a talented lady who sang solos at High Mass and wrote a comic opera which was put on at Drury Lane but 'damned at the first night'.[4] Having followed the law as his profession and become a successful Middle Temple conveyancer, as well as making a name for himself as a writer on legal and political subjects, Francis Plowden was well placed to voice his opposition to the Cisalpines of the Committee.

Ugbrooke

In 1788 the Committee prudently decided to add three clerics to its membership. The three chosen included Bishop James Talbot of the London District. James Talbot was conciliatory. He was Lord Shrewsbury's uncle and so was related to many of the Cisalpine grandees and understood their 'polite unenthusiastic' brand of Catholicism.

Lord Petre and two other members of the Committee had an interview with the Prime Minister, Pitt, who expressed himself willing to allow a Bill for Catholic relief to come before Parliament. However, as a preliminary, the Government wanted the Catholics to make a public declaration renouncing what Charles Dormer called 'some absurd doctrines generally imputed to us'[5] – notably the idea that the Pope would dispense Catholics from their allegiance to a heretic prince. The Committee saw nothing against this declaration, which came to be known as the Protestation, but the bishops felt it was unnecessary and that the 'absurd doctrines' had already been satisfactorily repudiated. Even Bishop Thomas Talbot of the Midland District, a peacemaker like his brother, objected.

The bishops had to defer to the Committee – for after all, the Faith was kept alive in country districts by men like Lord Petre and his friends, who maintained chaplaincies – and all four Vicars Apostolic eventually agreed to sign the Protestation. Among the total of 1,500 signatories were most of the great names; not only names from the Cisalpine south like Shrewsbury, Petre, Dormer and Throckmorton, but names redolent of the more rugged Catholicism of the north: Lawson, Tempest, Charlton and Strickland. The Duke of Norfolk's heir, Bernard Howard, signed, and so did young Thomas Stonor; so did Maria Fitzherbert's brother-in-law Basil Fitzherbert of Swynnerton and so did the elderly convert Shropshire baronet Sir Richard Acton. Lord Arundell and Lord Clifford signed and so did Thomas Weld, though not without many misgivings. No fewer than 240 priests signed, but not Father Charles Plowden; though his brother Francis did.

A further and more acrimonious controversy arose when the Bill was drafted; for it gave Catholics the curious designation of 'Protesting Catholic Dissenters', to which the bishops and others took exception. The bishops also objected to the wording of the Oath drawn up for Catholics to take in order to qualify for the relief granted by the Bill, which in their view appeared to deny even the spiritual powers of the Pope. The Committee, on the other hand, regarded this Oath as acceptable.

Relations between the Committee and the bishops worsened after the death in 1790 of Bishop James Talbot. His successor, Dr James Douglass, a priest by no means sympathetic to the Committee, joined with two of the other Vicars-Apostolic in condemning the Oath in an encyclical which brought a protest from Lord Petre and his colleagues, who described it as 'imprudent, arbitrary and unjust'. The

The scene at the old Tichborne House in the seventeenth century, when the Tichborne Dole was being distributed

Plowden brothers rallied to the bishops' defence; Father Charles publishing 'A Refutation of the Principles, Charges and Arguments advanced by the Catholic Committee against their Bishops'; Francis writing of 'the unwillingness of the Committee to abandon any one of their own fond conceits'.[6]

The bishops had prepared the encyclical at Lulworth, which has been described by a descendant of Lord Petre as 'the storm centre of opposition to the Committee'.[7] Thomas Weld's opposition was not just negative; he belonged to the great world and so was able to go and see Pitt himself and tell him of his co-religionists' 'horror of the title Protesting Catholic Dissenters'.[8]

The changing of this offending title to 'persons professing the Roman Catholic religion' and some further amendations to the Oath which satisfied Bishop Douglass put an end to the controversy and the Bill became law in June 1791. The Mass ceased to be illegal and could be celebrated openly; Catholic churches could be built. It was no longer necessary to speak of 'Prayers', though needless to say the habit died hard. Catholic schools were allowed and Catholic barristers could plead in court. Catholic squires could sit on the Grand Jury and thus play an active part in the

Thomas Weld, holding the plan of his new chapel
at Lulworth

affairs of their county. This may have been unfortunate in the case of the Tichbornes, for in 1794 Sir Henry Tichborne was persuaded by his county neighbours to discontinue the Tichborne Dole, on the grounds that it attracted vagrants; although Dame Mabella Tichborne was said to have put a curse on the family if it were discontinued: Tichborne House would fall down, there would be no male heir.

After the passing of the Relief Act, the Committee was dissolved; but a few months later some of its former members founded a club in order to meet and to watch unofficially over Catholic interests. To a nucleus of old Committee stalwarts such as Petre, Throckmorton, Jerningham and Towneley were recruited others, including Lord Shrewsbury, Bernard Howard, Charles Dormer and Basil Fitzherbert. The club was named the Cisalpine Club, which was provocative, to say the least; even Lord Petre had misgivings and it is perhaps significant that Lord

Clifford and Sir John Lawson both refused to join; though Clifford's cousin Henry Clifford did so and served as secretary. Thomas Weld not only refused to join but told Henry Clifford that he did not even want to know who the members were.

In 1786 Thomas Weld had built a large chapel at Lulworth, a short distance from the Castle. Unlike most other Catholic churches and chapels built in England since the Reformation, which were discreetly incorporated in houses, it was freestanding. He made it circular, with a dome, which may have been more than just a matter of taste; for in this way the suspicions of potential trouble-makers could have been set at rest by reports that he was building a temple or a mausoleum. The fact that he moved the coffins of his Catholic ancestors from the parish church to a vault in his new building gave substance to the latter theory.

By February 1787 work was sufficiently advanced for the altar to be set up. This had been made in Rome under the direction of the invaluable Father John Thorpe, with whom Thomas had doubtless been put in touch by Lord Arundell. It was designed by Quarenghi, who had designed the altar at Wardour, and was of

Thomas Weld's chapel at Lulworth

ormolu, as were the candlesticks, in which Thorpe took a particular pride; their shape, he told Thomas, 'was judged in the line of taste superior to whatever stands upon any altar in Rome' and they had been seen and admired by the Pope.[9]

Towards the end of 1790, Thomas's new chapel really came into its own; for no fewer than three bishops were consecrated in it, each on a separate day. They included Bishop John Carroll, first Bishop of Baltimore and father of the United States hierarchy. At one of these ceremonies, the preacher declared: 'I speak within walls equally known to, equally respected, and that have been equally honoured by Pius VI and George III'.[10] Whereas the Pope had done no more than take an interest in the building of the chapel and grant it privileges, the King had actually visited it. Following his second attack of insanity in 1788, George III had convalesced at Weymouth – bathing in the sea while bystanders sang God Save the King – and in August 1789 he and Queen Charlotte and some of the Royal children came over to Lulworth, landing in a ship at Lulworth Cove and driving up to the Castle in state with outriders.

Eight of the Weld children 'dressed in uniform' lined the steps leading up to the hall door, where Thomas received his Royal guests before entertaining them to 'an elegant collation, served up on a gold plate prepared for the occasion, richly embossed and each piece with the motto of "God Save the King"'. The King and Queen were then shown the new chapel and 'were highly delighted with an anthem, which was excellently performed, both vocal and instrumental'.[11]

A great crowd followed the Royal family into the church but, as Thomas reported to Lord Arundell of Wardour, there was 'no kind of noise or bustle or disturbance', though the Royal attendants and the sailors from the ship had all been well entertained and the 'populace' treated to beer. When someone remarked on how 'the populace were neat and cleanly dressed', the reply came that 'Mr Weld always living in the country spent his money amongst the people about him which enabled them to live comfortably and dress themselves cleanly.'[12] The King so enjoyed himself that he stayed longer than he had intended and was late for a command performance of a farce at the theatre in Weymouth that evening; he showed consideration for the other playgoers by sending a message desiring that the performance should start without him. This was the first of four visits which George III and Queen Charlotte paid to Lulworth between 1789 and 1792.

Thomas Weld and his wife Mary had fifteen children, of whom the eldest son, also called Thomas, was sixteen at the time of the first royal visit. Thomas was generous to his children, giving each of the boys and girls £100 a year when they reached the age of eighteen, even though they were still living at home; and he showed his affection for them in his account books by putting 'Dear' before the

Sir John Acton. An engraving by Bartolozzi

names of those children to whom he was making payments. When they misbehaved, he fined them. The fines were not large except for lying and for prolonged sulks. For 'talking loud when Papa is talking', the fine was a penny.[13]

In 1791, a few months after the passing of the Relief Act, the elderly convert Sir Richard Acton died. The heir to his baronetcy and to the Aldenham estate in Shropshire was his fifty-five-year-old bachelor cousin John Acton, son of Edward Acton the medical doctor at Besançon who had married a French Catholic bride and turned Catholic himself. The new baronet, after a training both military and naval, had become a general in the service of the Grand Duke of Tuscany and had commanded the Tuscan fleet. Then in 1778 he had been given the task of reorganizing the navy of King Ferdinand IV of Naples and within four years had become to all intents and purposes prime minister of the Neapolitan kingdom. His rapid rise to power was due to his efficiency and integrity, which appealed to the Queen, the intellectual and highly energetic Maria Carolina, sister of Marie Antoinette. The Queen influenced the easy-going King, who spent his time shooting and fishing, and Acton influenced the Queen. Such was his influence over her that he was rumoured to be her lover but while she was more than a little in love with the slim, personable Englishman with his piercing blue eyes, his grave expression and his perfect manners, he remained insensible to her charms and behaved towards her with the strictest propriety.

Acton managed to survive the jealousies and intrigues of the Neapolitan court. He evaded assassination plots and triumphed over the French and Spanish factions who wished to get rid of him because of his determination to free Naples from the influence of France and Spain. To achieve this object, he tried to bring the Neapolitan kingdom closer to Britain, and made friends with the British envoy Sir William Hamilton, who regarded him as 'still an Englishman at heart', despite his French upbringing and his years in Italy.[14] Hamilton was one of the few friends Acton had, for he mixed little in Neapolitan society; though he kept open house and was excellent company.

After the outbreak of the French Revolution, Acton was put in charge of foreign affairs in addition to his other duties; and he tried to form an Italian league backed by Britain against France. Having always mistrusted the French, though he was half French himself, he now mistrusted them more than ever. His succession to Aldenham and the baronetcy in 1791 came as a welcome distraction. His friend Hamilton, who had just married the beautiful Emma Hart, reported that he was 'not a little proud' of being Sir John and that he was 'meditating his retreat from an elevated but perilous situation to his quiet family seat in Shropshire'.[15] But his sense of duty kept him at his post in Naples, endeavouring to preserve the kingdom against the forces of revolution. For a long time he had looked old for his age; he now fairly wore himself out with work and his health was undermined.

Francis Fortescue Turville and his wife Barbara avoided the horrors of the Revolution by returning to England early in 1789 and settling down to a peaceful life in Leicestershire at Bosworth Hall, which they enlarged to accommodate their fast-growing family by building a plain but commodious three-storey block on to the back of the old gabled house; the new, like the old, being of red brick. Barbara's cousin Charles Browne Mostyn stayed on in Lyons and was there in July 1789 when eighty people were killed in rioting and a mob took over the Customs House and drank all the wine in the bonded store. In October 1790 he ventured into Paris where he found everybody, even the beggars, armed with swords, guns or pistols.

Edward Jerningham the poet was in Paris in 1792. 'Sacchini's music makes one bear French singers' he wrote. 'As for the French tragedy, it is so pompous.' He met the youthful Madame de Staël and saw 'not the least pedantism about her'.[16]

That summer, his sister-in-law Frances Lady Jerningham and her daughter Charlotte took the waters at Spa. Charlotte had lived up to the promise which she

A print showing the old Bosworth Hall, with Francis Fortescue Turville's eighteenth century block below it

had shown as a schoolgirl at the Ursulines. She was tall and beautiful, with large blue eyes and black hair; she danced well. She was a talented artist, she had a taste for literature; her uncle the poet would send her books such as *L'Homme de Qualité* and Thomson's *Seasons*. Her eldest brother George, who had stayed behind at Cossey with their father Sir William, kept her up-to-date with Norfolk news. Sir Richard Bedingfeld of Oxburgh was ill, his son, young Richard, had grown very fat. They were all 'violent against the Jacobins', except for 'some rascals at Norwich'. Everything in Charlotte's room, her brother assured her, was just as she left it; even the bats in the closet.[17]

Despite its proximity to the theatre of war, Spa was crowded with the fashionable world. And indeed, Frances's main reason for coming was to be near her son William who was serving in the Low Countries with the Austrian army. In November, having migrated to Brussels, she and Charlotte drove out to visit him at the front. He came out and sat in their coach and they chatted for half an hour until 'suddenly a firing began at the outposts' and he had to go. A month later, Brussels was occupied by the French. The Jerninghams had three French soldiers billeted on them and three rooms in their house were commandeered for keeping the French general's supply of bullion.

Frances and Charlotte managed to get back to England without any trouble, arriving soon after Christmas. Martha Swinburne, wife of Henry Swinburne the traveller, was less fortunate. Having been in Paris, where she tried to persuade Marie Antoinette to escape by changing clothes with her, she had the greatest difficulty in reaching Boulogne, where a mob surrounded her carriage, believing her to be the mistress of Philippe-Egalité, Duc d'Orléans. She saved herself by putting her head out of the window and declaring that she was neither young nor beautiful. Meanwhile in quiet Northumberland her husband's nephew, the renegade Sir John Swinburne, was calling himself Citizen Swinburne having espoused the cause of the Revolution; and his wife Emilia, the Duchess of Northumberland's niece, was lisping out 'All for equality!' as she drove in her carriage with the four greys and the two powdered footmen.

While Martha Swinburne risked her safety in France, the young Viscount Montagu, a connection by marriage of her husband, was travelling with a friend in the Rhineland. The two young men thought it would be fun to shoot the falls of Schauffhausen, near Basle, in a flat-bottomed boat; the local magistrate tried to dissuade them, and even had guards posted on the river bank to stop them; but they managed to get past and pushed off into the current. They safely negotiated the first of the two waterfalls but going down the second they disappeared and were never seen again. Lord Montagu died in happy ignorance of the fact that, three weeks earlier,

William Jerningham

his family home in Sussex, Cowdray House, had been burnt to the ground. The monk's curse of fire and water on the posterity of his forebear Sir Anthony Browne had taken effect. The title passed to a distant cousin Mark Anthony Browne, a friar at Fontainebleau, and was to die with him; even though, not being a priest, he had married in what proved to be the vain hope of having an heir.

Lord Montagu was the second English peer to die in Germany during that inauspicious year of 1793. In January, a few days before the execution of Louis XVI, Lord Clifford's travels in search of health ended with his death in Munich; he was laid to rest amidst the rococo splendours of the Jesuit college there and his pretty wife made her way sadly back to England. At that time she was not the only member of the Clifford family on the Continent. Her brother-in-law Robert Clifford, who had given up his career in the French army as an officer in the Dillon Regiment because he refused to serve under the Revolution, was living at Liége,

Cowdray House, before the fire

where he had made friends with the Prince-Bishop. Robert's sister Charlotte was also at Liége, as a novice at the convent of the English Canonesses, where another of the young nuns was their first cousin Anne Clifford. Anne had a brother, George, who was a boy at Liége Academy, where their cousin Walter Clifford was studying for the priesthood.

The Academy was still run by the English Jesuits, though the Society of Jesus had been suppressed by the Pope twenty years earlier; but under the threat of revolutionary France many parents were taking their boys away. Among them was Thomas Weld, who, accompanied by Father Charles Plowden, came to Liége in 1793 when the city was in Austrian hands and stayed several months; leaving with his three schoolboy sons in May 1794. Before he left he offered Stonyhurst, the Elizabethan mansion in Lancashire which the Welds had inherited from the Shireburns, to the 'Gentlemen of the Academy' should they be driven out of Liége. But they still hoped to remain there.

The English Canonesses were less sanguine. As early as January, they had felt sure that the French, who had already occupied Liége and been driven out by the Austrians, would soon be back; and they had taken a house at Maastricht to which they sent some of their valuables. Towards the end of May they decided to leave and slipped out of their convent at three o'clock on a very wet morning, 'all crying most bitterly'. The nuns had been promised a comfortable barge to take them down the Meuse; but as is recorded in an account of their adventures which Anne Clifford helped to write, they found 'nothing but a coal boat covered in with a few boards so filthy and so small that only one half of us could get into it'.[18] By dint of putting some of their baggage into another boat they were somehow squeezed in and reached

Maastricht safely. Eventually they proceeded to Rotterdam, where they took ship for England. Not until they reached London did they manage to get rid of the fleas which they had picked up when staying in a former military hospital at Roermond.

The English Benedictine nuns at Cambrai had a worse time than the Canonesses. In October 1793 they were ordered out of their convent at a quarter of an hour's notice and taken off in carts on a journey that was to last five days. As they passed through various towns, the rabble cried out 'Aristocrates à la guillotine!' or thronged around their carts threatening to tear them to pieces or bury them alive in their religious habits. They were fortunate in being protected by an escort of hussars, who unlike the populace, showed them some humanity and politeness.

Eventually the nuns reached Compiègne, where they were confined in a former convent, now used as a prison. In the following January, most of them went down with a fever, of which two of them died; the seventy-nine-year-old Dame Elizabeth Anselma Anne, aunt of the Yorkshire squire George Anne of Burghwallis, and Bishop Walmesley's half-sister Dame Teresa Walmesley. Then, because the nuns had no money to pay for their one meal a day, they were put on bread and water.

In June some French Carmelite nuns were lodged in the prison before being taken to the guillotine; as they left they cheerfully waved goodbye to the English nuns, who fully expected to suffer a similar fate. Eight days after the Carmelites died came the fall of Robespierre and the English nuns were henceforth better treated, though they suffered greatly during the exceptionally cold winter that followed. In the spring of 1795 they managed to get permission to return to England. To pay for their journey, they were able to draw money on Edward Constable of Burton Constable, the nephew and heir of William Constable, the collector, who was also a nephew of Dame Elizabeth Frances Sheldon, one of the nuns.

Escaping from the Continent was much easier for Thomas Weld's cousin Mary Simeon Weld, Abbess of the English Franciscan nuns at Bruges, and her community which included Thomas's twenty-year-old daughter Juliana as well as the two Plowden sisters and their cousin Mary Dormer and three daughters of Thomas Ferrers of Baddesley Clinton in Warwickshire. When in June 1794 the French were getting close to the town, the nuns left their convent and took shelter at a farm near the sea shore, from where they were able to board a ship. In the same month as the Franciscan nuns left Bruges, the English Augustinian Canonesses of Louvain, led by their Prioress, Mother Mary Benedict Stonor, set out for England with all their belongings piled into three coaches, eventually taking ship from Rotterdam to Gravesend.

Mother Mary Benedict's niece, the younger Mary Stonor, was now herself a nun; having forsworn 'powder and pomature' at the age of twenty in 1788 and returned to the convent of the English Augustinian Canonesses in Paris, where she was at school. With the Revolution imminent, her brother Thomas came to Paris to try and persuade her to return home but she insisted on staying and took her vows three weeks after the storming of the Bastille. She and Thomas were very close and they wrote to each other frequently. They somehow managed to keep up their correspondence during the fateful years that followed, though at one time they had to address their letters to 'Citoyen' or 'Citoyenne' Stonor.

For the next three years Mary and the other nuns continued their life of prayer and teaching in the face of threats and alarms, braving the guillotine by offering Conventual Mass for Louis XVI on the morning after his execution. In the July of that year, twenty-one men with drawn swords burst into the convent searching for priests and in December, during the Terror, the convent was commandeered as a prison for women. The nuns, however, were allowed to stay and brought consolation to the prisoners, among whom were three of Mary's cousins, Mrs Blount of Mapledurham and her two daughters who had been at the school. Many of the prisoners, though not the Blounts, were taken to the guillotine; and one night in July 1794 word came that all those who survived were to die in a general massacre. Next day Robespierre suffered the fate of his victims and the prisoners were soon afterwards released, their place being taken by other nuns who had been turned out of their convents, including the English 'Blue Nuns'.

In the spring of 1795 the Blue Nuns left for England, but the Augustinians, including Mary Stonor, remained in Paris. The most illustrious of the Blue Nuns, their former Abbess Lady Anastasia Stafford-Howard – who would have been Baroness Stafford in her own right but for her great-grandfather's attainder – also stayed behind. This seventy-three-year-old cousin of Sir William Jerningham was well looked after, though she was to complain to her relations in England that she did not get enough to eat and that her shifts were 'almost quite gone, every wash I am forced to put patch upon patch'.[19]

Having lingered at Liége until a fortnight before the French occupied the town in July 1794, the Gentlemen of the Academy left in barges as the Canonesses had done in the previous May. The boys from the school who went with them included George Clifford. Since Thomas Weld had offered them Stonyhurst as a new home, the main party of Jesuits and boys went by sea all the way to Hull and from there headed straight for Lancashire, losing no time in taking possession of the great house which had stood empty for long. Having been the last out of Liége Academy, George Clifford was determined to be the first to arrive at Stonyhurst. Wearing his travel-stained Liége school uniform and with the soles of his boots coming away from the uppers, he ran up the avenue ahead of everybody else, passed under the gate

Stonyhurst, as it was in 1794

tower into the quadrangle and forced open the door into the old banqueting hall.

As well as giving Stonyhurst to the Jesuits, Thomas Weld gave a house at Winchester to the Franciscan nuns from Bruges. And while both these benefactions could be said to have helped his family – his three younger sons were able to continue their education at Stonyhurst, his eldest daughter was one of the Franciscan nuns and his cousin was their Abbess – his motives were entirely disinterested when in 1794 he established a community of French and English Cistercian monks on a farm at East Lulworth. His idea was to rebuild the ruins of the old Cistercian Abbey of Bindon nearby and found a monastery there, but the scheme was not a success.

Other Catholic magnates provided new homes for the refugee religious, though in most cases they were only temporary. The Canonesses from Liége were lent Holme Hall in Yorkshire, which Lady Stourton had inherited from her father, the last Lord Langdale. When the nuns arrived, some of the villagers 'were greatly alarmed to see so many persons dressed in a peculiar manner', thinking they were 'Frenchmen dressed in womens' clothes'.[20]

When the President of the English Seminary at St Omers, Dr Gregory Stapleton, brother of the Yorkshire squire Thomas Stapleton of Carlton, arrived in England in

1795 with ninety-four students, having been imprisoned by the revolutionaries in the citadel of Dourlens, he did not have to find temporary shelter in a nobleman's house. He was invited by Bishop Douglass of the London District to establish himself and his students at Old Hall Green in Hertfordshire where Douglass had started a school for Catholic boys after the Relief Act of 1791. This was now enlarged to become the College of St Edmund, both a seminary and a school.

Among the boys who started at Old Hall Green before the arrival of the St Omers contingent were Francis Fortescue Turville's two elder sons, George and Charles. Charles had gone there at the age of six and soon after he arrived a master had complained to his father that he had 'practised indecencies in word and deed, which he admitted were common in his former school'. As a 'method of correcting a vice that would lead to the boy's downfall', the master had whipped him until he bled.[21] Charles and also George had better reports from Dr Stapleton after he had taken over; Charles eventually wrote a mathematical thesis which he dedicated to Charles Dormer. Before the two Turville boys left the school it was in financial difficulties and Lord Petre was criticizing its cleanliness. Stapleton wondered how he could do so when he had gone no further than the refectory.[22]

The Jesuits from Liége and the secular priests from St Omers were not the only Catholic schoolmasters to arrive in England at this time; there were also the Benedictine monks who had run schools at Douai and at Dieulouard in Lorraine. Maria Fitzherbert's cousin Sir Edward Smythe, who was an old boy of Douai and devoted to the Benedictines, gave both communities a refuge at his family seat in Shropshire, the handsome, Ionic, Acton Burnell Hall, which was then empty as he was living at his father-in-law's house in Warwickshire. Meanwhile, Maria herself befriended the Benedictine nuns from Montargis who arrived destitute at Shoreham on the Sussex coast, collecting money for them and driving over from her house at Brighton to meet them.

Since 1786 the Prince and Maria had spent much of their time at Brighton, he living officially at Marine Pavilion which Henry Holland had rebuilt for him in the Classical style – the oriental pleasure-dome still belonged to the future – she in a house nearby where she had a small oratory for Mass. But as in London, he used his own residence just for entertaining, with Maria as hostess, and her house was his real home. Maria's marriage had gone surprisingly well, given the hazards of its illegality and the impossible character of her Royal husband. There had been a crisis in 1787 when Charles James Fox, in order to persuade Parliament to pay the Prince's debts, denied his marriage – almost certainly at the Prince's instigation. Maria was so angry that she threatened to leave the Prince, but soon forgave him.

She put up with the Prince's drunkenness, waiting up for him when he came

Acton Burnell Hall

home late from his roisterings; hiding behind the furniture or even under the sofa to avoid his drunken companions, only to be discovered by him and brought forth. As a boring repetitive joke he would search the room for her with drawn sword. However, he drank less in her company than he did with anybody else and she sometimes managed to prevent him from saying foolish things in his cups.

The knowledge that he continued to love her would have helped her to put up with his faults; this and the fact that she almost certainly loved him. And her marriage, for all its trials, had obvious compensations. She occupied a high place in fashionable society, she enjoyed the respect and friendship of the Prince's brothers, particularly of the Dukes of York and Clarence. Even the King and Queen looked on her with kindness, realizing what a good influence she was, and indeed, it was largely through her that the Prince was reconciled with his father.

But over the marriage hung the black cloud of the Prince's debts, which since being paid by Parliament had mounted once again to the alarming figure of £375,000. The King was willing to pay them on condition he married a German princess. The Queen, realizing that it would take more than just money to make him give up his Maria, subjected him to the wiles of the elderly but seductive Lady Jersey. The plan worked. One morning in June 1794 Maria received an affectionate letter from the Prince, beginning 'My dearest Love'. That evening he sent her a note saying that he never intended to see her again. In the following April he reluctantly married his cousin Caroline of Brunswick, a jolly, hoydenish princess whose aversion to soap and water made her particularly distasteful to her fastidious bridegroom, since she was not like Maria 'sweet by nature'.

A month before the break-up of Maria's marriage to the Prince, the Duke of Norfolk's cousin and heir Bernard Howard was divorced from his wife by Act of Parliament, an unusual occurrence for those days. 'Barney', as he was known, had married the beautiful Lady Elizabeth Belasyse, daughter of the erstwhile Catholic Earl Fauconberg, in 1789 but she was then already in love with Lord Lucan's son and heir, Richard Bingham. Her parents forced her to marry Barney, who as well as being a future duke was a kind and amiable young man, though he was short and of no particular looks. Lady Elizabeth told her maid that 'she would rather go to Newgate than live with him'[23]; and having endured him long enough to bear him a son in 1791, she became the mistress of Bingham, who up till then had kept away and tried to forget her. Barney, who blamed neither her nor her lover and stated that he did not question the legitimacy of his son, divorced her to enable her to marry Bingham, which she did within the month. He himself never married again. In order to do so he would, as a practising Catholic, have had to get an annulment from Rome, which might have been possible on the grounds that Lady Elizabeth had married him against her will. But as a strong Cisalpine he might have disliked having to invoke the power of the Papacy to solve his matrimonial problem. And he may still have loved Lady Elizabeth.

CHAPTER 4

Trying to serve King George

ARLY in 1795 Sir Richard Bedingfeld, known as 'Hooknose', died. Since the death of his wife, a sister of the Lord Montagu who conformed and then made a death-bed repentance, he had lived in melancholy retirement at Oxburgh Hall, his ancestral seat in Norfolk, a moated medieval house of tawny brick with a tall gate tower and a courtyard. Sir Richard had modernized the old house, pulling down the great hall and adding an Adamesque saloon. Before taking to his bed for the last time, he went round this room in a wheel chair, gazing long at each of the pictures.

In the following June his twenty-seven-year-old son Sir Richard, the new baronet, married the beautiful Charlotte Jerningham. It was a suitable if somewhat obvious match; Charlotte's father Sir William being the other Catholic baronet in Norfolk. The Bedingfelds were as ancient a family as the Jerninghams, though less well off. Charlotte's old cousin Lady Anastasia Stafford-Howard wrote from Paris that Richard Bedingfeld was 'the very man I had in my noddle picked out for her'.[1] Richard, like all the Bedingfelds, was shy and reserved but very good-hearted. He was certainly very much in love with his 'Corry', as he called her; three months after they were married, when she had gone to visit her mother at Cossey, leaving him on his own at Oxburgh, he wrote to her:

> You, my dear Corry, are *everything to me* . . . I have very often been alone in this house before, but I never felt as I do this time, perhaps you will say it's foolish in me, when you are only gone for a few days, but I can't help it.[2]

Charlotte settled down happily to a peaceful country existence at Oxburgh, delighting in the picturesque antiquity of the house and giving birth to four sons and four daughters as the years went by. Richard carried out his duties as a country squire

Oxburgh Hall

– sitting on the Grand Jury from which until 1791 he had been debarred – with driving four-in-hand as his chief recreation. He occasionally went to Newmarket Races and to the Races at Yarmouth, where he and Charlotte had a seaside house, presenting a gold cup when Nelson arrived with the Fleet.

Apart from their migrations to Yarmouth, Richard and Charlotte stayed with her parents at Cossey and occasionally visited other country houses. They stayed at the Jacobean Haughley Park in Suffolk and at the Elizabethan Sawston Hall in Cambridgeshire which both belonged to old Catholic families, the Sulyardes and the Huddlestons respectively; Frances Sulyarde being about to marry Charlotte's eldest brother George. While they were at Sawston they went into Cambridge with the younger Huddlestons for a Commencement Ball. One summer, Richard drove Charlotte in his curricle all the way to North Wales and back, a trip lasting seven weeks. Only seldom did they go to London, where they had no house of their own but stayed with Charlotte's parents.

While Charlotte's father, Sir William Jerningham, disliked London, her mother Frances had something of a salon at their house in Boulton Row. The *émigré* French nobility gathered there together with the English Catholic world – the 'Cats'

The former Charlotte Jerningham, now Lady
Bedingfeld, by Opie

as she called them – so that she came to be known as 'Her Catholic Majesty'. She
also gave hospitality to the *émigrés* at Cossey. 'I like to have several people in the
house', she told Charlotte, 'and a multitude cannot be had cheaper than with the
unfortunate French: no servants, no horses, no drinkings'.[3] To help entertain the
French there was often Sir William's 'French Brother' Charles, the Chevalier, who
having been a general under the *ancien régime* had escaped to England after the attack
on the Tuileries. But when staying at Cossey one Holy Week he found the 'fasting
and praying' too much for him and left on Maundy Thursday; although as a Knight
of Malta he should have been used to religious exercises.[4] The atmosphere at Cossey
was for a time even more religious when Frances gave shelter there to the Blue Nuns
from Paris. She admitted to Charlotte, 'Your poor father has been a little impatient
about them'.[5]

Though Frances purported not to like large gatherings – she declared that she 'entirely enjoyed not going' to the Duchess of Devonshire's ball, the Duchess having failed to invite her, not realizing that she was in London at the time[6] — she gave 'routs'. At one of them the hundred-odd guests were entertained by 'the two Damianis, Miss Wynne who has a very fine voice . . . and Miss Le Tourneur on the harp'.[7] She went to a ball at Lady Hardwicke's and to 'a most violent ball' given by Lady Kenmare, the wife of a Catholic peer from Ireland, at which there were four or five hundred people. 'Half of them were in masks', Frances noted, 'but as there were a very great assemblage of Cats that all knew one another intimately, it was really very pleasant.'[8] Her daughter-in-law the younger Frances Jerningham, George's bride, frightened her by dancing a great deal, for she was pregnant; but she was none the worse for it next day.

The two Frances Jerninghams went frequently to Court, as did Sir William. The elder Frances described the dress which she wore at a Drawing Room as 'not at all dismal and very fashionable, the petticoat is white crêpe, and a drapery up and down, one of white satin, the other of drab crêpe like the gown, and tassels of large white beads'.[9] The King and Queen were always very gracious to the Jerninghams; when the younger William came back to England, having fought the French on the banks of the Rhine as an officer in the Austrian service, the King said to the Austrian who was with him, 'Son père, le cher Jerningham, est le plus honnête homme que je connaisse'.[10]

The Queen often asked after her namesake Charlotte Bedingfeld. 'I want to see your *own* daughter, what can she be doing always in the country?' she demanded of the elder Frances, who had brought her daughter-in-law to a Drawing Room. On being told that Charlotte was 'lying in of a son', the Queen replied, 'That is very well, but I want to see her here'.[11] As a young girl, Charlotte had danced before the Queen in minuets and had clearly made a good impression on her. Moreover, the name Bedingfeld stood high at Court thanks to the courage of Richard's cousin John Bedingfeld. When, at the opening of Parliament in 1795, an angry mob surrounded the King's carriage clamouring for peace and for the dismissal of Pitt, he sprang single-handed to the defence of his Sovereign and kept the mob at bay with his sword. The 'Tall Cousin', as John was known in the family, had been thanked personally by the King and also by the Queen and the Princesses, though his parents felt that the Royal gratitude might have taken a more tangible form.

The tall and gallant John was the eldest son of Richard Bedingfeld's uncle Edward, who like Charlotte's uncle Edward Jerningham was a minor poet. His works include some verses *On the Victory off the Mouth of the Nile*:

Imperious Fame now Nelson's triumph lends
Not where the stream began, but where it ends.

His talent, such as it was, had been inherited by his second son Thomas, a lawyer who died young in 1789 and who wrote, among other poems, *The Triumph of Beauty*, addressed to the Duchess of Devonshire on her successful canvass for Charles James Fox.

Edward Bedingfeld and his wife Mary, who was a Swinburne, lived in York and their daughter Mary had married into the Yorkshire Catholic gentry. Her husband, Thomas Waterton of Walton Hall near Wakefield, came of a family as much noted for its adherence to Catholicism as for its antiquity. Walton Hall, a somewhat gloomy eighteenth century block on an island in a small lake joined to the mainland by a bridge, stood on the site of an older house which the wife of a seventeenth century Waterton had defended against the Roundheads after the Battle of Marston Moor.

Charles, the eldest son of Thomas and Mary Waterton, was one of the first boys to be educated at Stonyhurst, where his love of natural history was encouraged by the Jesuits who made him rat-catcher and fox-taker to the school. One of them, believing that young Waterton would be a traveller and that drink would get him into trouble in far countries, made him take the pledge. He was to keep it as long as he lived, just as he did a later promise to his father to give up hunting.

After the Peace of Amiens, Charles Waterton was sent to Málaga where two of his Bedingfeld uncles, Peter and the younger Edward, had established themselves in business. Here he learnt Spanish and nearly died in an epidemic of the dreaded 'black vomit', a form of yellow fever which killed one of his uncles. Like his uncle John Bedingfeld, this uncle was very tall and his coffin was too big for the plague pit in which he was buried; so his body had to be taken out and thrown on to the heap of bodies in the pit. His family seems to have derived some consolation from the fact that 'a Spanish marquess lay just below him'.[12]

While the two Bedingfeld brothers were building up their business in Málaga, the seventh Earl of Traquair had applied for a concession to work some coal mines in Spain and hoped to obtain a Spanish Grandeeship. But his Spanish venture brought him tragedy, for his wife died in Madrid in 1796. According to one of the family traditions regarding the closed gates at Traquair House, her husband refused to open them again until there was another Countess of Traquair; which as it turned out, there never was.

More successful than Lord Traquair was Henry Stonor, an uncle of Thomas and of Mary the Canoness, who became a wine merchant at San Lucar near Seville, exporting sherry to England. After his death in 1792 only one of his four surviving sons had stayed on in Spain. This was Charles, who obtained a commission in the Spanish army and thus became the second Stonor of his generation in the service of a foreign prince; the other being his cousin Henry, brother of Thomas and Mary. At the age of seventeen, Henry Stonor had become a lieutenant in the army of the Elector of Bavaria through the influence of one of the Irish Wild Geese who was a general in the Bavarian service. Unfortunately this general had married off his thirteen-year-old daughter to the eighteen-year-old Henry; the girl's dowry consisted only of 'the clothes on her back, a new bed and a gold-headed cane'[13] and she was to prove unfaithful.

The marriage had aroused the indignation of Henry's eldest brother Thomas, whose own matrimonial affairs had turned out much more satisfactorily. Having wanted to marry Thomas Weld's beautiful daughter Clare, who was determined to become a nun like her two elder sisters, he had settled for Kitty Blundell, a daughter of the collector Henry Blundell of Ince Blundell in Lancashire. Kitty's late mother was a Mostyn, which made her a first cousin of Lord Shrewsbury and of Barbara Turville.

During the early years of their marriage, while Kitty bore him two sons, Thomas carried out improvements at Stonor, redecorating some of the rooms and the interior of the chapel in Georgian Gothic. He made good his mother's depredations; his great-uncle Monsignor Christopher Stonor, who was for many years agent in Rome for the English Vicars Apostolic, had given him a sum of money to furnish one of the empty rooms and a French *émigré* priest who was a chaplain at Stonor bought back some of the family portraits and presented them to him. Thomas also made a deer park, cutting down the woods which had surrounded the house and been admired by the greatest English Catholic poet of the eighteenth century, Alexander Pope. Frances Jerningham heard of these alterations from one of her sons, who did not approve of them. 'He says that the brown shades, celebrated in Pope's letter, are terribly devastated' she told her daughter. 'The venerable house is deposed . . . it appears that the present owner is so different in taste from his ancestors.'[14]

Thomas's taste was trusted at any rate by his father-in-law Henry Blundell, who made him his agent for buying Classical sculpture. Blundell was able to add greatly to his collection after 1800, when pieces plundered from the Vatican by the French came up for sale at Christie's and elsewhere. It was certainly a tribute to Thomas that Blundell should have relied on him in preference to his mentor and former collaborator Charles Towneley; but Towneley's health began to fail in 1803 and even before that he may have become more concerned with saving his soul than with buying antiquities. 'He has been for many years a *bel esprit*, had too much wit to

Ince Blundell Hall, with Henry Blundell's Pantheon on the right

pray' Frances Jerningham wrote of him in 1800. 'His mind now is reformed and he is become particularly regular.'[15]

In 1802 Blundell started building a miniature version of the Pantheon in Rome to house his growing collection; it stood alongside the early-Georgian Ince Blundell Hall but was not actually joined to it. He had already built a temple in the garden to contain some of his earlier purchases. He continued buying pictures as well as sculpture and by 1803 his collection included nearly 200 pictures and drawings.

Blundell was now nearly eighty and had long been a widower. His portrait shows him to have been tight-lipped and rather desiccated; one suspects that he now bought works of art as a distraction from the loneliness and unhappiness of his old age. His only son Charles was a bitter disappointment; he was lethargic, interested in nothing and refused to marry; as the years went by he grew increasingly corpulent and eccentric. 'He takes no field sports, neither shooting, coursing, nor hunting' Blundell lamented to Thomas Stonor. 'He visits few . . . What a different life I led at his years!' Blundell also complained that Charles had 'expressed a violent dislike to both his sisters'.[16]

Blundell's younger daughter Elizabeth was married to Stephen Tempest of Broughton Hall near Skipton in Yorkshire, not far from the Lancashire border. Tempest, an old boy of the Jesuits at Bruges and Liége, was head of another landowning family that had always been Catholic. He was intelligent as well as handsome, with a high forehead and distinguished features, wearing better than Elizabeth who in middle age was portly with a double chin and beefy arms. What Elizabeth may have lacked in looks she made up for with a dowry of £8,000 which would have been a help to her husband in his improvements at Broughton, even though he was reasonably prosperous himself. Since before his marriage he had been gradually redecorating the interior of the house, which was originally Elizabethan but had been remodelled in about 1730. It was splendidly situated on the side of a wooded hill.

To the south was a deer park from which in 1802 a buck escaped and was killed by the Skipton hunt, a pack of hounds supported by the townsmen of Skipton. Tempest, who supported the more respectable local hunt, the Craven, was not at all pleased and a row ensued. The Skipton followers sent him anonymous letters and put up rude notices, including a particularly offensive one accusing him of drunkenness. This was unkind since the Tempests had always prided themselves on their sobriety. And having been warned off his land, they broke down his fences and put hounds into the deer park. Eventually the hunt apologized, after Tempest had started legal proceedings for trespass.

With the threat of a Napoleonic invasion, Tempest joined the Militia, like so many other country squires. Although the Relief Act of 1791 had done nothing specific to enable Catholics to hold commissions in the armed forces, this depended rather on the attitude of individual commanding officers: whether or not they made the officers under them take the prescribed oath against Popery. Hitherto, all commanding officers had insisted on this oath, which had effectively debarred practising Catholics from holding commissions; but after the outbreak of the Revolutionary Wars an increasing number were prepared to waive it.

So William Jerningham, having returned to England after serving in the Austrian army, was able to get a commission in the 57th Foot in 1800. George Turville, having completed his education at Old Hall Green, became a captain in the army stationed at Dover Castle. After the renewal of hostilities in 1803 he told his family that he expected an invasion night and day. This did not prevent him and his brother officers from giving a fortnightly ball and putting on a play every other night; and he gave so many supper parties that he overspent his allowance, much to the annoyance of his father, who said that he would soon have to leave the regiment. He promised to do better, assuring his father that he never played cards for money. He

Broughton Hall, as it eventually became

also had a good excuse for being hard up, for in the previous winter he and his brother officers had contributed a month's pay to buying flannel waistcoats for the men.

His younger brother Charles tried to get into the Royal Military Academy at Woolwich through the influence of their uncle Lord Shrewsbury. He was turned down not on account of his religion but because he was over the age of fourteen. Eventually he joined the local Volunteer corps in Yorkshire, where he was articled to a solicitor. Their cousin Charles Browne Mostyn was made a Lieutenant-Colonel of Volunteers, but managed to 'escape' this appointment. Another cousin Charles Talbot was in the Oxfordshire Militia as was Evelyn Dormer, the younger half-brother of Charles Dormer who succeeded as the ninth Lord Dormer in 1804.

While Henry Stonor led his Bavarians into battle against the French – he was later to fight on the side of Napoleon, when Bavaria helped the French against Prussia – his brothers Thomas and John soldiered at home with the local Volunteer Horse. Two of Thomas Weld's younger sons, Humphrey and James, were commissioned in 1803 in the Dorset Yeomanry, which Thomas Weld himself and

Charles, sixth Lord Clifford of Chudleigh

Thomas his eldest son had helped to raise in 1794. But then the King had refused to sign their commissions, believing that to have done so would have been contrary to the oath against Popery which he had taken at his Coronation. So the elder Thomas had retired from the Yeomanry while Thomas the younger served for a time as a sergeant. The fact that the King was on friendly terms with the Welds and therefore knew they were Catholics was to their disadvantage; for in the ordinary way he would have signed the commissions without having any idea as to the religion of the gentlemen in question. In the case of James and Humphrey Weld, nine years later, the King had then barely recovered from one of his bouts of insanity so that their commissions were most probably signed not by him but by the Lord-Lieutenant of the county.

It was probably on account of being known to the King that Charles, the sixth Lord Clifford of Chudleigh failed to obtain a commission, though he served

Robert Clifford, by Mather Brown

throughout the war years as chairman of the committee for the internal defence of Devon and raised the Teignbridge Yeomanry and many Volunteer corps. He wore an unofficial uniform, half naval, half military, specially designed for him, which suited him well, for he looked very much the military man. Unlike his elder brother Hugh, Lord Clifford, whom he had succeeded in 1793, he enjoyed excellent health.

Lord Clifford's handsome and clever younger brother Robert, who had returned to England from Liége shortly before its capture by the French, had also failed to get a commission in the British army. But the British High Command was sensible enough to take advantage of his interest in military affairs and the first-hand knowledge of French tactics which he had acquired as an officer in the Dillon Regiment under Louis XVI, employing him unofficially for purposes of intelligence. Of particular value was his knowledge of cartography, a science of increasing military importance in which the French led Europe; he was able to make a series of up-to-date maps of Southern England. He also passed on information on French troop movements which he received from his friend the Prince-Bishop of Liége, now in exile.

The Peace of Amiens saw Robert Clifford back in Paris, where under cover of studying mineralogy he collected French maps which might be of use to the British when war broke out again as he was sure it would; his letters to his military friends were full of warnings of an invasion by Bonaparte. When in the spring of 1803 it became clear that war was imminent, he left for Calais, his three travelling companions and his baggage having gone ahead of him, but he only arrived there after war had been declared and after the Dover packet had already cast off. There was still time for him to board the packet by following it in a small boat but he then found he had lost the pass which had been issued to him by the local French Commissary. So he had to go back to the Commissary who fortunately believed his story and gave him a duplicate pass.

What happened next is told in his own words:

> Off I set, was in a boat to follow the packet, when my servant called me from the pier to say that the captain had refused to take my baggage on board. Then all was over, I had the provisions, the keys, part of the baggage with me and my companions gone.[17]

However, he now found his original pass – it had been all the time in his waistcoat pocket – and he took it back to the Commissary who was so impressed with his honesty that he gave him permission to sail in an English ship which had come to fetch the British Ambassador's horses. He was lucky in that almost immediately afterwards the French stopped all remaining British from leaving and had he been stopped he would have been in serious trouble for he had with him a large box of maps. Even if he had not been taken for a spy, he might have languished for several years as a civilian prisoner of Napoleon, like Sir Henry Tichborne and Sir John Throckmorton's brother Charles, both of whom were caught in France at this time. While Sir Henry Tichborne was in captivity, it seemed that Dame Mabella's curse was starting to take effect: the old Tichborne House partly collapsed and his trustees replaced it with a plain Regency house.

A report actually reached England that Robert Clifford and his companions had been hanged on gibbets in the fort at Calais for espionage. There was a debate about it in the House of Commons. Charles James Fox, having 'expatiated on the virtues of Bonaparte' said 'that the execution of the unfortunate gentlemen, the subject of the debate, ought in no shape to be attributed to a cruel or savage temper in the Chief

The new house at Tichborne

Consul, but to Necessity, State Necessity, the law of the wise and the good in every age'. Another member even more enamoured of Revolutionary France maintained that 'the Sovereignty of the People and its Majesty' had shown mercy in not having allowed the severed heads of Robert and his companions to be 'borne about the streets and their bodies mangled in a thousand pieces'.[18]

While the debate was going on, Robert was actually in London, having arrived safely just in time to go to a party at Lady Kenmare's. His companions were also safely back in England. Contrary to what was believed by Fox and his friends, Robert Clifford was no spy; the maps he had brought with him from France had not been obtained by any breach of faith, but purchased from Paris booksellers. He had simply made use of his talents and his contacts to help his country, as other noblemen did, receiving no pay for what he had done.

Of the help given by English Catholics to their country in the struggle against Revolutionary France, perhaps the most valuable was Sir John Acton's secret order for the provisioning of Nelson's fleet at Syracuse on its way eastwards before the Battle of the Nile. Acton was still King Ferdinand's right-hand man, 'killing himself with overwork', as Sir William Hamilton observed.[19] Together with

Nelson and Hamilton he had supervised the removal of the Court and treasury to Sicily when Naples was overtaken by revolution and then, after the defeat of the so-called Parthenopian Republic, he had worked with Nelson in meting out dire punishment to the revolutionaries. The unsatisfactory peace with France in 1801 made him plan to retire and he spoke of being 'on my way to Shropshire'[20]; but the King insisted that he should stay on. Even the newly-arrived French Ambassador recognized that he was the only man capable of administering the Kingdom but was later to complain to Bonaparte that 'in the Sicilian Cabinet Chevalier Acton' was 'only a member of the British Cabinet'.[21] Bonaparte himself, writing to the Queen – who to add to Acton's troubles was now estranged from him, as well as from the King – remarked sorrowfully, 'What must I think of the Kingdom of Naples when I see at the head of its entire administration a man who is alien to the country?'[22]

Though his troubles were increasing, Acton now at least had a wife to comfort him. In 1800 he had surprised the Court by marrying a daughter of his brother Joseph, who was a Neapolitan general having served in the French army before the Revolution. At the time of the marriage, Acton was sixty-four and his bride Marianne barely fourteen. It is said that when he came to propose to her, resplendent in Court uniform, she had to be coaxed from under the sofa with a box of chocolates, later she tried to run away dressed in boy's clothes. However, the marriage turned out successfully. Acton was an affectionate husband; Marianne bore him two sons and a daughter and proved equal to being the chatelaine of his palaces in Naples and Palermo.

At about the same time as Sir John Acton obtained a Papal dispensation to marry his niece, a Papal brief was sent to Maria Fitzherbert, informing her that her marriage to the Prince of Wales was valid in the eyes of the Church. The Prince, having fathered the infant Princess Charlotte, had left Caroline of Brunswick and wanted Maria to take him back, which she was only prepared to do if assured by Rome that she was his lawful wife. So a priest had travelled out from London to state her case and when an answer came that was favourable, she and the Prince had been reunited. On the day when she had first admitted him once again to her London house she had invited the whole of Society to a breakfast so that everybody could see them together. Years later, she was to admit to her cousin, the then Lord Stourton, that 'she hardly knew how she could summon resolution to pass that severe ordeal, but she thanked God she had the courage to do so'.[23]

She was also to tell Lord Stourton that 'the next eight years were . . . the happiest of her connection with the Prince. She used to say that they were extremely poor, but as merry as crickets'.[24] Their poverty did not prevent the Prince from enlarging the Brighton Pavilion and building a fine new house for Maria on the nearby Steyne. As

Marianne, Lady Acton at Palermo with her sons Richard and Charles (afterwards Cardinal Acton) and her daughter Elizabeth (afterwards Lady Throckmorton). By Robert Fagan

before, she insisted on having a separate establishment; but whether in London or in Brighton he made her house his home and used his own residences merely for entertaining, when she would sit as his wife and act as hostess for him. Maria also entertained for the Prince in her own houses. At one of her parties her sister Frances, wife of the Northumberland Catholic baronet Sir Carnaby Haggerston, dressed up as a milkmaid and having promised the Prince cream for his syllabub treated him to the sight of 'her neat ankle' beneath 'her tucked-up gown' as she sat down to milk what she thought was a cow but which turned out to be a bullock.[25]

As in the earlier years of her marriage, Maria tried hard to prevent the Prince from

drinking too much. This was not easy when he was with cronies such as the Duke of
Norfolk, who would come over to Brighton every year from Arundel Castle, which
he had restored in the fashionable Gothic style as his principal family seat. When the
Duke, who was known as 'Jockey' because of his adventures on the Turf and after
his ancestor 'Jockey of Norfolk' in Shakespeare's *Richard III*, was staying at the
Pavilion in 1805, the Prince, at Maria's bidding, pretended that he had urgent letters
which needed answering after dinner so as to avoid drinking with him.
Unfortunately he did this two nights running and Jockey took umbrage.

Such was Jockey's addiction to the bottle that he formed a special friendship with
a Cumberland neighbour for the reason that when they drank together, it was he
who first lost the use of his legs whereas the other gentleman first lost the use of his
tongue. So the other gentleman could get up and ring the bell for the servant and the
Duke, from his chair, could order more wine. As might be expected, given the
intermarriages of the Catholic families, Jockey was a connection of Maria's. His
mother was a Brockholes of Claughton in Lancashire whose nephew had married a
sister of Maria's second husband. In this way, Claughton had been inherited by
Maria's brother-in-law William Fitzherbert-Brockholes.

Despite his public renunciation of Catholicism, Jockey had kept in touch with
Catholics and was always ready to use his influence on their behalf. In his cups he
would claim to be still a Catholic at heart; which was harmless enough compared
with when, at the height of the war against Revolutionary France, he had staggered
to his feet at dinner and drunk to 'the majesty of the people', an indiscretion that had
cost him his Lord-Lieutenancy. It was one of the many contradictions of his nature
that while taking an immense pride in his ancestry he was in politics almost a
republican. He had named his farms at Greystoke in honour of the American
revolutionary leaders and their victories, rebuilding them in the Gothic taste which
he associated with the ancient liberties of England.

His enthusiasm for Gothic, which he used for his additions to Greystoke Castle
itself as well as at Arundel, sprang also from a genuine antiquarian interest. He was a
Fellow of the Society of Antiquaries and a generous patron of scholars, artists and
writers – on hearing that Shelley and his bride were living half-starved at Keswick,
he invited them to Greystoke for the rest of their honeymoon. All this made up for his
less attractive traits, his coarseness, his drunkenness, his aversion to soap and water.
He was once driving from London to Arundel with the wife of his cousin Henry
Howard – who like him, had conformed to Anglicanism – and her small son
Henry. When she mentioned that they were on the Hog's Back, the boy piped up
'That's why there's such a nasty smell', causing his mother to fear for their prospects
of inheriting Greystoke.[26]

'Jockey', eleventh Duke of Norfolk, in old age

The inner court of Arundel Castle, as remodelled by Jockey

Jockey was ahead of his time in buying back family heirlooms which had been dispersed; his example in this respect was to be followed by subsequent Dukes of Norfolk. There was, however, one historic inheritance which could not be recovered, namely the thirteenth century barony of Mowbray, premier barony in the Peerage of England, which had come to the Howards with the heiress of the Mowbray Dukes of Norfolk in the fifteenth century. On the death of the ninth Duke of Norfolk of the Howard line in 1777, the Mowbray barony had not gone with the dukedom to his second cousin, Jockey's father, but had fallen into abeyance between his great-nephew Charles Stourton, son of his elder niece, and his younger niece Lady Petre. The ninth Duke had endowed Charles's father the sixteenth Lord Stourton with lands in and around Leeds; so that having lived in Essex and elsewhere after uprooting themselves from Stourton in Wiltshire at the beginning of the eighteenth century, the Stourtons had finally come to rest in Yorkshire where, at about the time of Trafalgar, Charles bought Allerton Park which became the principal family seat. He built a simple chapel with a Georgian Gothic interior

Charles, seventeenth Lord Stourton

adjoining the pedimented house.

Charles, who had succeeded his father as the seventeenth Lord Stourton in 1781 and had been a member of the Catholic Committee, had other Yorkshire connections. His wife Mary was a daughter and heiress of the last Lord Langdale; he was himself a cousin of Philip Langdale of Houghton, the last of the untitled branch of the Langdales; and of a Yorkshire baronet who was the last of his line, Sir Thomas Vavasour of Hazlewood. The estates of these two families would eventually be inherited by two of Charles's younger sons.

While the Stourtons were recovering their former prosperity – even though Charles had lost £3,000 gambling – their erstwhile neighbours in Wiltshire, the

Arundells, were in financial difficulties. The eighth Lord Arundell of Wardour had overspent himself in building the new Wardour Castle with its magnificent chapel which he had since enlarged to the design of the brilliant young architect John Soane; by 1804 he was in trouble with his creditors and his effects at Wardour were being seized by the bailiffs. He and Lady Arundell were angry with their son-in-law Lord Clifford, who was one of the trustees.

Robert Clifford, having escaped from the French, had to act as go-between. Robert feared that Lord Arundell and his cousin and heir James Arundell – who was also his son-in-law – would 'pass for swindlers in the eyes of the world' if they went ahead with a scheme which he regarded as 'a mere juggle between him and Mr A not to pay the creditors'; he tried to persuade Lady Arundell 'to put a stop to these manoeuvres'.[27] The long-suffering Robert also tried to arrange for Lord Arundell to see a doctor, for he was no longer young and afflicted with gout and other maladies. Lord Arundell expressed his willingness to send for a doctor of Robert's recommendation and to pay the thirty-guinea fee; the doctor made arrangements for travelling down to Wardour and awaited his summons, but heard no more. 'His Lordship may find worms more inexorable than his creditors' Robert observed drily, 'Though he seems to wish to put them off in the same way.'[28]

To raise money, Lord Arundell was selling Chideock, an estate in west Dorset, to his friend Thomas Weld. The property was heavily encumbered and the negotiations dragged on for years. Robert Clifford considered that Thomas, who claimed to be acting in Lord Arundell's interest as well as his own, was not living up to his reputation for piety and generosity. He wrote in 1807:

Mr Weld may call himself a friend of either party of the Trust, but a more mortal enemy could not easily be found . . . To have saved £30,000 to a noble family in distress, on which the religion of some hundreds depends, would, I hope, without rash judgement, be more meritorious than saying the priest's breviary at four o'clock in the morning. But everybody has their own method of seeing things, as the Welshman said when he kissed his cow.[29]

Thomas Weld eventually acquired Chideock, which was destined for his son Humphrey. He planned to leave estates to each of his six surviving sons, except for John who was a priest. The younger Thomas would get Lulworth, James an estate in Oxfordshire, George part of the Stonyhurst estate and for Joseph, a keen yachtsman, he bought the estate of Pylewell on the Solent. His generosity to his sons was by no means limited to their future prospects; he made them handsome allowances, which encouraged some of them to be extravagant and bought them a

Courtfield

pack of hounds so that they could hunt one day and shoot the next.

Of Thomas's daughters, Juliana the Franciscan nun had died in 1800; Mary – always referred to by her father as 'my dear sweet Mary' when making payments to her[30] – was a nun at the Visitation convent at Shepton Mallet in Somerset where 'little Clare', Thomas Stonor's old flame, planned to go. Catherine, who was as pretty as Clare and known as the 'Dorset Rosebud', was married to the seventeenth Lord Stourton's eldest son Edward, whose sister Charlotte was married to her brother Joseph. Teresa was married to her second cousin William Vaughan of Courtfield in Monmouthshire, whose grandfather, one of the two Vaughan brothers exiled after the 'Forty-Five', had become a Spanish general. Courtfield, until recently let to a farmer, was now lived in by the family once again; William having rebuilt the house in a simple Classical style.

In 1809, when he was not yet sixty, Thomas Weld's health began to fail, perhaps his habit of getting up at four in the morning to say the Divine Office was too much for him. In the summer of 1810 he went to Stonyhurst to make a retreat, after which he and his sons joined the Community and the boys at dinner on the feast of St Ignatius, founder of the Jesuits. At the end of dinner, while he was entertaining the company by singing a comic song, he collapsed with a stroke, of which he died next day.

Lytham Hall

In spite of having borne him fifteen children, Mary Weld was to survive her husband by twenty years. She spent most of her widowhood at the Visitation convent at Shepton Mallet, where she had rooms for herself and her maid and her two daughters Mary and Clare who were nuns in the Community. She kept in touch with her other children by going on visits to them.

Mary Weld's roots were in Lancashire. Her father was Sir John Stanley-Massey-Stanley of Hooton, head of the Catholic senior branch of the family of the Earls of Derby; her mother was a Clifton of Lytham. The Cliftons were one of the richest of the Lancashire Catholic families. Mary's uncle Thomas Clifton had employed John Carr of York to rebuild Lytham Hall in grand style, with an Ionic façade of brick and stone and a magnificent staircase. Her cousin John Clifton, the next squire of Lytham, was a great patron of the Turf; his horse 'Fyldener' won the St Leger in 1806 in a record field; his jockeys, wearing the brown and yellow Clifton colours, were cheered on every racecourse.

Mary's nephew Sir Thomas Stanley-Massey-Stanley was married to the daughter of Maria Fitzherbert's sister, the would-be milkmaid Frances Haggerston. By the time of the Regency, the days were past when the Prince of Wales put up with

Frances's nonsense for Maria's sake. Since 1808 his relations with Maria had been poisoned by another woman, the clever and powerful Marchioness of Hertford. Lady Hertford had been brought on the scene to prevent Lord Hertford's orphaned niece Minney Seymour, whom Maria had adopted, being taken away from her on account of her Catholicism – though she was bringing up the child a Protestant – and her apparently irregular matrimonial status.

Thanks to Lady Hertford's influence, Maria was able to keep her adored Minney, but at the cost of her husband. Though she was no beauty, Lady Hertford managed to gain an ascendancy over the weak-minded Prince, playing on his fear that Maria's unpopularity as a Papist would affect his position as Regent, which he expected to become at any time now that the King was hopelessly insane. For Maria, the next couple of years were wretched, with the Prince still spending his mornings with her but ignoring her in public for the sake of Lady Hertford.

During those years, Maria was frequently on the point of ending what had become an impossible situation; but was dissuaded by members of the Royal Family. The final break came in the summer of 1811, six months after the Prince had assumed the Regency, when he invited her to a great dinner at Carlton House given in honour of the exiled Louis XVIII. Hitherto, on all occasions when he and she were together, it had been customary to arrange the seating without any regard to precedence, so as to enable her to be treated as the chief lady even though she had no official rank. But she heard that at the forthcoming dinner precedence was to be observed. When she asked the Prince about it, he said 'You know, Madam, you have no place'.

'None, Sir,' she replied with dignity, 'but such as you choose to give me'.[31]

She refused his invitation to the dinner and she never again opened her doors to him.

CHAPTER 5

'It is really become fashionable to be a Catholic'

MORE ambitious than Lord Stourton's chapel at Allerton was the chapel which Sir William Jerningham built at Cossey in 1809, joined to the house by a conservatory. It was designed by Sir William's youngest son, the popular and talented barrister Edward, who had the satisfaction of hearing it described by a stranger on the Bury coach – an old Anglican clergyman who had no idea who he was – as 'the precise model of King's College Chapel'.[1] Sadly Sir William, who had been ill for some time, died just before the dedication of his new chapel, which took place on the eve of his funeral.

Edward Jerningham the poet, who was staying at Cossey at the time of his brother's death, appeared 'very light and thoughtless', though he had 'burst into violent and loud weeping' at the sight of his sister-in-law Frances, who was herself suffering from gout, sitting by her husband's death bed. Charlotte Bedingfeld hoped her uncle Edward 'might be touched by the awfulness of the event and return to the ancient faith – but he did not'.[2] The old poet was incorrigibly frivolous. In one of his letters to her he described a dinner party which he had attended as 'an assembly of virgins', it having consisted entirely of maiden ladies and unmarried gentlemen like himself; together with their host's tom cat 'whom they assured me had never been out of the cloister'.[3]

In 1812 old Edward fell seriously ill and Charlotte became more than ever concerned about the state of his soul; as was her brother Edward who watched 'with anxiousness for some happy moment to mention the dreadful subject of religion'.[4] But the poet insisted that he found more mercy in Anglicanism than in Catholicism. 'My dear niece, if you ever write, do not touch this *ground*' he told Charlotte in his last letter to her, written a month before he died. 'There is no combatting with your side:

Cossey Hall with the new chapel. A sketch probably by Charlotte, Lady Bedingfeld

the Catholic comes with the axe of Infallibility, and instead of fighting with Lady Bedingfeld I am engaged with a female *tomahawk*.'[5]

While Edward the poet lay dying the younger Edward Jerningham was electioneering. Since the death in 1807 of their cousin, the illustrious old nun Lady Anastasia Stafford-Howard, the Jerninghams had been much concerned with what the elder Frances referred to as 'the grand affair of the *Title*' – the dormant barony of Stafford, the right to which had passed to Sir William and then on to his son Sir George. Whereas 'the Title' itself remained elusive – a reversal of the seventeenth century attainder being unlikely in the still predominantly anti-Catholic political climate of the time – the estates in Staffordshire and Shropshire which went with it had been inherited by Sir William, giving his family a Parliamentary 'interest' in the borough of Stafford. In the autumn of 1812 Edward tried to help Richard Brinsley Sheridan fight the seat. 'I am straining every nerve for him', he told Charlotte. 'I have declared open hostility against every tenant who holds, and against every man who expects to hold land, and who opposes Sheridan'.[6] But the ageing Sheridan arrived at Stafford too late to make an effective canvass and spent the election loitering at the inn.

Edward Jerningham was a born politician and an active member of the Catholic Board which had been formed in 1808 to work for full Catholic emancipation; a larger and more influential body than the Cisalpine Club, which still existed. As in the days of the old Catholic Committee, there was the question as to whether in return for emancipation the Catholics would offer the Government a veto on the appointment of bishops, which the Government particularly wanted now that Pope Pius VII was a prisoner in the hands of Napoleon. 'Government has only to signify that it is their wish that the King in future shall have the nomination of the Catholic bishops' Sir John Throckmorton, the chief survivor of the old Cisalpines – the ninth Lord Petre having died in 1801 – had stated optimistically in 1807,[7] an assertion that shocked the Irish Catholic bishops no less than Bishop John Milner, the Vicar Apostolic of the Midland District, who was their agent in England.

A pugnacious Lancastrian stalwart of middle-class origin, Milner was strongly opposed to aristocratic lay influence in Church affairs, while being himself a member of the Catholic Board and on friendly terms with some of the Catholic grandees such as the Welds and the Jerninghams. Matters came to a head in 1813 when an abortive Bill for Catholic relief was brought before Parliament; Milner regarded the Bill as obnoxious because it provided 'securities' with regard to the appointment of bishops. Thomas Stonor and Lord Clifford, who were both on the Catholic Board, invited Milner together with other members, including Lord Shrewsbury, Sir Richard Bedingfeld, Robert Clifford and Edward Jerningham, to a meeting which appeared to bring about a reconciliation. But Milner was soon denying this and accusing the Board of falsehoods. The Board retaliated by expelling him from its select committee on the resolution of George Silvertop, a coal-owning Northumberland squire whose late uncle Sir John Lawson had always stood out against the more extreme Cisalpines. 'Spare no false doctrine or profane novelty,' Milner wrote in the *Orthodox Journal* under a pseudonym, 'whether it is broached by a friend or a stranger, whether by a *Mr Silvertop* or a *Mr Copperbottom*'.[8]

Milner had to wield his own pen in his defence, unlike the bishops of 1791 who had an eloquent advocate in Francis Plowden. But when Milner was battling with the Board, Plowden had his own battles to fight; his polemics had landed him in a libel action, which resulted in damages against him of £5,000. To avoid paying, he eventually fled to France. His eldest son, a captain in the army, was also unfortunate, being killed in a duel in Jamaica where he was ADC to a general.

The number of Catholic army officers was very much on the increase. Wellington, who had known Catholic officers since his Indian days, when Jarrard Strickland of the Sizergh family was his ADC at the battle of Seringapatam, is said to have maintained that nearly half his officers in the Peninsula were Catholics.

Edward Jerningham of the Catholic Board

Though this was an exaggeration, the Catholics among them were quite numerous; they included Thomas Clifton of the Dragoons and his brother Edward of the Coldstream, sons of the sporting squire of Lytham and Major Thomas Ferrers, younger son of Edward Ferrers of Baddesley Clinton in Warwickshire and nephew of the three Ferrers nuns formerly at Bruges. There was also Lord Clifford's eldest son, Hugh, who served under Wellington as a 'Gentleman Volunteer'.

Among the military sons of the English Catholic families who were in Paris both before and after the Hundred Days, one came from the opposite direction. This was Colonel Henry von Stonor, who marched to Paris at the head of his Bavarian troops, Bavaria being now on the side of the victorious Allies. He entered the city ahead of his battalion with a corporal and ten men in order to protect his sister's convent against the marauding Russians. He found Mary looking well and happy, having managed to remain in Paris throughout the upheavals of the past twenty-five years.

Michael Tasburgh, the nephew of another valiant nun, Dame Elizabeth Anselma Anne, came to Paris at the end of 1814 with his young wife Maria. Michael, squire of Burghwallis in Yorkshire, was by birth Michael Anne; he had changed his name on marriage because Maria had inherited the estate of the Tasburghs, a Norfolk Catholic family. For both of them, a trip to France might have seemed rather like tempting Providence, for not only had his aunt Elizabeth died a prisoner of the French, but Maria and her father had been caught in France when hostilities were resumed after the Peace of Amiens and for several years had been interned in the fortress of Verdun. Eventually Maria was smuggled back to England in a coffin labelled as containing the body of a dead nun.

This macabre journey should have led to a brilliant future, for she was a niece by marriage and a god-daughter of Maria Fitzherbert, who wished to bring her out in Society; but unfortunately her incarcerated father did not know the true facts about Maria Fitzherbert's ménage and forbade the young Maria from having anything to do with her. So at the age of seventeen she had been married off to Michael Anne, who though descended in the direct male line from Sir William de Anne, Constable of Tickhill Castle in the time of Edward II, was not so great a catch; moreover he was fifteen years older than her and rather austere.

While they were in Paris, Michael took Maria to see the Catacombs. This was injudicious, for she was seven months pregnant and the expedition was tiring as well as harrowing. 'I was unaware of the extent or horribleness of these mansions of the dead' he wrote in his diary.[9] However, Maria suffered no ill-effects; doubtless inured to such horrors by her journey in the coffin. What was more serious, they were still in Paris when Napoleon returned from Elba; but they were more fortunate than Maria and her father had been in 1803 and managed to get out in time.

Edward Jerningham and Everard Arundell — son and heir of James, now the ninth Lord Arundell of Wardour — went to Calais with their respective wives to see Louis XVIII land. 'I do not much like this Calais expedition, as it is for *Edward* taking two violent emetics' his mother wrote. But although Edward was indeed 'very sick upon sea', he was 'well on landing and in great spirits' and could not resist 'running on to Paris for a fortnight'. He was, however, 'quite miserable' about the 'murderers and rogues' in the new French Senate.[10]

Thomas Weld the younger and his wife Lucy, a cousin of Lord Clifford, attended the fête given by the city of Paris in honour of the return of Louis XVIII; at whose request the Prince Regent was to make Lucy's brother Thomas Clifford a baronet – the first time an English Catholic had been made one since the seventeenth century. Thomas and Lucy Weld were a pleasant and pious couple; both good-looking, though she dressed badly and did not hold herself well. He was musical and artistic, as well as being a keen horseman. They were popular in Paris, where they stayed six months. Unfortunately, while they were there, Lucy went down with a very severe fever; the effects of which may have had something to do with her death less than a year later. 'Dear Lucy departed this life at about half past three in the evening, after receiving all the rites of the Church in the most edifying manner', her husband recorded on that sad day, a fortnight before Waterloo.[11]

The Last Rites of the Catholic Church were not apparently availed of by Jockey as he lay dying at Norfolk House in the following December; six months after giving a great dinner in his new Barons' Hall at Arundel to commemorate the six hundredth anniversary of Magna Carta. He was succeeded as twelfth Duke by his Catholic cousin Bernard Howard, known as Barney. The new Duke of Norfolk was a quiet and conscientious little man of nearly sixty with a touch of melancholy in his kindly eyes; he had not got over the misery of having been deserted by his wife, whose name was never mentioned in his presence.

Barney followed his predecessor's example in supporting the Whigs, who favoured the cause nearest to his heart, namely Catholic Emancipation. In attaining this great object, the Catholics could look to him as their undoubted leader; for as Premier Duke his standing in the country was far higher than that of the ninth Lord Petre in 1791. And while like Lord Petre he was a Cisalpine, he was too good a Catholic to antagonize the bishops. There was, however, one substantial fly in the Catholic ducal ointment: his only son the Earl of Surrey had a Protestant wife. She was Lady Charlotte Leveson-Gower, daughter of the rich and powerful Marquess of Stafford – whose title, incidentally, was quite different from that which the Jerninghams claimed – and of his even more powerful Marchioness. 'Old Mother Stafford . . . will make the young one turn Protestant', the lawyer Henry Brougham predicted.[12]

Whereas Jockey and those of his predecessors who had turned Protestant all had Catholic heirs, the 'young one' already had a son of his own, the infant Lord Fitzalan, who seemed likely to be brought up in the religion of 'Old Mother Stafford'. And the next heir was the Duke's Protestant brother, 'the naughty Henry', as Frances Jerningham called him, to whom Jockey had left Greystoke despite his son's tactlessness on the Hog's Back. In making this bequest, Jockey was in no way penalizing his Catholic successor, for Greystoke was traditionally the seat of a cadet branch of the Howards and Barney, before coming into the great Norfolk inheritance, already had two properties of his own, Glossop Hall in Derbyshire, the seat of his branch of the family, and Fornham Hall in Suffolk which he had bought. Even after he had inherited Arundel, Fornham continued to be his favourite residence and he carried out various improvements there.

The Chinese pagoda at
Alton

The monument at Alton,
based on the Choragic
Monument of Lysicrates,
with a bust of the fifteenth
Earl of Shrewsbury

The Duke's architect at Fornham was Robert Abraham who on his
recommendation worked for other Catholics, notably for the fifteenth Earl of
Shrewsbury. Having in his younger days spent so much money on Heythrop, Lord
Shrewsbury, now in his sixties, his long and distinguished face topped with a
reddish-brown wig, had transferred his attentions to Alton, his estate in the wild
hilly country of north Staffordshire. He had fallen under the spell of the Romantic
Movement and so had his wife, who came from outside the world of the Talbots.

She was Elizabeth, daughter of James Hoey, a Dublin printer; he had married her in Bordeaux in 1792 just as she was about to take the veil.

By 1815 the old Alton Lodge had been transformed into Alton Abbey. Heythrop was being stripped of its contents to furnish it; all the wine out of the cellar was sent to Staffordshire, even the glass from the conservatory. The latter was destined for one of the conservatories being built at Alton, where Lord and Lady Shrewsbury were turning the valley below the house into a vast landscape garden replete with follies, which were eventually to include a Gothic temple, a Chinese pagoda and a thatched cottage inhabited by a blind Welsh harper. Lord Shrewsbury's nephew George Turville, when he came to stay at Alton, was not impressed; though this may have been due to the fact that his uncle only allowed him to shoot over a part of the estate which was heavily poached.

Lord Shrewsbury had an unmarried sister who was ugly but cheerful. She lived in Bath, as did old Mrs Edward Ferrers of Baddesley Clinton and her two unmarried daughters, the sensible Hester and the mentally-defective Frances. Another daughter, Elizabeth, was married to the brother and heir of the Lancashire baronet Sir William Gerard; another, Anne, to Lucy Weld's brother Henry Clifford. Mrs Ferrers was soon to suffer a tragedy when her younger son Major Thomas Ferrers, who had served all through the Peninsular War, fell to his death from the ramparts of Cambrai. She had already lost her elder son; Baddesley Clinton now belonged to her grandson Edward who, like Lord Surrey, had recently married the daughter of a Protestant marquess. But the girl's father, Lord Townshend, was nothing like as rich as Old Mother Stafford's husband; which was perhaps a pity, for the Ferrers were not well off.

Other Catholics living in Bath around the time of Waterloo included the Bedingfelds. Sir Richard and the delectable Charlotte and their family had come here a few years before, having let Oxburgh; with four sons and four daughters to educate – even though Charlotte had taught them herself when they were young – it had been necessary to retrench. While they were in Bath their eldest daughter Frances, known to her family as Fanchon, was married to the young eleventh Lord Petre. Fanchon became the chatelaine of Thorndon but though her marriage was outwardly brilliant, it did not bring her much happiness. Her husband was inclined to be difficult and suffered from a 'periodical disorder' so that she had to spend her time nursing him. Soon after Fanchon's wedding the Bedingfelds went to live abroad, having found Bath too expensive; they made for the Low Countries, which Charlotte had known as a girl.

While Richard Bedingfeld was living sedately with his family in Ghent, his cousin Charles Waterton was exploring the jungles of Guiana. Having first

Fanchon Bedingfeld, who married the eleventh Lord
Petre

travelled out to that part of the world in 1804 at the age of twenty-two to look after
plantations in Demerara belonging to his two uncles Charles and Christopher
Waterton, he returned there several times and undertook long and hazardous
journeys into the interior, spurred on by his passion for natural history. Among other
adventures, he found himself struggling to keep afloat in the Orinoco river while
holding on to a venomous snake which he had ambitions to stuff; and he rode on the
back of a ten-foot cayman which he likewise planned to stuff for his collection.
'Should it be asked how I managed to keep my seat,' he wrote, 'I would answer, I
hunted some years with Lord Darlington's foxhounds.'[13]

He became an accomplished taxidermist and claimed to have invented a new
method of preservation which kept the true colours of tropical birds. To demonstrate
his skill, he moulded a monkey's skin into a semi-human creature of his own
invention which he called 'The Nondescript'. He included a picture of it in his
Wanderings in South America as a joke on the British public; but the joke rebounded

on him, affecting his reputation as a naturalist. Some accused him of having killed and stuffed an Indian; while a Yorkshire baronet on seeing the picture remarked, 'Dear me, what a very extraordinary-looking man Mr Waterton must be.'[14]

While he brought back 200 specimens of birds from one trip alone, he felt sorry about killing them; writing of how a bird which he had shot 'left his little life in the air, destined to become a specimen, mute and motionless, for the inspection of the curious in a far-off land'.[15] This was no mere sentiment, for his love of birds and other wildlife was such that he turned his park at Walton into one of England's first bird sanctuaries.

In between his South American wanderings, Waterton spent part of 1817 and 1818 in Rome. Happening to meet an old schoolfellow who, like him, had been keen on tree-climbing, the two of them shinned up the façade of St Peter's and left

The Bedingfeld family *en voyage*. A sketch by Charlotte, Lady Bedingfeld

Charles Waterton riding a live cayman

their gloves on the lightning conductor. Pope Pius VII was not amused.

Among the more decorous English visitors to Rome in 1817 was Waterton's fellow-Yorkshireman Stephen Tempest who was touring Italy with his wife Elizabeth and their three eldest children. They had their own coach and horses with them and were away two years, collecting pictures and objects to take back to Broughton which they had enlarged in 1810 by adding Ionic wings to the original block. The house now had rooms in perfect Regency taste with furniture by Richard and Robert Gillow, the famous Lancaster cabinet-makers who were themselves Catholics of good family. They could afford to pay for all this, since Elizabeth's father Henry Blundell had left her and her sister Kitty Stonor £3,000 a year each when he died in 1810. Their brother Charles had roused himself from his lethargy to contest the will, but had been unsuccessful.

While the Tempests were in Italy, they heard that the tenants at Broughton were dissatisfied at their being away so long. Times were bad on account of the agricultural depression following the end of the Napoleonic Wars and the people knew they would receive more help from the Squire if he were at home. The slump was to affect even the wealthy Thomas Weld; though in 1817 his lawyer assured him that he need not worry about money. Thomas was then making arrangements to let Lulworth, not for reasons of economy but because he had decided, soon after Lucy's

'The Nondescript'

death, to become a priest. He left for Paris in the autumn of that year to begin his theological studies, knowing that his only child, the black-eyed Mary Lucy, was happily settled; for she was about to marry her cousin Hugh Clifford, the son and heir of the sixth Lord Clifford of Chudleigh.

At about the same time as Thomas Weld started at Abbé Carron's establishment, another Thomas, the elder son of Thomas and Kitty Stonor, started at Paris University. In a letter to his father, the young man mentions dining with the Welds and the Cliffords and also with the Dormers – presumably with the bachelor Charles, now the ninth Lord Dormer, who spent a great deal of time in Paris. His enjoyment of these and other dinner parties was hampered by what he called the 'unnecessary regulation' of the seminary where he was boarding which obliged him to be in at half past nine.[16]

Young Thomas's days were filled with lectures and sightseeing and with lessons in the piano and the flute. Once or twice a week he visited his aunt Mary at her convent and he also found time to go riding. If he 'happened' to run into a hunt, so much the better; in 1818 he had a long run with the Duke of Wellington who was out with the two nephews of Louis XVIII, the Duc d'Angoulême and the Duc de Berry; the beautiful Duchesse de Berry following in her carriage.[17]

While Wellington and young Stonor were chasing the stag, Byron was writing *Don Juan*, in which there appears Aurora Raby, the beautiful Catholic girl staying in a fashionable country house party.

> Aurora Raby, a young star who shone
>   O'er life, too sweet an image for such glass
> A lovely being, scarcely form'd or moulded,
> A rose with all its sweetest leaves yet folded;
> She was a Catholic too, sincere, austere,
>   As far as her own gentle heart allow'd,
> And deemed that fallen worship far more dear
>   Perhaps because 't was fallen: her sires were proud
> Of deeds and days when they had fill'd the ear
>   Of nations, and had never bent or bow'd
> To novel power; and as she was the last,
> She held their old faith and their feelings fast.

The fact that Cecily Nevill, mother of Edward IV and Richard III, was known as the Rose of Raby, could be a clue to Aurora's identity, if indeed she is based on a real person. In Leicestershire, the next county to Byron's own county of Nottinghamshire, there was an ancient Catholic family of Nevill: the Nevills of Nevill Holt, neighbours of Francis Fortescue Turville at Bosworth. Cosmas and Maria Nevill had three daughters, Maria, Anne and Christina, who were the same age as Byron and likely to have attracted him being partly Italian.

Since inheriting Nevill Holt in 1767, Cosmas Nevill had made many alterations to the rambling medieval house; putting in sash windows, giving the great hall a coved ceiling painted with the Battle of the Giants and the state bedroom a ceiling of Adamesque plasterwork. He was a man of culture, like so many of the Catholics a Fellow of the Society of Antiquaries. He was also very pious, having originally intended to be a Jesuit like his brother Charles. His wife Maria came from outside the Catholic world; her brother was a popular Anglican preacher in Bath. But she was a convert and as pious a Catholic as her husband.

Unlike so many of the Catholic families, such as the Howards, Talbots, Cliffords and Ferrers, who boasted of an unbroken male descent from great medieval nobles, the descent of the Nevills from the historic medieval house of that name had passed twice through the female line. The second time was in the eighteenth century when Cosmas's grandmother Mary Nevill, the heiress of Nevill Holt, married the London bullion-broker Cosmas, Count Migliorucci, and their son took the surname of Nevill. The changing of patronymics to revive surnames traditionally associated with particular estates was a practice by no means peculiar to Catholics, though it happened to be prevalent among the Catholic families in the early and middle years of the nineteenth century when two of the younger sons of the seventeenth Lord Stourton changed their names from Stourton to Vavasour and Langdale respectively; while William Wright took the name of his maternal grandfather Sir John Lawson on inheriting the Lawson estates. In 1821 Lucy Weld's brother Sir Thomas Clifford took the name of Constable having inherited Burton Constable from his bachelor cousin Francis, who had himself changed his name to Constable from Sheldon. Francis and his elder brother Edward had inherited Burton Constable from their maternal uncle William Constable, the collector, whose father had changed *his* name to Constable from Tunstall, a Tunstall having married the original Constable heiress.

At the beginning of 1821 Michael Tasburgh, who had changed his surname from Anne to Tasburgh on his marriage, set out with his wife Maria and their four children in the family coach from the Yorkshire seat of the Annes, the many-gabled Burghwallis Hall. Their destination was Paris, where they proposed staying several years. This time there were no wars, but Providence was not entirely kind to them. They were to lose a younger son, born during their French sojourn, and soon after their arrival their youngest daughter Barbara – whose birth during the Hundred Days could so easily have likewise occurred in France – nearly died of a fever. It was attributed to the diet of cold meat and salad, hard boiled eggs and gruyère cheese, which was inflicted on the girls by their mother to accustom them to convent school fare.

The girls were sent to Mary Stonor's convent. Mary was now its Prioress, tall and severe with failing eyesight; according to Barbara she made her abstain contrary to doctor's orders, 'saying that her own soul would be imperilled if any child under her charge failed to observe an abstinence enjoined by the Church'.[18] Though the school was now predominantly French, there were a few English girls there as well as the Tasburghs; one of them was Mary Tasburgh's best friend Louisa Riddell from Northumberland. She died and the nuns gave her a solemn requiem which was too much for the thirteen-year-old Mary who was carried out swooning.

A happier episode was when the Tasburghs were all presented to Charles X after his accession. 'My heart beat fast for fear I should make a wrong reply if I were good-naturedly spoken to' Barbara, who was eleven at the time, afterwards recalled.[19] This was not the family's only encounter with French royalty; Michael and Maria used to go to Chantilly for the St Hubert festival as guests of the Duc de Bourbon, father of the ill-fated Duc d'Enghien. Their royal host was grateful for the hospitality given to his sister, a Benedictine nun, at the Tasburgh house in Norfolk when she was an *émigrée*.

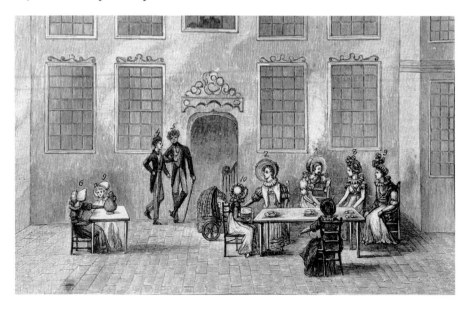

A tea party in Ghent in 1820. A sketch by the young Matilda Bedingfeld, who sits at the left-hand end of the larger table with her mother, Charlotte, Lady Bedingfeld, three places away from her. Next to Matilda sits the Duchess of Clarence, the future Queen Adelaide, whose sister, the Duchess of Saxe-Weimar, and their mother, the Duchess of Saxe-Meiningen, are on either side of Charlotte

The Bedingfelds and Jerninghams were also consorting with royalty, at home as well as abroad. Charlotte Bedingfeld made friends in Ghent with Princess Adelaide of Saxe-Meiningen, soon to be married to the Duke of Clarence, the future William IV, whose younger brother the Duke of Sussex, the most pro-Catholic of the Royal Dukes, was friendly with Charlotte's brother and sister-in-law Sir George and Frances Jerningham and also with Edward Jerningham. In August 1819 he paid a visit to Cossey, where he admired the portrait of Mary Tudor in the library and was 'delighted' with the chapel where the organist played God Save the King as he entered.

God Save the King again pealed out in the chapel two years later when his cousin and brother-in-law the Duke of Gloucester came to stay. The Jerninghams' twenty-one-year-old daughter Charlotte had to act as hostess on this occasion, for her mother was laid up with a severe cold; according to her cousin Henry Bedingfeld, who was one of the party, she 'looked vastly handsome at the top of the table'. Henry, the eldest son of Richard and Charlotte Bedingfeld, was himself a very handsome young man and, according to his uncle Sir George, 'perfectly at his ease' with the Duke. The Duke, who was known as Silly Billy, did not greatly impress young Henry, who thought him 'rather foolish and prosing'.[20]

While Henry Bedingfeld was helping to entertain the Duke of Gloucester, his younger brother Edward, a midshipman in the Navy and known in the family as the Little Seaman, was in HMS *Phaeton* escorting George IV back from a visit to Hanover. After the new King's accession in the previous year, Edward Jerningham had organized a petition for full Catholic emancipation signed by 20,000 Catholics and presented by the Duke of Norfolk. It was somewhat overshadowed by Queen Caroline's unexpected return from the Continent and her subsequent trial, during which she made her celebrated remark that the only time she had ever committed adultery was with the husband of Mrs Fitzherbert. The elder Frances Jerningham was in London during the riots in support of the Queen, when the mob threatened to break every window that was not illuminated in her honour. Frances, however, did not illuminate her windows and they were not broken. The Catholic peers were more fortunate than the Queen at the King's Coronation, for they were allowed to be present in the Abbey. 'Who is it that overtops the Barons as they march? The Catholic Lord Clifford', George Canning said of the ceremony.

A month after the Coronation, the younger Frances Jerningham went to stay with the Petres at Thorndon. She found Lady Petre – her husband's niece Fanchon – 'as usual *most* delightful'; but Lord Petre appeared to be 'not in good humour' with her, for he had allowed her only one candle on her dressing-table. When her maid asked for more, she was informed, 'My Lord only allows *one*.' Frances 'took care to burn it down to the socket', as she told her sister-in-law Charlotte Bedingfeld, Fanchon's mother.[21]

Poor Fanchon died a few months later giving birth to a daughter who was her fourth child; she already had two sons and an elder daughter. 'Poor dear William's state of mind it is impossible to express', Lord Petre's mother wrote to Charlotte Bedingfeld; however, he was to marry again after little more than a year. His maternal uncle the Duke of Norfolk was more constant; his divorced wife had died in 1819 but he was showing no sign of remarrying. When he heard of her death 'he shed tears and was very melancholy'.[22]

In 1822 Edward Jerningham was involved with Canning's unsuccessful Bill to allow Catholic peers to sit and vote once again in the House of Lords. This was Edward's last effort for Catholic emancipation, for within a month he had succumbed to a disease which also proved fatal to his wife. Soon afterwards Bishop Milner was at Cossey and as he stood in the chapel above the spot where Edward lay, he exclaimed, 'Ah, poor Edward! If I thought, Sir, that his spirit hovered above this vault, I would get up at midnight to commune with it.' With his mind full of such thoughts, the good Bishop set off, having been given a plentiful supply of cold roast beef by the Jerninghams' housekeeper to sustain him on the road.[23]

Edward Jerningham's death was followed a year later by the marriage of his niece Charlotte, daughter of Sir George and the younger Frances. A raven-haired beauty of singularly sweet disposition, with legs and feet so perfect she would occasionally raise her skirts to display them, Charlotte had found a suitor from outside the English Catholic cousinhood, the young Highland chief Thomas Fraser of Lovat and Strichen, who would have been Lord Lovat but for the attainder of his kinsman Lord Lovat of the 'Forty-Five'. Fraser's immediate forebears had been Presbyterian but his father, encouraged by the local Presbyterian minister, had married the daughter of a distinguished Scottish Catholic family, the Leslies of Balquhain in Aberdeenshire. He had died soon after his son was born and the minister had helped his widow to bring up the child a Catholic.

The wedding at Cossey was a great event. The village was adorned with flower-decked triumphal arches; the bridal party drove in a procession of ten carriages from the chapel, where the Catholic ceremony took place, to the parish church where the Bishop of Norwich performed the still-obligatory Protestant ceremony. After the wedding breakfast the bride and bridegroom set off in their travelling chariot for Inverness-shire. For Charlotte and her family, it was as if she were going away to a strange and distant land; she took comfort in the thought that the marriage settlement stipulated that she should be allowed to visit her old home at least every other year. A local poet bade her farewell in eight stanzas:

> Oh, weep for the pride of the valley! She's flown
> To glad with her smiles the far mountains and towers:
> Lovely groves! Her lost beauties, once crowning thine own,
> Now bereave thy sweet wreath of the best of its flowers.[24]

Writing to Charlotte Bedingfeld, who had come over from Ghent for the wedding, the bride's mother gave her news of the happy couple. They had arrived in Edinburgh after travelling 124 miles in one day; but young Charlotte had not been too tired to walk to Mass next morning, for it was Sunday. 'A sermon before the Mass in broad Scotch, *on the different kinds of love* ... next Sunday the sermon will be in Gaelic; how very odd.'[25]

When Charlotte Bedingfeld was in London before the wedding, she was visited by her son Edward, the Little Seaman. It turned out to be their last meeting, for three months later he fell overboard from the deck of his ship during the night and was

'Barney', twelfth Duke of Norfolk

never seen again. Of the other two younger sons of Sir Richard and Charlotte, Felix became a lawyer and Charles followed his uncle William Jerningham into the Austrian army – a rather surprising choice for a young English Catholic in the eighteen-twenties.

'It is really become fashionable to be a Catholic', the elder Frances Jerningham had remarked in 1819;[26] and as a sign of this, 'the grand affair of the Title' was happily settled at last in June 1824, only just in time as far as she was concerned for she was to die a few months later. The attainder was reversed and Sir George Jerningham became the eighth Lord Stafford. It had been by no means plain sailing, for the title had recently been claimed by an impostor named Stafford Cooke who had started legal proceedings to eject Sir George from the estates which went with it; he had actually tried to take formal possession of the Staffordshire estate. Even after Cooke's case had been dismissed and when he and his brother were awaiting trial for conspiracy, the two of them were bold enough to appear at a Levee at which Sir

Sir Charles Throckmorton, seventh Baronet

George happened to be present. The pair of impostors beat a hasty retreat, but had the last word by getting the flunkeys to bawl out, 'Lord Stafford's carriage!'[27] It was doubtless to celebrate his elevation to the peerage that the real Lord Stafford embarked on vast red-brick Tudor-Gothic additions to Cossey; he employed Chessell Buckler as his architect though the design was largely influenced by Lady Stafford, as the younger Frances Jerningham now was.

Sir George's success over the Stafford peerage was followed a week later by another step along the road to Catholic emancipation. As a Catholic, the Duke of Norfolk was unable to exercise his hereditary office of Earl Marshal; his Anglican brother, Henry of Greystoke, had acted as Deputy Earl Marshal since his accession. On Naughty Henry's death in June 1824 a private member's Bill was introduced in the Lords to enable the Duke himself to officiate in future as Earl Marshal regardless of his religion; it was passed, despite the furious opposition of the King's brother, the Duke of York.

In 1825 yet another Bill for Catholic relief was introduced in the Lords and was defeated. Among the peers who voted against it was Charles Dormer's younger half-brother Evelyn, now the tenth Lord Dormer. He had turned Anglican and taken his seat in the Lords in 1823, four years after succeeding to the title; his defection put an end to the chaplaincy at Peterley, his Buckinghamshire seat, which had been maintained even though the family had long ceased to reside there. Like the Stourtons, the Dormers had been somewhat peripatetic during the eighteenth century, deserting Peterley for Idsworth in Hampshire which was sold in 1789. Then the eighth Lord Dormer, father of Charles and Evelyn, had settled at Grove Park near Warwick, which like Peterley and Idsworth had been in the family for many generations.

Evelyn Lord Dormer died in 1826 and was succeeded by a Catholic kinsman. His death came soon after that of another Warwickshire landowner, Sir George Throckmorton, younger brother and heir of Sir John of the Catholic Committee. Sir George, like Sir John, had no children and was succeeded by a third childless brother Charles, the one-time prisoner of Napoleon, now a widower of nearly seventy. Like other Catholic younger sons in the days before the 1791 Relief Act he had chosen medicine as a career.

The ancient Warwickshire seat of the Throckmortons, Coughton Court, with its priests' hiding places and its tall early-Tudor gatehouse tower, had for many years been neglected by the family in favour of Buckland in Berkshire, though Sir Charles's grandfather old Sir Robert had modernized it in Georgian Gothic and Sir John had opened up the courtyard and made a new chapel. Sir Charles now decided to make his home at Coughton and handed over Buckland to his nephew and heir. He came here from Buckland in the early summer of 1827, accompanied by a housekeeper, a cook, an under-butler, a laundry-maid, an under-housemaid and a kitchen-maid. A mile from the town of Alcester he was met by most of his tenants and many of the local tradesmen, all on horseback and wearing white scarves and sprays of laurel. They escorted him to Coughton and when they reached the manor boundary they 'hurra'd' and took the horse from his carriage and pulled it up to the house. Over the first gate was inscribed 'May happiness enter with you'; a little further on was a flowery arch with the legend, 'Proceed and prosper'. Over the gatehouse tower flew a banner with 'Long live Sir Charles'.[28]

Sir Charles's nearest neighbour in Warwickshire, when he was at home, was Lord Hertford, son of the Lady Hertford who broke up Maria Fitzherbert's marriage. In 1825 Lord Hertford's young cousin Minney Seymour, Maria's adopted daughter, had married the younger son of an Irish earl; he was handsome and well-connected and like her a Protestant, but Maria considered him not good enough for her beautiful Minney. In 1828 her other adopted daughter, the Catholic Marianne

Marianne Smythe, who married Edward
Jerningham, second son of Sir George Jerningham,
eighth Lord Stafford

Smythe, married the Staffords' second son Edward Jerningham, a good-looking
subaltern in the 6th Dragoon Guards. Maria was as pleased with this marriage as she
had been displeased with Minney's. 'Everything we could wish for or desire except
for that odious commodity money', she wrote.[29]

Since Edward was one of eleven, money was certainly short; Maria proposed
giving Marianne £20,000 but would not consent to the marriage unless the Staffords
gave Edward more than his younger son's portion of £5,000. The Staffords agreed
to come up with more which might suggest that they believed, as some did, that the
mysterious Marianne, who was supposed to be the natural daughter of Maria's
brother Jack Smythe, was in fact Maria's own child by the King. As further

The Catholic Emancipation Act of 1829 receives the Royal Assent. The twelfth Duke of Norfolk can be seen in his robes to the right of the throne. To the left of the throne are members of the Clifford and Arundell families, invited by the Duke of Wellington to witness the occasion

evidence of this belief, Maria referred to Edward as 'my son-in-law' but never spoke thus of Minney's husband, even after she had become entirely reconciled to him.[30]

At seventy-two, Maria kept her youthful radiance, lavishing her affection on her adopted daughters and also on her pretty and lively young nieces Louisa and Georgina Smythe. Louisa and Georgina – known as Cou – were the daughters of Maria's brother Wat Smythe and his Protestant wife; they had been brought up as Protestants and Maria seems to have made no attempt to alter this state of affairs. The two girls may sometimes have gone with their Aunt Fitz to Mass, because Cou was to remark, after attending Morning Service at Salisbury Cathedral, 'I was enchanted with it, so like a Catholic service'.[31]

Maria's family, adoptive or otherwise, had become her chief concern. Yet she still received the fashionable world at her houses in London and Brighton, where, now that the King and his friend Lady Conyngham had more or less deserted the Pavilion, she was the undoubted queen. People treated her like royalty, called her 'Ma'am' and stood longer in her presence than in the presence of anybody else. In January 1829 she gave a fancy dress ball which was described by a newspaper as 'the most splendid party . . . probably ever seen in Brighton'. There were more than two hundred present, 'including all the Fashionables now residing in the town'. Maria, who 'looked in excellent health and spirits', wore 'a rich dress of white satin'. Minney and Marianne both wore black, one with 'a head-dress of diamonds', the other with a richly ornamented stomacher'. Louisa Smythe wore a Turkish dress, Cou 'a simple white fancy dress with a veil confined with a chaplet of white roses'.[32]

While Maria Fitzherbert was enjoying herself, her royal husband, now bloated and ill, was having hysterics at the prospect of giving his assent to Catholic emancipation, which he regarded as an infringement of his Coronation oath. But the Government – not the Duke of Norfolk's Whig friends, but a Tory Government led by Lord Clifford's friend the Duke of Wellington – was determined to bring in full Catholic emancipation at last. The Bill was passed by Parliament and on 13 April 1829 the King reluctantly gave it his assent. All the remaining disabilities, with some few exceptions, were swept away. On 28 April the Duke of Norfolk, Lord Clifford and the new Lord Dormer took their seats in the House of Lords; they were joined on 1 May by the eighteenth Lord Stourton, son-in-law of Thomas Weld the elder, by Lord Stafford and by poor Fanchon Bedingfeld's husband, Lord Petre. Someone who saw the Catholic peers walking together in the House of Lords a few months later, with the tall, erect, venerable figure of Lord Clifford and his equally tall and handsome nephew by marriage the tenth Lord Arundell of Wardour among them, said, 'What a pity we have so long excluded from our deliberations such a fine-looking set of men!'[33]

CHAPTER 6

Red hats and coronets

EVERARD, tenth Lord Arundell of Wardour, was an Arundell on both sides; his father, whom he had succeeded in 1817, was the cousin and heir of the eighth Lord Arundell, his mother was the eighth Lord Arundell's daughter. At the time of Emancipation, he was in his early forties. Tall and handsome in a Byronic way, he was scholarly and pious, though not as pious as his good-looking and accomplished wife Mary, the convert daughter of a great magnate, the Marquess of Buckingham. Mary Arundell had become a Catholic a couple of years before the death of her mother, who had herself converted as a young woman. Lord Buckingham had at first insisted on his wife's Catholicism being kept secret and had only allowed her to see a priest once a year. Later the exiled Comte d'Artois, the future Charles X, had come to stay at Stowe, the Buckingham seat, and with the house full of French court chaplains Lady Buckingham had been able to attend daily Mass in her own home.

From a worldly point of view, Mary Arundell could have made a better marriage; for as a girl she had been much sought after. The Arundells were chronically poor; the sales of land begun by the eighth Lord Arundell had been continued by Everard's father, so that the family income was greatly reduced. At the time of Emancipation, Wardour was closed up and Everard and Mary were living in Rome to economize. Apart from its material shortcomings, the marriage had proved childless and Everard was not the easiest of husbands. He was moody and continually changing his mind; while they were in Rome he alternated between staying there for ever and returning immediately to England. 'He refused to buy more of a wine that was offered him because he could not drink it all this winter and could not take it to England if he went in the spring', Mary told her sister-in-law. 'In a week after he was buying a house here, and a week after that altering Wardour.' She had learnt to pay no heed to what he said, attributing it to 'his state of biliousness' at

Everard, tenth Lord Arundell of Wardour and Lady Mary Grenville, his wife

the particular time. 'If he was to tell me he wished to hang himself and was going to do it, I would give him a rope and dance a rigadoon . . . knowing he meant no such thing, but would alter his tone the next moment.'[1]

Everard's health and spirits were affected by money worries and also by the prospect of Parliamentary Reform, which as a High Tory he dreaded; one reason for his remaining abroad was to escape the Reform Bill troubles. He and Mary both liked Rome; the Pope, Leo XII, was kind to them. They received 'a magnificent present of game' from him and shared it with their clerical friends as being 'the properest persons to eat Papal game'. The Arundells entertained ecclesiastics from Ireland as well as from England at their 'clerical Sunday dinners' and once a week the Rector of the English College, Dr Wiseman, brought twenty of his students to 'a merry luncheon' and to practise singing motets in Mary's drawing room.[2]

Mary gave 'Sunday soirées' at which Cardinals and the Roman nobility mingled with German princelings, ambassadors and ambassadresses and visiting English. Chief among the English Catholics then in Rome were the new Earl and Countess of Shrewsbury, who lived in style in the Palazzo Colonna. 'Good humoured dear Lord Shrewsbury', as Mary Arundell called him, had succeeded his uncle as the

John, sixteenth Earl of Shrewsbury and Maria, his wife

sixteenth Earl in 1827. He rather allowed himself to be ruled by his wife, who was Irish like the previous Lady Shrewsbury but better born; in fact she came of a distant Irish branch of the Talbots. For all that, she was, according to Mary Arundell, surprisingly vulgar; overfond of 'diamonds and going out and great dinners and driving with her four horses in the Pincio instead of enjoying the beauties of Rome'. She 'talked of her riches and estates and of all the Kings and Queens she knew, describing the dull formality of a German court *as so delightful* and so superior to the rude manners of an English country house.'[3]

What Mary found particularly annoying about Lady Shrewsbury was that, though a good Catholic herself, she had 'no *esprit de corps* . . . no wish to patronize Popery, will not visit half the Papists here because they are not fine enough, throws away all her dinners and balls on heretics'. To please the 'heretic' Lady Westmorland, she gave a ball on New Year's Day, although in Rome it was not done to dance before Epiphany. Everard spoke about it to Lord Shrewsbury, who agreed with him but could not stop his wife from having her way. As might have been expected, the ball was a flop; the Romans would not enter the ballroom, but 'sat in state' in another room; the English Catholics also refused to take the floor.[4]

Adela Petre

Although the Talbots of the previous generation were now all dead, Lord Shrewsbury's uncle by marriage Francis Fortescue Turville was still alive, a fine old gentleman of nearly eighty wearing the silk coats of an earlier age and with the courtly manners of the *ancien régime* acquired during his years in France before the Revolution. He would sit in the breakfast room in the new block which he had added to Bosworth forever taking snuff – getting through handkerchiefs at such a rate that he kept more than three hundred of them in a drawer in his room – and reading medical books which made him imagine he had gout. He attended Divine Office as well as daily Mass in the chapel in the old Tudor part of the house; his responses to the prayers were sonorous and portentous.

His grandchildren were relegated to this part of the house, as far away as possible from his own quarters in the new block. Here they could explore the garrets, where there was a priests' hiding place, and they would lie awake at night listening to the squeakings and scratchings of the rats behind the wainscot. On Sundays, from their nursery window, they would greet the people coming to Mass.

Francis Fortescue Turville's second son Charles, who was to die through falling between the train and the platform at Rugby station, achieved distinction as a lawyer and was for many years secretary of the Cisalpine Club. The club was dissolved in 1830, not long after Lord Stourton's brother Charles Langdale had proposed Daniel O'Connell as a member, in recognition of all he had done for Catholic emancipation; his seconder was Thomas Stonor. But he was blackballed, a sign of the growing estrangement between the Catholic worlds of England and Ireland.

Charles Langdale and Thomas Stonor's son, the younger Thomas, were among the first Catholic members of the House of Commons after Emancipation; the very first being, as was fitting, the Duke of Norfolk's son Lord Surrey who was still a Catholic despite the fears expressed at the time of his marriage to the Protestant Lady Charlotte Leveson-Gower. Others included Lord Petre's half-uncle Robert Petre as well as Philip Howard, son of Henry Howard of Corby in Cumberland. The Howards of Corby were descended, like the Earls of Carlisle, from a younger son of the ill-fated Elizabethan fourth Duke of Norfolk but whereas the Carlisles were Protestant, the Corby Howards had remained Catholic. Corby Castle, their seat overhanging the River Eden, had been transformed by Henry Howard into a foursquare Grecian block of red sandstone, with the original peel tower hidden behind its façades.

In 1830, the year when Philip Howard became an MP, his sister Adela was married to Henry Petre, a grandson of the ninth Lord Petre whose Lancashire estate of Dunkenhalgh had passed to him. Henry Petre was a widower with children and somewhat older than the dark, vivacious Adela; he was her first cousin since his mother was her father's sister. Nevertheless, it was very much a love-match.

However, when he and she set off on a tour of the Continent some months after their marriage, it was not quite a second honeymoon for they went in a party that included her parents and his half-uncle Robert Petre, who had recently married the Staffords' daughter Laura Jerningham, together with the two sons of Lord Erskine, the British Minister in Munich on whose staff Adela's brother, the younger Henry Howard, was serving. On their first evening at Ostend, as Adela wrote in her diary, Henry and Robert Petre 'let off some most spirited fireworks, Catherine wheels and squibs, which had the prettiest effect and appeared to cause real amusement to a large crowd that collected'.[5] From Ostend they went to Brussels and visited the field of Waterloo, Henry Petre having been present at the battle. They then went on to Cologne and as they entered the city the postilions sounded their bugles, a Prussian custom which delighted Adela.

Having ordered cases of eau-de-Cologne to be sent to them in England, they sailed up the Rhine and in Frankfurt Adela acquired 'a piping bullfinch which had long been an object of my wishes'.[6] In Baden they consorted with royalty, the widowed Amalie Duchess of Baden being an old friend of the elder Henry Howard. They were joined here by young Henry Howard, who accompanied them to Munich, where Adela admired the pictures and drove in the English Garden. Young Henry was found to be 'most deeply inamorato' with the Erskines' daughter Sevilla, whom he was to marry before the year was out.

'I am now entering on a task which only a Walter Scott should attempt, that is, the description of scenery too enchanting even to fancy', Adela wrote in Upper Bavaria. And in the Tyrol she wrote, 'I defy even the powers of a Byron to have described it'.[7] They returned to England by way of Switzerland and France, where the July Revolution had just taken place. 'Everything appears to have suffered since the last "glorious revolution" (as it is termed)', Adela noted. At Fontainebleau, the old concierge who showed them the Palace 'appeared to feel most deeply for the ex-Royal Family, with whom he said he had been to England during their previous exile, he was all but in tears in talking of them'.[8]

At the start of this second exile, Charles X and his family rented Lulworth for three months. 'Voilà! La Bastille!' the old French King exclaimed as the castle, with its massive round towers, came into sight. Joseph Weld, whose brother Thomas had made over Lulworth to him in 1827, greeted the royal party at the foot of the steps. Mary Arundell, now back in England, lost no time in coming over to welcome the King, whom she knew well from when he stayed at Stowe. She felt sick with emotion at the prospect of meeting him again in such melancholy circumstances; but he was 'quite composed and cheerful and led her to the window holding both her hands as she sobbed'.[9] According to Mary, the castle was too small for the French Court, but she would have been prejudiced, as she and Everard had hoped that Charles X would take Wardour.

At the time when Thomas Weld made over Lulworth to his brother Joseph, he was already a bishop, having been ordained priest in 1821. But for various reasons he had delayed taking up his episcopal appointment, which was in Canada, and he eventually accompanied his daughter Mary Lucy and her husband Hugh Clifford to Italy, hoping that the climate would benefit Mary Lucy's failing health. In January 1830, soon after his arrival in Rome, he heard that the Pope was to make him a cardinal. Considering his relatively modest position in the Church, this was a tremendous and unexpected honour; he was the first Englishman to be raised to the Sacred College since Cardinal Howard in the seventeenth century. It was a tribute to him as a *grand seigneur* prelate rather than to his ecclesiastical career; it was also taken as a gesture of goodwill towards Britain after Catholic emancipation. Mary Arundell claimed to have had a hand in his elevation and would refer to herself afterwards as a 'cardinal-maker'; possibly she helped to influence Dr Wiseman, the Rector of the English College, on his behalf.

He quickly settled down in Rome, his one complaint being that he could no longer take exercise riding or walking, but as a Prince of the Church was expected to go everywhere in his state carriage with the red silk trappings and the gilt buckles on the harness. Mary Lucy and Hugh and their children lived with him; Rome suited not only Mary Lucy's health but also Hugh's finances; for unlike his forceful father he was hopeless as far as money was concerned. But his piety and charm made him a success in Rome and though incapable of looking after his own finances, he was good at managing his father-in-law's household, particularly since he could speak Italian, which his father-in-law could not.

The new Cardinal had the sense to realize that at this stage he could learn neither the language nor the ways of the *Curia* and was happy to rely on a good theological adviser and on equally good secretaries. His uprightness, his humanity and his Anglo-Saxon efficiency made up for his inexperience of high ecclesiastical business, added to which he was courteous and hospitable. In the words of Dr Wiseman, 'His apartments in the Odescalchi Palace were splendidly furnished, and periodically filled with the aristocracy of Rome, native and foreign, and with multitudes of his countrymen, every one of whom found him always ready to render him any service.'[10]

Having been a cardinal for less than a year, Thomas Weld took part in the Conclave which elected Gregory XVI in succession to the short-lived Pius VIII. He had with him as his secretary Father William Riddell, younger son of Ralph Riddell of Felton in Northumberland and brother of poor Louisa who died as a schoolgirl in Paris. In this Conclave, Cardinal Giustiniani, a cousin of both Mary Lucy and Hugh Clifford, nearly became Pope, but his election was vetoed by the Court of Spain. Giustiniani's great-grandfather was a Clifford who married the Countess of Newburgh in her own right. On the death of the last Radcliffe Earl of Newburgh in 1814 the Scottish earldom had passed to the Cardinal's eldest brother Prince Giustiniani. But he had taken no steps to claim the title, which was assumed by his cousin the Derbyshire Catholic squire Francis Eyre of Hassop on the grounds that it could not be inherited by a foreigner. The same false argument had been used to block the claim of the French-born priest Abbé Charles Edward Drummond to the Earldoms of Perth and Melfort, although at the time he was living in England and had written an ode on the death of Nelson.

There was a myth current among the English that Thomas Weld was made a cardinal because of his connection with the King; his uncle Edward Weld having been Maria Fitzherbert's first husband. If George IV ever felt inclined to regard

Cardinal Weld

Thomas's Red Hat as a vicarious compliment to himself, he did not live long to enjoy it. Towards the end of June 1830 he became desperately ill, scarcely able to breathe; on hearing that he was dying, Maria wrote him a letter. When given it, he seized it, read it with emotion and put it under his pillow. Maria said afterwards to her cousin the eighteenth Lord Stourton that nothing had so 'cut her up' as not having received one word from him in answer.[11] But she did have an answer, only it was from the grave; she was told that the King was wearing a miniature portrait of her round his neck when he died, and that he had asked for it to be buried with him.

The new King, William IV, came to see Maria at Brighton and offered to make her a duchess. But in the words of Lord Stourton, in whom she confided – he was her cousin through his maternal grandmother, who was a Smythe – 'She replied that she did not wish for any rank; that she had borne through life the name of Mrs Fitzherbert; that she had never disgraced it and did not wish to change it.'[12] The King accepted her reason for declining the honour, but said that he would insist on her servants wearing the Royal livery. He invited her to the Pavilion and when she arrived he 'came himself and handed her out of her carriage' and introduced her to Queen Adelaide and to the other members of the Royal Family who were present, 'as one of themselves'.[13] William IV and Queen Adelaide were to treat Maria as a King's widow as long as she lived.

On King William's accession, Queen Adelaide made her friend of Ghent days, the recently-widowed Charlotte Bedingfeld, a Woman of the Bedchamber. 'I am in dread of my royal summons', Charlotte wrote and she felt quite ill when she set out for Brighton to go into waiting for the first time, but the journey did her good. 'I descended from my dark carriage into the blaze of a seemingly enchanted palace, the Pavilion can neither be described nor guessed at, it is the dream of some Chinese Poet (if there be such a thing)', she told her son Sir Henry, as he now was. The housekeeper led her up 'between nodding mandarins' to her apartment. 'Presently my trunks were brought up and I began to undress when a lady entered gently and was close by me before I was aware of her presence, it was Her Majesty!'[14]

Charlotte wrote from the Pavilion a few months later, 'My life is a strange tissue here and I am in a Palace surrounded with grandeur and bowing pages and scarlet footmen asking my leave for this and for that. I often wish they would all vanish!'[15] Yet she enjoyed Court life and grew very attached to the Queen's young invalid niece Princess Louisa of Saxe-Weimar. And there were quite a few familiar Catholic faces at the Pavilion, not only Maria Fitzherbert and her relations but at one dinner party when Charlotte was in waiting the guests included the Duke of Norfolk as well as various Jerninghams and Petres.

Charlotte's son Sir Henry had married in 1826 Margaret Paston, the last of the Pastons who in the fifteenth century wrote the celebrated letters. She was a delightful girl and a Catholic: she had a fortune of some £50,000 so that she and Sir Henry were able to carry out repairs and improvements at Oxburgh, which had become so dilapidated during his parents' absence abroad that when they first came to live here he facetiously headed a letter The Ruin.

For their alterations to the house, which were intended to restore its original Tudor and medieval character, they employed as their architect Chessell Buckler who was working for Sir Henry's Stafford cousins at Cossey. Sir Henry also built a chapel across the moat: he was as pious as his mother and followed his great-uncle the Chevalier Jerningham into the Order of Malta, which having formerly been limited to celibates was now open to married men as well. In the garden, Sir Henry built a wall with five small towers, said to commemorate his five children, and he built another wall along the public road 'to keep the village out'.[16] This wall may have been built as a result of an incident on 5 November 1830, when 'a number of

Charlotte Jerningham, wife of Thomas Fraser of
Lovat (afterwards the fourteenth Lord Lovat)

these Oxburgh wretches', as Margaret Bedingfeld called them, 'arrived to beg
money to burn the Pope'. Sir Henry refused to give them anything and sent his dog
'to hasten their departure', whereupon they set fire to one of his barns.[17]

Three years after Sir Henry Bedingfeld married, his cousin Charles Waterton also
took a wife. He was forty-eight, his clean-shaven face furrowed with the tropical sun
and rain: his bride, Anne Edmonstone, was a convent girl of seventeen, an orphan
whose maternal grandmother was an Indian from the forests of Guiana. He married
her at four in the morning in the church of the convent in Bruges where she was at
school and took her off to see the collections of stuffed animals in Antwerp, Ghent
and Paris by way of a honeymoon.

He then brought her home to Walton where thanks to his efforts the house had
been cleared once and for all of the rats that had formerly infested it. But while the rats
– which had particularly offended his Catholic susceptibilities, being, as he

believed, Hanoverian rats – had gone, some of his taxidermical efforts might have been no less disturbing to his young bride. In the entrance hall she was greeted by an object meant to represent a nightmare, consisting of a human face with horns, elephant's ears, bat's wings and the tail of a serpent. The cayman which he had ridden stood stuffed at the head of the stairs, from which a door led to a room full of stuffed snakes. It is to be hoped that Anne was able to laugh at his caricatures of famous Protestants, made out of the component parts of lizards and toads.

Poor Anne died in 1830 after less than a year of marriage, having given birth to a son. 'She was a week ill, persuaded of her danger, and evinced the greatest sentiments of piety and resignation, beautiful young creature!' Charlotte Bedingfeld told her son Felix, who had written a letter of condolence to Waterton but had received no answer.[18] Anne's unmarried sister came to live at Walton, to bring up the child. Waterton, who was heartbroken, henceforth led the life of an ascetic, dedicated to his wife's memory. To symbolize his separation from all other women he never again entered a bed, but slept on the floor with a hollowed-out beech block for a pillow.

Matilda Waterton, daughter of one of Waterton's two uncles who owned plantations in Demerara, was married to Edmund Jerningham, son of William formerly of the Austrian army. Edmund and Matilda were staying in Inverness-shire with Thomas and Charlotte Fraser of Lovat and their children in September 1831 when Charlotte's brother Edward Jerningham came to stay. 'I was rather sickened with deer-stalking', Edward confided to his diary, 'and felt more happy by the peat fire, sipping my *toddy*, than scrambling over the hills'.[19] When not on the hill he fished for salmon without success and shot partridges: one day he shot a valuable dog which fortunately seemed likely to recover. He also attended a dinner of 300 in Inverness after the Cattle Show, and while he was there heard Mass and was not impressed by the set-up, 'A small mal-ordered chapel . . . with a sermon of the most Irish description'.[20] He also went to a chapel which had been designed in the Norman style by his mother Lady Stafford and built by his brother-in-law.

Fraser not only built churches; he carried out many improvements to his estates, draining fields, making roads and planting several million trees, not all of which survived the depredations of squirrels descended from a pair brought from Norfolk by the beautiful Charlotte to remind her of home. He planned to build a Scottish Baronial castle to take the place of the modest eighteenth century house where his family had lived since their ancestral castle was burnt in the 'Forty-Five'.

As well as working hard in the management of his estates, Fraser was very active in the affairs of his county. Having at first been mistrusted on account of his Catholicism, he came to be respected for his judgement and commonsense and was eventually made Lieutenant and Sheriff Principal, even though he was a poor speaker owing to a stammer and deafness caused by an illness in childhood. The fact that he accepted the spurious claim of the two brothers who called themselves Sobieski Stuart to be the grandsons of Bonnie Prince Charlie, and established them on an island in the River Beauly near his home, was not held against him. He brooked no quarrels under his roof: he was a generous host: the drink flowed freely at his table though he himself drank nothing stronger than ginger beer.

Less successful than Fraser in establishing good relations with his county was Everard Arundell who in 1831 nearly caused a mutiny in the Sarum Troop of the Wiltshire Yeomanry, which he commanded, by voting against the Reform Bill in the House of Lords; he was the only Catholic peer to do so. He took the unruly behaviour of his yeomen very much to heart and resigned in the following year. Feelings ran high in Wiltshire when Everard was in the Yeomanry owing to the so-called 'Wiltshire Machine Riots', caused by the introduction of new farm machinery.

In Lancashire, at the same time, there was industrial unrest. Adela Petre wrote in 1831 of the weavers near Dunkenhalgh being at starvation level and breaking their frames in protest. Adela and her husband had now settled down to married life in Lancashire after their Continental tour. In 1832 they made alterations to the Tudor and Regency Gothic house at Dunkenhalgh and laid out gardens, and in August of that year she announced the birth of 'a nasty animal, a boy'.[21] But she never really recovered from his birth and died a year later of scarlet fever.

The Petres' improvements at Dunkenhalgh were modest compared with the palatial house which another Lancashire Catholic, the young racing baronet Sir John Gerard, had recently built for himself at Garswood: it was in a rich Classical style, with an Ionic centre flanked by pavilions resembling triumphal arches. The Gerards had become very wealthy through coal-mining on their estates, though Sir John's younger brother Robert had been obliged to refuse the offer of a commission in the Life Guards because it was such an expensive regiment. This must have been hard for him, for he was quite a young buck. While in Dieppe, he had drunk nothing but the best claret and burgundy: he had helped to found a cricket club and had taken full advantage of the French custom whereby a gentleman could ask any lady to dance whether he knew her or not.

The Industrial Revolution also benefited the Traffords, whose principal seat, Trafford Park, with its elegant eighteenth century house, was close to Manchester. A sister of Thomas Trafford of Trafford was married to John Clifton, younger son of another wealthy Lancashire Catholic, the sporting John Clifton of Lytham, whose eldest son Thomas shocked the Catholic world in 1831 by turning Protestant. A local Catholic priest reckoned he did so because his wife was a

Protestant of Jewish origin and because he and she were both gamblers. The priest also blamed Thomas Clifton's 'ruin' on the fact that his father was himself by no means an exemplary Catholic. He had 'suppressed a mission' and lived 'at variance with his wife'.[22]

The wife with whom old John Clifton lived 'at variance' was Elizabeth Riddell, aunt of the Northumberland landowner Thomas Riddell and of Father William Riddell who was Cardinal Weld's secretary at the Conclave. Thomas Riddell, who had two estates in Northumberland, Felton and Swinburne Castle – originally belonging to the Swinburnes but bought by the Riddells in the late seventeenth century – was, like John Clifton, a considerable figure on the Turf. He owned a string of racehorses, the most famous being Dr Syntax, winner of twenty Gold Cup races. Much local money was wagered on the 'Catholic Horse', as he was known, and at least two public houses in Northumberland were named after him. Another famous horse of Thomas Riddell's was Gallopade, winner of the Doncaster Gold Cup in 1832, yet another was the aptly-named Emancipation.

The year 1832 was a bad one for Everard and Mary Arundell. Not only did it see the passing of the Reform Bill, which Everard had dreaded and opposed but their finances continued to deteriorate. At the beginning of 1833, having let Wardour, they went abroad once again; they spent a year travelling slowly southwards, during which time they both suffered recurring bouts of illness. In Munich they heard that the tenant at Wardour was giving up. 'Everard is undone', Mary lamented, though there was a chance of another tenant who 'had a sober household, no London footmen'. But then their agent let the place to this person 'for nothing'.[23]

They arrived back in Rome in June 1834 when the temperature was a hundred degrees in the sun, but the heat seemed at first to suit Everard, who started working for Cardinal Weld. The Cardinal's daughter Mary Lucy had died in 1831, but her husband Hugh, now the seventh Lord Clifford of Chudleigh, and their children continued to live with him. The Romans had grown accustomed to the sight of a cardinal driving out in his carriage with a little grand-daughter.

When they had been in Rome a few days, the Arundells visited the Jesuit church, the Gesù; and as they were leaving Everard said in a whisper to Mary, 'I wish to be buried in front of the gate of the chapel of the Sacred Heart. Fr Glover's confessional is close to it and he would remember to pray for me.' At the time he was quite well, but he was taken ill that evening and a couple of days later it was clear that he was dying. The Pope sent a message; Cardinal Weld and Hugh Clifford came: his Jesuit friend Father Glover heard his confession and gave him the Last Sacraments. Everard remained conscious almost to the end and said calmly, 'We shall meet again in a better world, and then, Mary, we shall never be parted more, and praise God

Ambrose Lisle March Phillipps

together in happiness eternal.'[24] Seeing that Mary was on the point of breaking down, he said cheerfully, 'Come, Mary, make no scene.' But when he breathed his last as morning broke, the Roman morning with its brilliant blue sky, Mary's screams were terrible. He was buried in the Gesù as he wished, with a simple memorial tablet on which the name Wardour was misspelt.

Rome, so unkind to the Arundells, brought happiness, at least on the face of it, to Lord and Lady Shrewsbury, whose younger daughter, Lady Gwendaline Talbot, was married in May 1835 to the eldest son of Prince Borghese, head of one of the greatest families of the Roman nobility. Richard Monckton Milnes, the young English man of letters who had become a popular figure in Roman society, wrote a sonnet on the marriage:

> . . . may the cool northern dew
> Still rest upon thy leaves, transplanted flower!
> Mingling thy English nature, pure and true,
> With the bright growth of each Italian hour.

Lady Gwendaline herself had literary aspirations and would hand round the red and gold morocco volume of her own verses among her friends, smugly discussing their merits with Monckton Milnes.

A year earlier it had looked as if the Shrewsburys' elder daughter Mary would make an even more brilliant match, at any rate in the eyes of Lady Shrewsbury, with her love of German courts. She became engaged to Prince Frederick of Saxe-Altenburg. The match had been proposed to the Shrewsburys through the Queen of Bavaria and the Queen of England: the King of Bavaria had already made Mary a princess in anticipation of it. 'We came over to see him, and on approval Mary took him', Lord Shrewsbury wrote to a friend.[25] The engagement, however, was eventually broken off: Prince Frederick never married.

The friend to whom Lord Shrewsbury wrote about his daughter's engagement was the young Ambrose Lisle March Phillipps, son of the wealthy Leicestershire landowner Charles March Phillipps of Garendon Park and Grace Dieu Manor. In 1825 at the age of sixteen Ambrose had shocked his father and his uncle who was an Anglican bishop by becoming a Catholic. But such was the charm and sincerity of 'this young saint', as Mary Arundell, who was also a friend of his, called him,[26] that his family became reconciled to his conversion and on his marriage in 1833 to Laura Clifford – a first cousin of Hugh Clifford – his father had given him the romantically-named estate of Grace Dieu and had built him a new manor house here in the Tudor style. It had, of course, a chapel, with an Angelus bell, 'at the sound of which', Ambrose told a fellow-convert, 'all the neighbouring parsons are said to quake'.[27]

From the moment he became a Catholic, Ambrose Lisle March Phillipps devoted his life to bringing England back to the Old Faith and his optimism in this respect knew no bounds. Having, with Lord Shrewsbury's help, established a Catholic school in Leicester, he wrote, 'This will be the grand means of converting England.'[28] When the aristocratic Anglican clergyman George Spencer, a younger son of Earl Spencer, was received into the Catholic Church while staying with him at Grace Dieu, he saw it as 'a sign that God has grand designs on our wretched country'.[29] The advent of seven other prospective converts in his local town caused him to declare, 'I do believe in 30 years there will not be a Protestant in Leicester'.[30] Not content with building churches and chapels and gathering around him a band of missionary priests – including Spencer, who became a Passionist Father – to preach Catholicism to the country people and the urban poor, Ambrose set about founding a Cistercian monastery. In 1835 he bought some land in Charnwood Forest that had traditionally belonged before the Dissolution to the Cistercian abbey of Garendon, of which his ancestors, the De Lisles, were benefactors, and he gave it to the Cistercian Order for the proposed Abbey of Mount St Bernard.

As well as coming into contact with the old Catholic world through his wife Laura, Ambrose Lisle March Phillipps saw it in his own county at Nevill Holt. When he first visited 'the ancient and beautiful residence of the Nevill family', as he described it, the octogenarian Cosmas Nevill and his wife Maria were still alive and would spend 'whole hours within the venerable chapel in prayer and meditation every day'.[31] But their son Charles and his wife Lady Georgiana – daughter of the Duke of Norfolk's divorced wife by her second husband the Earl of Lucan – was more worldly. After Cosmas's death in 1829 they were in no hurry to come and live at Nevill Holt, preferring London where they lived beyond their means and Charles lost money gambling. When they finally did settle down in Leicestershire, they proceeded to carry out elaborate alterations to the house to make it more Gothic: the red brick Georgian façades were plastered over: the sash windows replaced with oriels: the skylines enlivened with battlements. Inevitably, Charles found himself in financial difficulties.

Another house where all was not well at this time was Burghwallis in south Yorkshire, to which Michael and Maria Tasburgh had returned in 1830 after their lengthy sojourn in France. In 1833 Maria had inherited an estate and she and Michael had proceeded to quarrel violently over its future so that in 1835 there was a complete rift between them. Henceforth they lived separately, though under the same roof; she in the old part of the house, he in the new. But while he continued to go about his affairs she incarcerated herself in her room and took to the bottle. But whenever he hoed the flower beds beneath her window – for he was fond of gardening – she would lean out and spit on his head.

Very different from the unhappy atmosphere at Burghwallis was that at Courtfield in Monmouthshire, where John Vaughan and his beautiful wife Eliza lived a life of conjugal bliss and Catholic piety in the pedimented house among woods overhanging the River Wye which his father had rebuilt at the beginning of the century. Eliza, the daughter of another Monmouthshire squire, was originally not a Catholic: John Vaughan, though an extremely devout Catholic himself, had made no attempt to convert her when they became engaged. One Sunday during their engagement, she had accompanied him to Mass and had afterwards announced that she wished to be received into the Catholic Church. Then, having become a Catholic, she had announced, to her fiancé's dismay, that she wished to become a nun. He had talked her out of it and she duly married him in 1830: two years later their eldest son Herbert was born, the first of a family of eight sons and five daughters.

There is a tradition that Eliza would spend an hour each day praying in the chapel before the Blessed Sacrament that all her children should become priests or

at Stonor; he was a founder of Henley Regatta; he was an excellent shot; always shooting in a tall hat and white duck trousers. The new Lord Camoys had followed his father's example in going to Lancashire for his bride. Just as his father had married a daughter of the collector Henry Blundell, so had the younger Thomas married Frances Towneley, daughter of Peregrine Towneley of Towneley who was a first cousin of Charles Towneley, the other great Catholic collector of antiquities. 'Owd Peregrine', as he was known in his part of Lancashire, was rather different from the dilettante Charles; he dressed like a tramp, so that he was once mistaken for a poacher by his own under-keeper and imprisoned in his own ice-house.

There were great celebrations at Stonor when the peerage was called out of abeyance. One of the tenants recited a poem of his own composition which ended: 'Yea, may his tenants 'midst their other joys, Say "Bless the Queen which made him Lord Camoys"'.[37] At the time, nobody seems to have regretted that Camoys had superseded the proud designation of Stonor of Stonor.

CHAPTER 7

The good Earl John and the converts

IN 1839 Barbara Tasburgh became engaged to the twenty-eight year old William Charlton. Her engagement was at first 'much approved of': William was heir to lands in Cumberland as well as to Hesleyside, his ancestral estate in Northumberland where the Charltons had been seated since medieval times, when they were chieftains of the most powerful of the four 'graynes' or clans of North Tyndale. As well as being of ancient lineage, the Charltons had always been Catholic. Moreover William was a likeable young man who had travelled and spoke German and Italian.

No sooner had Barbara and William become engaged than their two fathers proceeded to fall out over the marriage settlement and went on wrangling for nearly five months, until the young people decided to settle matters by eloping. Just before midnight Barbara lowered herself by knotted sheets from her bedroom window at Burghwallis and joined William who was waiting for her outside. They posted to Gretna Green where they were made man and wife by the blacksmith, who, knowing that William was the heir to great estates, charged them the exorbitant fee of £20, so that Barbara had to pawn her jewels in Carlisle. They then returned to London where they were married in an Anglican church and also by a Jesuit.

The family lawyers now made the happy discovery that Barbara's father had no control over the estate which her mother had inherited, so that her mother was able to provide for the young couple. Maria Tasburgh was also able to move into the house on her estate, thereby ending her voluntary incarceration at Burghwallis. She never again saw her husband, who after their parting lived mostly abroad.

Barbara's new home, Hesleyside, was isolated amidst the moorland slopes of its Border valley. It was a house of different periods, with handsome eighteenth century façades and elegant rooms. What struck her about it more than anything else when she first came to live here was the cold and the damp. 'The long passages had no heat,

Hesleyside

the outside doors were never shut, the hall and corridors were paved with flagstones . . . Even in my early years at Hesleyside funguses grew on the passage woodwork.'[1]

Her impression of the house would not have been helped by the presence of her parents-in-law, with whom she and William had to live. She described the elder William Charlton as a gloomy recluse 'buried in his books' and as having 'the most sarcastic, disagreeable, sneering mouth I ever saw'. His wife Katherine looked 'like a frightened hare' and was mentally unstable: Barbara attributed her state to the cruelty of *her* mother-in-law, William's formidable grandmother, who used to say to her, 'My son, remember, only married you because you looked to be a good breeder'.[2] William's grandmother had disapproved of Katherine from the very start, although she came from a perfectly respectable family of the Yorkshire Catholic squirearchy, the Cholmeleys of Brandsby; probably suspecting even then that she was not quite right in the head.

Barbara was put off her meals by her mother-in-law's 'disgusting way of eating' and, apart from the home-killed mutton, she found the Hesleyside food hard enough to stomach at the best of times, 'Bad beef, unsound bread . . . salt butter and diseased potatoes'.[3] There was nothing to drink but water, perhaps because wine had been the undoing of William's grandfather. But while the family abstained, the butler and his 'pantry cronies' most certainly did not. 'It was hardly possible to find a more drunken establishment' Barbara wrote. 'Hesleyside was simply a house of public refreshment'.[4] At the time she did not know what her eldest son was to reveal to her many years later, namely that the laundry at Hesleyside was 'nothing but a brothel'.[4]

As county neighbours, Barbara had her cousins the Swinburnes who were also cousins of William's. They lived at Capheaton, a house with a seventeenth century front which was said to have had no fewer than seven priests' hiding places in the days of persecution. Old Sir John Swinburne, who had conformed in 1787, then supported the French Revolution and more recently had been a patron of Turner, was still alive; according to Barbara, he preferred to forget his family's Catholic past. His daughter-in-law Lady Jane Swinburne came to Hesleyside 'to pay her visit of congratulation to the bride', bringing her small son Algernon Charles, 'a pretty-featured, carroty-haired spoilt boy'. The future poet 'paid his respects most unpoetically' by pricking Barbara 'with a large pin in a tender place'.[5]

In the same year as Barbara travelled north to Gretna Green, the Shrewsburys' elder daughter Lady Mary Talbot went south to marry. Having been made a princess in Bavaria and having nearly become a Princess of Saxe-Altenburg, she now followed her sister's example and became a Roman princess; her husband being Prince Doria-Pamphilij. 'If Roman Princes make happiness, what a happy woman she must be' Mary Arundell remarked caustically of Lady Shrewsbury,[6] though Gwendaline's marriage to Prince Borghese really does appear to have been happy. Poor Gwendaline was not married for very long, for she died in 1840; her three small sons all died within a few weeks of their mother.

The Shrewsburys were not too much parted from Gwendaline, when she was alive, and from Mary, for they spent every summer in Italy. This not only enabled Lady Shrewsbury to indulge her passion for the Roman nobility, but it also enabled Lord Shrewsbury to save money for his reigning passion, which was building Catholic churches and monasteries in England. As he explained to Ambrose Lisle March Phillipps, each summer abroad saved him £2,000, which represented 'half a small church or a whole monastery, or indeed all you want for your own church at St Bernard's'.[7]

Lord Shrewsbury's passion for church-building was fired not only by Ambrose Phillipps but also by another young Catholic convert and visionary, his architect Augustus Welby Pugin. Pugin's fanatical advocacy of the Gothic, which he regarded as the only true Christian architecture, had made his patron a Gothic enthusiast; as much a figure of the Gothic Revival as of the revival of English Catholicism. The churches which Lord Shrewsbury built to Pugin's design culminated in the magnificent St Giles's at Cheadle, with its soaring spire and its interior aglow with coloured glass, painted decoration, brasswork and encaustic tiles.

One suspects that the Good Earl John, as he came to be known among the Catholics of the English Midlands, would, if left to himself, have been content to build churches in the neighbourhood of Alton, his Staffordshire seat, without supporting more ambitious projects for the conversion of England. He had something of the mentality of the old English recusants with their innate conservatism and was even slightly Protestant in his outlook, thus he objected to people gardening on the Sabbath. But Ambrose Phillipps was always there with his convert's zeal and generally succeeded in winning his support for schemes on which he was at first inclined to look askance. Having doubted the wisdom of spending money on founding a Cistercian abbey in the heart of Charnwood Forest, rather than developing some existing Catholic centre, he ended by giving Ambrose £3,000 for building Mount St Bernard.

Ambrose had another scheme for which Lord Shrewsbury began by showing no enthusiasm. This was to bring some Italian priests to England as missionaries: an idea which had originated when Ambrose and George Spencer made friends in Rome with the Passionist Father Dominic Barberi, a priest of humble origin but great fervour who could neither speak nor write English yet was convinced that he was called to be a missionary in England. Lord Shrewsbury saw Father Dominic and tried to talk him out of the idea and having met Father Gentili, another of Ambrose's Italian priests, declared categorically that he was 'not suited for England'.[8] But Ambrose persisted in his plan: he brought Gentili to Leicestershire where in no time he was making converts by the hundred and founding missions: and Lord Shrewsbury paid the interest on a loan for building him a church.

Father Dominic Barberi also came to England with a few of his Passionists and in 1841 settled in a house near Stone, not far from Alton. Having struggled to learn the language, he began preaching in broken English and was soon attracting large crowds. By August 1843 he had made eighty converts and had some thirty more under instruction. With the Oxford Movement now in full swing, his fame spread beyond Staffordshire. Four years after embarking on what most people regarded as his crazy venture to convert England, Father Dominic had the brightest star in the firmament of Anglican Oxford, John Henry Newman, kneeling at his feet.

Soon after his conversion, Newman was invited by Lord Shrewsbury to Alton, where there was a large party of prominent Catholics, including Lord and Lady Camoys, Lord and Lady Dormer, Sir Robert Throckmorton and Sir Edward Vavasour. For Newman, it was something of an ordeal, 'A house full of company,

A twentieth-century impression of Alton Towers in
the days of the Good Earl John

and I looking like a fool'. But he found Lord Shrewsbury 'most kind'.[9]

Alton was now no longer Alton Abbey but Alton Towers, having been
transformed by Lord Shrewsbury with the help of Pugin into a Gothic fantasy on a
palatial scale. It had long galleries filled with works of art and an armoury in which
figures in armour were ranged round an equestrian statue of Le Grand Talbot.
There was a vaulted octagon with stained glass windows like a medieval
chapterhouse and, of course, a vast and splendid chapel. In contrast to all this
magnificence, Lord Shrewsbury's own private room was 'bare and austere as a
monastic cell'.[10]

In his novel *Coningsby*, first published in 1844, Disraeli paints an idealized picture
of Alton, which he calls St Geneviève:

Sir Edward Vavasour

In a valley, not far from the margin of a beautiful river, raised on a lofty and artificial terrace at the base of a range of wooded heights, was a pile of modern building in the finest style of Christian architecture . . . a gathering as it seemed of galleries, halls and chapels, mullioned windows, portals of clustered columns, and groups of airy pinnacles and fretwork spires.

When the eponymous hero of the book came to St Geneviève for the first time, in company with his friend Lord Henry Sydney and others, 'what interested them more than the gallery, or the rich saloons, or even the baronial hall, was the chapel, in which art had exhausted all its invention, and wealth offered all its resources'.

Coningsby's host at St Geneviève is not, however, meant to be Lord Shrewsbury but Ambrose Lisle March Phillipps, who is thinly disguised as Eustace Lyle and depicted as belonging to an ancient Catholic family rather than as a convert. Like the real-life Ambrose, he was brought up to be a Whig but has become an ardent Tory through the influence of Young England, that group of romantic and high-minded young men, mostly patrician but including, in real life, Disraeli himself, who gave a new sense of purpose to the Tory party. Ambrose was a close friend of Lord John Manners, one of the leaders of the group, on whom Lord Henry Sydney is based.

One of Newman's fellow-guests at Alton was the eighteenth Lord Stourton's younger brother Sir Edward Vavasour, who had changed his name on inheriting Hazlewood, the estate of the extinct Vavasour baronets in Yorkshire. Sir Edward, who had himself been made a baronet in 1828, was musical and a keen rider to hounds; but more interested in the bringing up of his own children and in the welfare of the Catholic poor. He had founded a school for training Catholic teachers and, being a widower, was planning to join a religious order as a lay brother.

Another Yorkshire Catholic baronetcy which was revived at about this time was that of Lawson. William Wright, who took the name of Lawson on inheriting the Brough estate from his maternal great-uncle, the last of the original Lawson baronets, in 1834, was made a baronet in 1841. Sir William Lawson, as he now was, shared Lord Shrewsbury's enthusiasm for Gothic: no sooner had he come into Brough than he started building a Gothic chapel of immense height in the park, though there was already an elegant eighteenth century chapel in the Elizabethan and Georgian house. His new chapel was a copy of the thirteenth century Archbishop's Chapel at York, and while employing the fashionable architect Ignatius Bonomi, he himself took great trouble to get the details right. When the roof went on, the workmen were treated to a dinner of boiled beef and plum pudding with three pints of ale each; and when the chapel was finished there was a service of dedication lasting three and a half hours.

Among the aristocratic builders of Gothic churches in the eighteen thirties and forties, the Dukes of Norfolk of the time were conspicuously absent. Barney actually spent an average of £7,000 a year — more, indeed, than what Lord Shrewsbury spent — on providing places of worship for the growing Catholic population; and he gave sites on his Sheffield estate for Anglican churches. But he believed that small chapels of the old-fashioned sort were more suited to English Catholic worship than 'large edifices'.[11] The building activities of Barney's son, who succeeded him as the thirteenth Duke in 1842, were of a more secular kind, such as improvements at Arundel, where his father had neglected the castle while almost doubling the size of the estate. People who stayed there in Barney's time spoke of 'that horrid, dismal, benighted castle' and remarked that it would be a more suitable place for the owls to

'Fitz', Earl of Arundel and Surrey, and his wife Minna, with their three elder daughters, Toria, Minna and Mary, in 1846. A water colour by Dartiguenave

live in than the keep.[12]

The new Duke and Duchess had an excellent excuse for doing up the castle when they heard that Queen Victoria and Prince Albert were to honour them with a visit in December 1846. They called in Morants, the fashionable decorators, to put up a new green and gold paper in the drawing room and to provide a white and gold state bed for the royal bedchamber. Lest it should offend the Queen, they removed the painted window in the dining room in which Barney's predecessor Jockey was portrayed as King Solomon with a buxom Queen of Sheba.

There was a different display of plate at dinner on each of the two nights of the royal visit; on the first evening Victoria and Albert were entertained with fireworks, on their second with music by 'Ethiopian Serenaders'.[13] On the day after their arrival, while Prince Albert went shooting with the Duke, the Queen toured the grounds and went to the keep to see the famous owls, which were named after eminent judges; so that on one occasion the butler had announced: 'Lord Thurlow has laid an egg'. The Queen and the Prince left next day after the inevitable tree-planting, and everyone agreed that the visit had been an unqualified success.

The Norfolks were close to the Queen; the Duchess's sister-in-law the Duchess of Sutherland was one of the Queen's greatest friends, and the Duke held various Court appointments. He was also a Knight of the Garter and his robes suited him, for he looked every inch a duke, unlike his father or Jockey. But he was rather a weak character, arrogant and foolish. In a speech at an agricultural dinner he suggested that the starving poor should eat curry since it was 'warm and comfortable to the stomach', which offended public opinion and earned him the nickname of Old Pepper and Potatoes.[14]

Of the Norfolks' three sons, the youngest, Lord Bernard Fitzalan-Howard – he and his brothers took the additional surname of Fitzalan to commemorate their descent from the Fitzalan Earls of Arundel – died suddenly in Egypt on his Grand Tour, a couple of weeks after his parents entertained the Queen. The eldest son, the Earl of Arundel and Surrey, known to his family as Fitz having starting life as Lord Fitzalan, was a young nobleman of many virtues. His powerful maternal grandmother had not in the end succeeded in making either him or his brothers Protestants; but he was originally a somewhat lukewarm Catholic. Mary Arundell, who took an interest in his spiritual welfare, though no relation – Arundell being quite different from Arundel – blamed this on his 'fool of a father', who had appointed an Anglican clergyman as his tutor and had sent him to Cambridge; though he had left the University after the head of his college tried to make him take a Protestant oath and attend chapel.[15] Like his father, he had married a Protestant, though from a less exalted background. She was Minna, daughter of Lord Lyons, a

Sir Richard Acton, looking as though he is just
about to set off for the gaming tables

distinguished naval commander who had been made a peer. It was agreed that the
daughters of the marriage should be brought up in their mother's faith.

During the eighteen-forties, Fitz paid several visits to France. The nineteenth
century French Catholic revival was then at its height: he made friends with the
Catholic writer and politician the Comte de Montalembert: he heard the sermons of
Père Lacordaire and of other great preachers of the time. Suddenly his Catholicism
underwent a change, so great that he told Montalembert, 'You must look upon me as
a convert'.[16]

Two somewhat older Catholic contemporaries of Fitz who also went to
Cambridge were the sons of Sir John Acton. After their father's death in 1811, his
young widow Marianne had uprooted herself from the Kingdom of the Two

The meeting between Pope Gregory XVI and the Tsar Nicholas of Russia, with
Cardinal Acton acting as interpreter

Sicilies, which she had never left before, and had gone with her three children to live at Aldenham, the family seat in Shropshire. Though she was herself to all intents and purposes a Neapolitan, despite her English ancestry, she had agreed to make her children English. The two boys had been sent not only to Cambridge – though like other Catholics of their generation had left without taking a degree to avoid the Protestant oath that was still obligatory for those doing so – but before that to a Protestant school at Isleworth near London, while the younger son Charles had, like Fitz, spent a period with an Anglican clergyman as his tutor.

For all his English upbringing, the elder son Sir Richard had been attracted back to the Continent, entering the diplomatic service of the Kingdom of the Two Sicilies and building himself the palatial Villa Acton overlooking the Bay of Naples. He had made a brilliant marriage to Marie, daughter and heiress of the Duke of Dalberg: he and she had led a fashionable cosmopolitan life, moving between her family schloss on the Rhine, the Hôtel Dalberg in Paris, the Villa Acton and Aldenham. But he had died suddenly in 1837, leaving a three-year-old son. According to the family legend, Marie, to punish him for his gambling, told the servants at the Hôtel Dalberg not to let him in when he returned one wintry night from the gaming tables; with the result that he died of pneumonia.

Sir Richard's younger brother Charles was also destined to spend most of his life abroad. After leaving Cambridge, he had gone to Rome to study for the priesthood and, though very modest and unassuming, he had risen rapidly in the Church, holding various high offices which kept him in Italy except when he was attaché to the Nuncio in Paris. When Cardinal Weld died, Monsignor Acton was marked out as the next English Cardinal: he received his Red Hat in 1842, at forty-one the youngest member of the Sacred College.

Though he had a chance of returning to the kingdom of his birth, King Ferdinand II of the Two Sicilies being very anxious to have him as Archbishop of Naples, he preferred to remain in Rome, where he devoted himself to English ecclesiastical affairs and working for the poor; making a brief foray into high politics in 1845 when he acted as interpreter and sole witness at the meeting between Pope Gregory XVI and the Tsar Nicholas of Russia. His mother lived with him and became well-known in Papal circles, Pius IX wrote her some New Year verses under the pseudonym of 'The Hermit of Castelgandolfo' a few months after he was elected Pope. She had to sell her jewels to help her son keep up the state required of him as a Prince of the Church and to provide money for his numerous charities.

Cardinal Acton's sister Elizabeth lived in England, married to Sir Robert Throckmorton who succeeded his uncle Sir Charles in 1840. At their wedding at Aldenham in 1829, the future Cardinal had officiated and one of the guests had drunk no fewer than twenty-three glasses of champagne. After the untimely death of her son the Cardinal in 1847, Marianne Acton was to spend much of her time with the Throckmortons at Coughton in Warwickshire.

Sir Robert's first cousin Mary Throckmorton was married to the racehorse-owning Thomas Riddell, whose ecclesiastical brother William died in the same year as Cardinal Acton. William Riddell, who was a secretary to Cardinal Weld at the Conclave which elected Gregory XVI, had been made a bishop in 1844 and appointed Coadjutor to the Vicar-Apostolic of the Northern District of England. Three years later he gave his life working heroically among the victims of a cholera epidemic in Newcastle.

In the year that William Riddell was made a bishop, Frederick Weld landed in New Zealand. He was twenty, tall but slight with brown hair and piercing blue eyes, the third of the four sons of Humphrey Weld of Chideock in Dorset who like his brother the Cardinal had married a Clifford. Frederick was thus a nephew not only of the Cardinal but also of his Clifford son-in-law: he was also a nephew of two Cliffords who ventured into distant lands before him as missionary priests.

As the younger son of a younger son – though his father was fortunate among younger sons in having an estate – Frederick had to make his way in the world on leaving the University of Freiburg where he had gone after Stonyhurst. Having, as he himself put it, 'bush instincts' – as a child he had always wanted to sleep out under a certain old tree when staying at Ugbrooke with his Clifford grandparents[17] – New Zealand attracted him with its promise of a life of pioneering; particularly as he already had two cousins there. One was Charles Clifford, son of George Clifford who had been the first boy at Stonyhurst; the other was Sir Edward Vavasour's son William. Clifford and Vavasour, together with Henry Petre – second son of the eleventh Lord Petre and of Fanchon Bedingfeld – had obtained a concession of 30,000 acres in North Island from the Maoris and at the time of Frederick Weld's arrival had just bought 500 sheep in Sydney.

Frederick helped them with the sheep and showed a talent for shepherding, so that when Petre decided to pull out in order to speculate in horses, he was offered his share in the partnership. Vavasour, too, did not stay, so that it became a partnership of Clifford and Frederick, with Clifford in Wellington handling the business side of the enterprise and Frederick at the sheep station, where he built a new house to take the place of the original Maori hut which was so subject to flooding that as often as not he had slept in a canoe moored alongside it. The new house had a room for his books, an essential amenity for he was cultured and had a taste for literature, which he regarded as being in no way incompatible with his love of the wide open spaces. 'It has been said that "three years in the bush unfits a man for the purpose of civilized

Frederick Weld

society"' he noted. 'I don't hold that doctrine, I consider that a man who is a gentleman by birth and education will always remain such, as long as he retains his self respect as a Catholic.'[18]

More important than bookshelves were his relations with the local Maoris, some of whom disputed the partners' title to the land. 'A sound thrashing is the only cure for the arrogance of some of these chiefs', he once angrily declared.[19] But while maintaining this old-fashioned attitude, and mistrusting the humanitarianism of the Aborigines' Protection Society – not only because it threatened his position as a landowner but because it was associated with Protestant missionary activities – he developed his own brand of humanitarianism. He and his Maori neighbours became firm friends.

The partnership was soon one of the most successful sheep enterprises in the colony. They acquired 200,000 acres in the north of South Island; one of their new

Stonyhurst, New Zealand

stations they named Stonyhurst, while a sheep-run was given the name of Ugbrooke. They had their own boat to carry meat and wool to Wellington and bring back supplies: they made a harbour for it under a cliff which Frederick named White Nose after a cliff near Lulworth. However much he may have grown to like New Zealand, Frederick could not help thinking of home. He expressed his feelings in a poem which he wrote in 1847:

> I sat upon a lofty hill
> Far below the Ocean lay
> The wind was hushed, and calm and still
> Glittered with trembling light the bay.
> Could I forget in such a scene
> Those cliffs that rise on Chideock shore?
> The world's wide waste may intervene
> I love them but the more – the more![20]

While Frederick Weld and Charles Clifford were raising sheep in far-away New

Zealand, the English Catholic world was shaken by the storm which suddenly blew up over the so-called Papal Aggression. In the autumn of 1850, Pope Pius IX restored the English Catholic hierarchy, replacing the Vicars-Apostolic with bishops of territorial sees. Although the names of these dioceses were not the same as those of the Anglican episcopate, the very idea that the Pope should presume to give his bishops titles taken from places in England outraged English public opinion. Feelings were further inflamed by the over-exultant pastoral letter, 'From out the Flaminian Gate of Rome', which Cardinal Wiseman, as he now was, issued on his way to take up his appointment as the first Archbishop of Westminster.

The Prime Minister, Lord John Russell, publicly condemned the restoration of the Catholic hierarchy as 'insolent and insidious' and 'inconsistent with the Queen's supremacy'. The Anglican bishops came out with such phrases as 'foreign intruders' and 'foreign bondage': *The Times* led the Press in denouncing what it described as 'one of the grossest acts of folly and impertinence which the Court of Rome has ventured to commit since the Crown and people of England threw off its yoke'.[21] There were demonstrations all over the country: Guy Fawkes' Day was celebrated with frenzied excitement, effigies of Wiseman and the Pope blazing merrily on every bonfire.

Even a few prominent Catholics, who still had the old Cisalpine mentality, joined in the outcry. 'The late bold and clearly expressed edict of the Court of Rome cannot be received or accepted by English Roman Catholics without a violation of their duties as citizens', Lord Beaumont declared in an open letter, and the Duke of Norfolk entirely agreed with him. Lord Beaumont and his brother John Stapleton subsequently left the Catholic Church and so to all intents and purposes did the Duke, who while making no formal renunciation of Catholicism ceased practising as a Catholic and received the Anglican Sacrament. Lord Camoys, the former Thomas Stonor, took a similar attitude, without going so far as to cease practising. He was now a Lord-in-Waiting and when sitting next to the Queen at dinner on Christmas Eve he told her that he regarded the restoration of the hierarchy as 'inopportune' and that it made him feel quite uncomfortable in Society. 'Poor man, so sensible', the Queen afterwards remarked.[22]

Very different was the attitude of the nineteenth Lord Stourton, who had succeeded his father in 1846. In a letter to *The Times* regretting his inability to attend a meeting of Catholics in Yorkshire to protest against the agitation over the new hierarchy, he wrote:

I most fully concur in the religious principles and opinions expressed by the Roman Catholics on that occasion, and I trust that those same principles, for the

The thirteenth Duke of Norfolk as a page at the Coronation of George IV

support of which my ancestors have suffered for so many generations . . . will be held sacred and inviolate by me to my dying breath.[23]

Lord Shrewsbury, having at first been in two minds about the restoration of the hierarchy, deplored the agitation and wrote from Naples expressing his approval of two pamphlets in defence of Wiseman and the Papal point of view which Ambrose Lisle March Phillipps had published. One of Ambrose's pamphlets was described by the naturalist Charles Waterton as 'the perfection of Catholicity . . . a masterpiece beyond all praise'.[24] The Pope's champions among the Catholic squirearchy also included John Herbert, formerly Jones, of Llanarth in Monmouthshire – who had recently reverted to the original surname of his family – and his distant kinsman and county neighbour John Vaughan of Courtfield. The two of them stood up in defence of the Pope at a public meeting at Usk, where the audience was largely hostile. 'We belong to two of the few Roman Catholic families in the neighbourhood who have survived three hundred years of persecution', John Vaughan said in his speech. His words were greeted with yells and hooting, but he kept on and eventually silenced the audience.[25]

Early in the following year, though the furore had by then largely died down, Lord John Russell – 'the unbelieving Minister', as Lord Shrewsbury called him[26] – insisted on bringing in his Ecclesiastical Titles Bill to forbid the assumption in England of 'ecclesiastical titles conferred by a foreign power'. In fact it was never actually enforced and was to be repealed some twenty years later. The Duke of Norfolk voted for the Bill in the House of Lords, while his son Fitz voted against it in the Commons, having hurried back from the Continent in order to do so. The Duke had made frantic efforts to keep his son away from the debate: he even tried to get the Queen to send him on a mission to Rome as 'honourable banishment'.[27] He had worked himself up into such a state that his doctors had feared that his son's arrival at Westminster would give him a stroke.

Fitz's friend Father Frederick Faber of the London Oratory expected the Duke to cut off his son's allowance. Fitz, who had been MP for Arundel, which despite the Reform Act was still regarded as one of the Duke's pocket boroughs, resigned his seat so as not to be beholden to his father and was adopted for an Irish seat instead. Attempts to reconcile father and son were made by Fitz's younger brother Lord Edward Fitzalan-Howard who was also an MP and shared his views, though in a more moderate way.

A few months before the restoration of the hierarchy, Fitz's wife Minna had become a Catholic. She wrote a letter to their friend Father Faber of the Oratory, himself a convert Anglican clergyman, asking him to receive her into the Catholic

Church. 'The Earl brought it himself and was literally too happy to speak', Faber told Newman.[28] Fitz wished to show his gratitude to the Fathers of the Oratory for their prayers by making them a gift of money, but Faber would hear of no such thing. 'St Philip . . . would not like us to take money for it.'[29] So Minna gave the Oratory a set of gold vestments. The religious upbringing of her three elder girls, Toria, little Minna and 'noisy' Mary, now changed from Anglican to Catholic, which at first caused the ten-year-old Toria some distress. But the seven-year-old Minna took the change happily enough and by the end of the year had decided that she wanted to become a nun.

'People are beginning to call and notice us because of Lady Arundel's conversion: how small!!', Faber wrote to Newman in February 1850.[30] The Catholic Church was to rise still higher in the estimation of such people with the conversion, a few months later, of the young Viscount and Viscountess Feilding. Lord Feilding was the son and heir of the Earl of Denbigh; the earldom dated from the time of James I and the family was believed to be descended from the Habsburgs, hence Lord Feilding's romantic Christian name of Rudolph, which went well with his extreme good looks. Even without their Habsburg origin – which was to be disproved at the end of the nineteenth century, so that they came to be known as 'Perhapsburgs' – the Feildings were of ancient lineage, going back in the direct male line to a thirteenth century knight.

Despite their Welsh title, the Denbighs' ancestral seat, Newnham Paddox, was in Warwickshire; but as it happened, Lord and Lady Feilding actually lived in North Wales; Lady Feilding, the former Louisa Pennant, having inherited the Downing estate in Flintshire. Here they were building an Anglican church, both being devout High Anglicans; even though Lord Denbigh had taken the precaution of sending Rudolph to Cambridge in order not to expose him to the dangers of the Oxford Movement. But by 1850, like their friend Henry Edward Manning, the Archdeacon of Chichester, they were experiencing the difficulties which had already brought Newman into the Church of Rome.

In the summer of that year, Louisa Feilding, who was consumptive, fell ill and Rudolph took her to see a famous specialist in Edinburgh. While they were there they made up their minds and planned to be received into the Catholic Church by the local Catholic bishop before they left. Rudolph wrote to his father informing him of their decision, which brought Lord Denbigh hot-foot to Edinburgh, together with Rudolph's much-loved twin sister Minnie and an Evangelical clergyman, in a last-minute attempt to prevent his son and heir from taking 'so dreadful a step'.[31] Rudolph and Louisa heard of their arrival just as they were setting out for their reception into the Catholic Church. They felt they could not keep the

Rudolph, Viscount Feilding, afterwards the eighth
Earl of Denbigh

bishop waiting, so by the time Lord Denbigh saw them they had already become
Catholics. Lord Denbigh threatened to consider Rudolph 'as worse than dead' and
proceeded to disinherit him.[32]

Rudolph and Louisa now decided that the church which they were building in
Flintshire would be a Catholic church: they were paying for it themselves and had
not yet made it over to the local Anglican bishop so could do what they liked with it.
But their decision caused a terrible outcry; Rudolph was burnt in effigy. Two local
Anglican vicars opened a subscription list for building a church to take the place of
that 'diverted to the Romish schism': subscriptions poured in from all over the
country so that in the end there was enough to build not just one church but two.

Cecil Marchioness of Lothian

For the sake of Louisa's health and also perhaps to escape from the row over the church, the Feildings spent their first winter as Catholics in Rome. 'O the delight to feel that at length this glorious building really belonged to one', Rudolph exclaimed after visiting St Peter's.[33] Also in Rome were Viscount and Viscountess Campden, who were both received into the Catholic Church on New Year's Day. 'They are so happy', Rudolph wrote. 'He already looks quite a different man.'[34] The Campdens were contemporaries of the Feildings: he was the son and heir of the Earl of Gainsborough: she was a daughter of the Earl of Erroll and a grand-daughter of King William IV, her mother being one of the King's illegitimate children by Mrs Jordan.

The conversion of the Feildings and the Campdens was followed in April 1851 by that of Manning and his friend James Hope-Scott, a cousin of the Earl of Hopetoun who was a leading parliamentary barrister. Hope-Scott was married to the grand-daughter of Sir Walter Scott and lived at Abbotsford, the Tudor and

Scottish Baronial house which Scott had built for himself in Roxburghshire. A few miles away was Monteviot, one of the seats of the young Marquis of Lothian to whom Hope-Scott was connected by marriage, his sister being the wife of Lord Lothian's clergyman uncle Lord Henry Kerr.

Lord Lothian's mother, the widowed Cecil Lady Lothian, a daughter of Lord Shrewsbury's remote Protestant kinsman Earl Talbot, was described as having 'a face and form resembling in stately elegance the recumbent figure upon some quattrocento sarcophagus in Venice or Verona'.[35] She was deeply religious, a High Anglican as Manning and Hope-Scott had been, but since Newman's defection to Rome she had suffered misgivings. Less than a month after the conversion of Manning and Hope-Scott, she decided to follow them.

In taking this step she was supported by her brother Gilbert Talbot and by her brother-in-law Lord Henry Kerr, both of whom were soon to go the same way as she. But she had to contend with the family trustees, who were determined that her seven children should remain Protestant. Of her five sons, the two eldest, Lord Lothian and Lord Schomberg Kerr, were grown-up and firm in their Anglican beliefs. Of the other three, who were still schoolboys, Walter was out of harm's way in the Navy, but John, the youngest, wanted to become a Catholic like his mother and Ralph was wavering. And the two girls, Cecie and Alice, insisted on becoming Catholics despite the efforts of an Anglican divine brought by the trustees from St Paul's in London to argue with them.

The trustees then planned to take Ralph and John away from their mother, but Lady Lothian heard of their plan from her friend the Duchess of Buccleuch, who had Catholic leanings. So at four on a winter's morning she did a flit from Newbattle Abbey, the principal family seat in Midlothian, taking John with her. Ralph at first did not want to go and stayed in bed, but the girls went into his room and told him to go and join their mother and John. So he got up and dressed and ran after his mother and brother as they walked along the icy road to where a cab was waiting.

They drove straight to the Catholic bishop in Edinburgh, who at once received John into the Catholic Church. Ralph was uncertain and was told by the bishop to go away and pray for enlightenment, but then suddenly decided that he, too, wished to be received; and as he came out of the sacristy he announced, 'Mama, I am a Papist now'.[36] Meanwhile at Newbattle the boys' tutor was told of Lady Lothian's nocturnal flit by the girls at breakfast. Dropping his fork, he rushed off to tell the young Lord Lothian, who was still in bed. 'By Jove, they've done us', Lothian exclaimed, and he burst out laughing.[37]

As a Catholic, Lady Lothian felt uneasy living at Newbattle, which had originally been a Cistercian monastery but had been granted to the Kerrs at the Reformation. When she visited Rome, she told Pope Pius IX of her scruples. 'Sta tranquilla, figlia mia' said the Pope, but she was not happy until he had given her a document under his sign manual authorizing her and her children to occupy their Scottish home in peace.[38]

In 1851, the year of Lady Lothian's conversion, Isabel Arundell, 'a quiet girl enough of the convent type . . . fair-haired and rather pretty',[39] saw the light in a different way. She was walking with her sister on the ramparts at Boulogne when a man came towards her. As she herself described him, he was dark and 'weather-beaten', with 'clearly defined eyebrows' and 'an enormous black moustache'. What struck her most about him was 'two large black flashing eyes with long lashes, that pierced one through and through'.[40] When they had passed him, Isabel said to her sister, 'That man will marry me'.[41]

The man was Richard Burton. He was then thirty, ten years older than Isabel, and back from India where he had soldiered, studied oriental languages, customs and philosophies, lived the life of a native, prayed as a Mohammedan, and shocked the authorities by writing an over-frank report on Indian eroticism. A few days after the encounter on the ramparts, Isabel met him at a *thé-dansant*. He waltzed with her once and spoke to her a few times. She left Boulogne without seeing him again and soon afterwards he set off on his pilgrimage to Mecca.

At twenty, Isabel was not entirely the innocent convent girl: she was already a confirmed smoker, having acquired the habit through stealing her father's cigars. She had done a London season, when one of her favourite dancing-partners had been Teddy Howard: the Duke of Norfolk's pretty little page at the Coronation was now a tall and handsome young officer in the Life Guards. The brilliant scene at Almack's contrasted with the simplicity of Isabel's home life in a rambling Essex farmhouse; for her parents were relatively poor. Her father, Henry Raymond Arundell, a nephew of the ninth Lord Arundell of Wardour, had been obliged to earn his living as a wine merchant. Isabel's mother, though a sister of the wealthy Lancashire baronet Sir John Gerard, had been provided for no better than her fashionable but impecunious younger brother Robert. But the sense of family obligation, strong in those days and particularly strong among the Catholics, ensured them a footing in the fashionable world. The eleventh Lord Arundell, who was Isabel's godfather, was always kind to his cousins and at one time had lent them a wing of Wardour as a country retreat.

Since succeeding his elder brother Everard in 1834, the eleventh Lord Arundell of Wardour had done much to repair the family fortunes: he was able to live at Wardour and had actually bought land rather than selling it, as his predecessors had done. As well as being a good manager he was a talented musician, playing the cello, the cornet and the trombone: he had a sense of humour and was very popular. He managed to lead a normal life in spite of being paralysed on one side, the result of some form of stroke which he had suffered when comparatively young. It was attributed to his having sat on cold marble when overheated during a visit to Rome.

Lord Arundell's second wife Frances was a daughter of Sir Henry Tichborne and a grand-daughter of the Sir Henry who discontinued the Tichborne Dole. Sir Henry had only daughters and at his death in 1845 was succeeded by his brother Edward who had taken the name Doughty having inherited the estates of a wealthy cousin; estates worth three or four times as much as the heavily-mortgaged Tichborne patrimony. Sir Edward Doughty had just the one daughter, Katherine, known as Kate, having lost his only son. After his son's death, the Dole had been revived, for it then seemed that the second part of Dame Mabella's curse was dangerously near to taking effect, there being only one male heir in the next generation, the small son of Sir Edward's younger brother James Tichborne. Since then James's wife had been blessed with a second son.

James Tichborne lived in Paris with his beautiful virago of a wife Henriette-Félicité, who was to all intents and purposes French though a natural daughter of a Wiltshire gentleman named Henry Seymour. But her mother was French and her nominal father was a Bourbon Conti, which gave her delusions of royal grandeur: she had, moreover, spent most of her life in France. She tried to bring up her elder son Roger as a Frenchman, so that he grew to adolescence without speaking any language but French. But when he was sixteen his father, very much against his mother's wishes, sent him to Stonyhurst, where though he was a stranger to English life and spoke English with a strong French accent, he settled down and was happy. And when he left school, a slim, elegant youth with large and melancholy eyes, he remained in England, obtaining a commission in the 6th Dragoon Guards, known as the Carabineers, a regiment with a high proportion of Catholics among its officers. He was popular both in the regiment and away from it: he liked field sports, though he also had literary tastes, despite his sketchy education: he stayed in houses like Burton Constable. He had two other good reasons for preferring England to France. He wished to keep away from his possessive and bad-tempered mother and he had fallen in love with his cousin Kate Doughty.

As the ultimate heir to the baronetcy and to Tichborne, which was then her home, Roger was on the face of it a very suitable husband for Kate. But her parents were not keen on the match because they had heard rumours that he drank. In fact, though he may have drunk and smoked more than was good for him, he was noted neither for drunkenness nor for any other vice. He also incurred their disapproval by

Henriette-Félicité, Lady Tichborne

being casual in practising his religion, though he was quite a good Catholic at heart. Eventually Kate's parents agreed to the marriage if the young people would wait three years and not see each other during that time. So Roger decided to leave the army and go travelling.

He sailed for Valparaiso in March 1853, when he was twenty-four, and spent nearly a year travelling in South America. In April 1854 he left Rio in a British vessel bound for New York. The ship was never seen or heard of again and was presumed to have gone down with all hands.

If Roger Tichborne was originally brought up to be French, his cousin by

Roger Tichborne. A Daguerreotype taken in
Santiago, when he was on his ill-fated travels

marriage Lord Dormer – the husband of Sir Henry Tichborne's daughter Eliza –
started life as a Hungarian. Joseph Thaddeus Dormer, the son of John Dormer who
became a general in the Imperial service, grew up in Hungary and followed his
father into the Austrian army. When in 1826 at the age of thirty-six he succeeded his
cousin Evelyn as the eleventh Lord Dormer he could not speak English. But he
settled down in England, married Eliza Tichborne in 1829 and soon afterwards
rebuilt Grove Park, his Warwickshire seat, in a rather dull Tudor-Gothic style.

Another of Sir Henry Tichborne's daughters married, as her first husband,
Colonel Charles Talbot. Her son Bertram became the seventeenth Earl of
Shrewsbury when his cousin died of malaria in Naples in November 1852. The
new Lord Shrewsbury, a young man 'of singularly mild and gentle disposition'[42]
and a Knight of Malta, was not yet twenty and unmarried when his cousin died;

Henry Clifford, VC

there was then no other male Talbot of the Catholic Shrewsbury line. Fearing that if Bertram were to die leaving no son the Shrewsbury estates would be claimed by his distant Protestant kinsman Earl Talbot, the late Lord Shrewsbury had made a remarkable will leaving them in that contingency not to his daughter or grandchildren in the Roman nobility, but to be divided between Ambrose Lisle March Phillipps and another convert. He also left Ambrose and the other gentleman an unconditional legacy of £40,000 each.

In 1853, the year when Roger Tichborne set out on his ill-fated travels, Eliza Vaughan died, leaving a heartbroken husband and a motherless family of thirteen. By that time, the eldest son Herbert was twenty-one and studying in Rome for the priesthood. He was a handsome and adventurous young man who later admitted that what he found hardest to bear on entering the religious life was giving up riding and shooting. He had announced his intention of becoming a priest at the age of sixteen, when his mother had exclaimed happily, 'I knew it, dear'. But it had been a bitter disappointment to his father, who had hoped that Herbert would become a soldier. He said, 'If Herbert goes, all the others may go, too'.[43] John Vaughan's prophecy looked like being fulfilled when, in the year of Eliza's death, his second son Roger, who liked shooting as much as Herbert did, became a Benedictine monk.

The outbreak of the Crimean War took John Vaughan away from his domestic sorrows. Though he was then forty-five, he decided to go to the front and, having settled his family in Boulogne, he served in the Crimea until the end of the war. Catholics of the younger generation in the Crimea included Francis Turville who sailed from Portsmouth with his regiment after 'a capital ball';[44] Lord Stourton's second son Everard who was in the Hussars and his eldest son Alfred who spent a winter campaigning at his own expense; and Lord Lovat's second son Alexander Fraser of the Scots Fusilier Guards. Alexander Fraser fought in all the battles and suffered hardships which permanently affected his health. His eldest brother Simon also wanted to fight but his parents would not hear of it, so he had to content himself with visiting the Scottish regiments and bringing them comforts.

Alexander Fraser's war record was surpassed by that of Henry Clifford, a younger son of Hugh, Lord Clifford of Chudleigh and a grandson of Cardinal Weld. Henry Clifford went through life, as he himself put it, 'endeavouring with God's grace to be a good Catholic and a good soldier'.[45] He had served with distinction at the Cape, where as well as campaigning against Boer rebels he had looked after the moral welfare of a brother-officer, a son of Thomas Clifton who had turned Protestant, keeping him 'more than once out of evil' and praying daily for his conversion.[46] In the Crimea, where he was ADC to a general, he showed outstanding courage at the Battle of Inkerman, leading a few of his men against a much larger body of Russians. For this, he was given the Victoria Cross – one of the first VCs to be awarded.

CHAPTER 8

'Papal hymns and soldier-songs'

WHEN Alfred and Everard Stourton went to the Crimea, their father, the nineteenth Lord Stourton, had just finished rebuilding Allerton Park, his Yorkshire seat: he could afford to do so, thanks to the coal on his estates near Leeds. The plain Georgian house was transformed into a vast turreted Tudor-Gothic pile dominated by a formidable clerestory tower which lit the great hall. Lord Stourton did not build a chapel to match the style and grandeur of the house, but kept the simple chapel which his grandfather had built, now engulfed by the service wing. This did not denote any lack of piety on his part, for he was a most devout Catholic. He and his wife Mary Lucy, a sister of Hugh Clifford, used to be seen walking every afternoon saying the Rosary: they were known as Pooge and Mooge.

While Lord Stourton made do with an unknown architect named George Martin for Allerton, Charles Scarisbrick employed Pugin to transform Scarisbrick Hall in Lancashire into a Gothic extravaganza in his Houses of Parliament manner. The work had started in 1837 and was completed after Pugin's death by his son Edward in the middle eighteen-fifties, when the clock tower, which reminded Gladstone of the Clock Tower at Westminster, was built. The interior of the house was encrusted with medieval Flemish woodwork brought by Charles Scarisbrick from Belgium.

The Scarisbricks had been at Scarisbrick since the thirteenth century: but — unlike the Stonors, the Traffords and other Catholic families — they could not boast of an unbroken male-line succession for Charles's father had started life as Thomas Eccleston and changed his name to Scarisbrick on marrying the Scarisbrick heiress. Since succeeding his brother in 1833, Charles had become a millionaire through buying the land over which the town of Southport was spreading. His wealth does not seem to have brought him happiness. There was melancholy as well as a certain

Allerton Park, as transformed by the nineteenth Lord Stourton

toughness and even meanness in his long and sensitive face.

The American writer Nathaniel Hawthorne, who was living in Southport when Charles Scarisbrick was finishing his new house, picked up the local gossip on him:

> He is an eccentric man, they said, and there seems to be an obscurity about the early part of his life; according to some reports, he kept a gambling house in Paris before succeeding to the estate. Neither is it a settled point whether or no he has ever been married. He is a Catholic, but is bringing up his children, they say, in the Protestant faith. He is a very eccentric and nervous man, and spends all his time in this secluded Hall, which stands in the midst of mosses and marshes; and sees nobody, not even his own steward.[1]

In fact he was never married to the woman with whom he lived, and he did indeed allow her to bring up the children he had by her as Protestants. It was also true that he was a recluse; his tenants could never get near him and a man who came all the way from London to see him on business returned without having obtained an interview.

Charles, nineteenth Lord Stourton (right) and Mary Lucy Clifford, his wife

In 1856, at about the time that Pugin's Scarisbrick Hall was completed, his other great Catholic house, Alton, ceased to be Catholic. The young Bertram, seventeenth Earl of Shrewsbury, whose health had always been delicate, died unmarried in Lisbon; the will of the previous Lord Shrewsbury was immediately disputed by the Protestant Earl Talbot. After a lawsuit lasting many months, the costs of which were so enormous that poor Ambrose Phillipps received only £11,000 out of his £40,000 legacy, Lord Talbot succeeded in claiming the Shrewsbury estates as well as the title. There was, however, some unsettled property which Bertram left to the infant Lord Edmund Fitzalan Howard, younger son of Fitz who had recently succeeded as Duke of Norfolk; he was a distant cousin of the Shrewsburys but Bertram had many closer relations, notably his two sisters. His elder sister Lady Annette had made a very suitable Catholic marriage in 1855. Her husband was Sir Humphrey de Trafford of Trafford, whose father had been made a baronet in 1841 and like other early Victorians had adopted the 'de' to give his surname a medieval flavour.

'Don't let Cecil hear of it, for she will be plotting with Jim Hope to keep us out of the succession', Lord Talbot had written on hearing of Bertram's death.[2] It is understandable that he should have feared the machinations of his Catholic sister Lady Lothian, who was now the head of a formidable group of Catholic Kerrs. Her youngest son John, who was going to be a priest, had died of pneumonia at Ushaw, the notoriously spartan Catholic school and seminary in County Durham but his place had been taken by her naval son Walter, who when he came home on leave in 1856 began by making fun of his mother's 'superstitious religion'[3] and then surprised everybody by becoming a Catholic himself. And the six children of Lady Lothian's convert in-laws Lord and Lady Henry Kerr, including their son Schomberg who was also in the Navy, had by now followed their parents into the Catholic Church.

The aristocratic converts continued to come in. The conversion of Lord Norreys in 1858 meant that there would be another Catholic earldom to make up for the loss of Shrewsbury, for he was the son and heir of the Earl of Abingdon, head of the junior branch of the Berties, of whom the senior line were Earls of Lindsey and had

Scarisbrick Hall

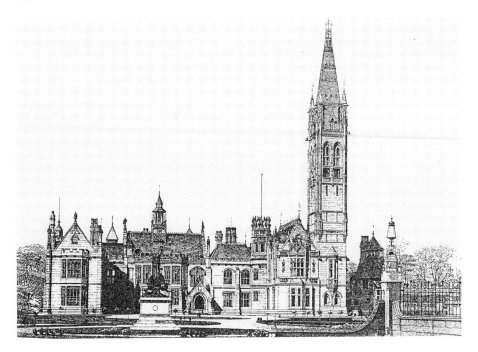

until 1809 been Dukes of Ancaster. An elegant young man renowned as a rider and as a whip – he could turn a coach-and-four on a threepenny bit, so to speak – Lord Norreys married Caroline, daughter of Charles Towneley of Towneley, in the year of his conversion.

By that time Rudolph Feilding, the first of the three convert heirs to earldoms of the eighteen-fifties, had also married into an old Catholic family. Poor Louisa had died in 1853. Her death brought about a reconciliation between Rudolph and his father, though Lord Denbigh still intended to disinherit him. Louisa left no children and in 1857 Rudolph married again, his second wife being the tall and graceful Mary Berkeley, daughter of Robert Berkeley of Spetchley Park in Worcestershire. The Berkeleys' ancestry was illustrious even by the standards of the Catholic aristocracy. They were descended from a younger son of a medieval Lord Berkeley. At Spetchley, a large Classical house which was always full of guests, Robert and Henrietta Berkeley and their sons and daughters devoted their lives to good works and music.

Rudolph and his new wife went to live in Flintshire at Downing, which Louisa had left to him. Mary was not at all jealous of her predecessor's memory: she treasured Louisa's possessions and put flowers in front of her portrait. She was an admirable

Sir Humphrey and Lady Annette de Trafford with their horses and hounds at Trafford Park. From a painting by Barrow

Walter Strickland

wife in other respects as well. She reorganized her husband's finances, which was most necessary since he was reckless and over-generous, and she joined wholeheartedly with him in looking after the welfare of the neighbourhood, learning Welsh so that she could get on better with the people. She kept a cauldron of 'good substantial soup'[4] always on the fire for handing out to the poor, while Rudolph took Christian charity still further and dressed the sores on the feet of tramps with his own hands. They also cared for the pilgrims – many of them blind or disabled – who came to the nearby St Winefride's Well, which had continued to be a place of pilgrimage for Catholics thanks to the presence in the neighbourhood of one of the few Welsh Catholic families of substance, the Mostyns of Talacre. Sir Pyers Mostyn and his wife Frances, a daughter of Lord Lovat, became close friends of the Feildings.

The year of Rudolph Feilding's second marriage was the year the Indian Mutiny broke out. The Mutiny saw the Crimean veteran Everard Stourton back in action, while another Everard, the second son of Ambrose and Laura Lisle March Phillipps, was killed at the Siege of Delhi and recommended for a posthumous V C. Lord Dormer's soldier son Jim — who had the impressive middle name of Charlemagne – was also serving in India at this time and so was George Turville, a brother of Francis who went to the Crimea and a son of George Fortescue Turville the squire of Bosworth. Young George, who was in the Indian Army, fell seriously ill with fever and dysentery in 1858. He was sent home, but died soon after returning to England.

Among the Catholics serving Queen Victoria at this time in other parts of the world was the young naval officer Lieutenant Walter Strickland, a cadet of the Stricklands of Sizergh in Westmoreland and a son of Jarrard Strickland who had been ADC to the future Duke of Wellington at Seringapatam. His ship was in the Mediterranean and took him frequently to Naples, where he was befriended by Sir John Acton's widow Marianne – now a diminutive but formidable old lady with a brown wig – as well as to Malta. One morning in 1857 an English Jesuit approached him on behalf of a Maltese nobleman offering him the hand of his daughter; the girl and her parents had apparently seen him in church and liked the look of him. On his next visit to Naples he consulted Marianne Acton who advised him to accept the proposal. In January 1858, at a ball on board his ship in the Grand Harbour of Valletta, he set eyes for the first time on his future bride, Donna Louisa Bonici. She turned out to be a beautiful, charming and cultivated girl who spoke English, French and Italian as well as Maltese; she was, moreover, a very considerable heiress. The fortunate Walter lost no time in marrying her.

Marianne Acton's clever grandson, the young Sir John Acton – known to his family as Johny – returned to England in 1858 having completed his studies in Munich under the liberal Catholic priest and scholar Ignaz von Döllinger. Apart from a period at Oscott, the Catholic school near Birmingham, his education had been entirely Continental; making him, in the words of a recent writer, 'an English gentleman brought up on German scholarship'.[5] In his character, which showed no trace of Neapolitan influence, the German scholar was uppermost: he was deadly serious and something of a prig. He saw himself as a missionary to educate English Catholic opinion and to lead the forces of Liberalism and Catholicism against Toryism, unbelief and what he saw as Papal obscurantism. He opened his campaign by taking a share in a Catholic periodical called the *Rambler* and becoming its editor.

Johny's mother, the fashionable Marie de Dalberg, had married as her second husband the English statesman Earl Granville, who had grown up in the charmed circle of the high Whig aristocracy known as the 'Devonshire House Set'. 'Pussy' Granville's light patrician touch, his easy-going and very English attitude to life, was in complete contrast to the Germanic seriousness of his stepson and was certainly good for him. To show young Johny that there were other worlds than Dr Döllinger's library, he had taken him as his secretary when he went to St Petersburg to represent Queen Victoria at the Coronation of the Tsar Alexander II, and Johny had got on surprisingly well in the glittering society of the Russian Imperial Court. He also helped Johny to enter Parliament.

Lord Granville was of course an Anglican but his sister Lady Georgiana Fullerton was a convert and one of a group of aristocratic Catholics devoted to good works, chief among whom were the new Duke and Duchess of Norfolk. Fitz, a cousin of Lady Georgiana through his mother, had succeeded his father – who had died reconciled with the Catholic Church – in 1856. Since then, he and his wife Minna had used their great position 'entirely for the service of God and the poor'.[6] To serve God, he built churches and chapels. Unlike Lord Shrewsbury and Ambrose Lisle March Phillipps he was immune to Pugin's fallacy that Gothic was the only true Christian architecture and was just as happy building a chapel in an Italianate Classical style for the London Oratory as he was building a Gothic chapel at Arundel.

He and Minna looked a homely couple, she by no means a beauty, he with rather bucolic features framed by the sort of whiskers known as a Newgate fringe. When not serving God and the poor they devoted themselves to their children; the two boys Henry and Edmund and the eight girls ranging from Toria who was almost grown-up to Anne, who was born a year after Fitz succeeded to the dukedom. And then a blow fell on the happy and godly family life of Arundel and Norfolk House. In 1858 Fitz contracted a painful and incurable disease of the liver: two years later he died, aged only forty-five. During the last six weeks, Father Faber spent most of his time at Arundel, giving spiritual comfort to his dying friend and keeping the younger children happy by telling them fairy tales. 'No Saint could have had a holier death', Faber wrote of Fitz when it was all over; while his other great friend Montalembert called him 'the most pious layman of our time'.[7]

Fitz's death was followed eight months later by that of another Catholic peer, the octogenarian Charles Stuart, eighth and last Earl of Traquair. He was the son of the Lord Traquair whose wife had died in Spain: he never married, but lived at Traquair House in Peeblesshire with his unmarried sister Lady Louisa Stuart. To a visitor who came here a few years before his death, the ancestral home of the Stuarts of Traquair, like the Stuarts themselves, 'seemed dying out, everything subdued to desolation. The old race, the old religion, the gaunt old house with its small, deep,

Traquair

comfortless windows, the decaying trees, the stillness about the doors, the grass overrunning everything.'[8]

While the Stuarts of Traquair were dying out, their cousins the Constable Maxwells, the other old Catholic family of the Scottish borders, flourished. William Constable Maxwell, tenth Lord Herries, was the eldest of five brothers; while he and his wife Marcia, a daughter of Sir Edward Vavasour, had no fewer than sixteen children. He was prosperous as well as prolific, having inherited not only the Carlaverock estate in Dumfriesshire but also the estate of Everingham in Yorkshire where he had built a fine Classical church adjoining the red-brick Georgian house. Both properties had come to him through the female line, for he was by male descent a Haggerston from Haggerston in Northumberland. One of his Haggerston ancestors had married the heiress of the Constables of Everingham, while Carlaverock came from his Maxwell grandmother as did the medieval Scottish barony of Herries which having been under attainder since his ancestor the Earl of Nithsdale took part in the 'Fifteen', was restored in 1858.

Lord Herries was devoted to his children. His wife Marcia was stricter than he was and would not allow the girls to waltz, so that they had to confine themselves to quadrilles and lancers. An exception was made for the eldest, also called Marcia, either because she was her father's favourite or because she looked so prim and proper as to be deemed immune from the dangers of waltzing. When the girls were at

Everingham in their parents' absence they would run wild, saddling up all the horses and galloping about the park. They did not, however, have any desire to hunt, even though hunting loomed so large in their brothers' lives that pink coats would be seen at weekday Mass in the Everingham church during the hunting season.

As well as sending his own five sons to Stonyhurst, Lord Herries paid for the two sons of his butler to be educated there. Believing these two boys to be unusually bright, he arranged for the Rector of Stonyhurst to come to Everingham to see them. On the Rector's approach, the boys hid in the bushes, either through shyness or because they did not wish to go to a boarding school. But they were discovered, approved of by the Rector and duly packed off to Stonyhurst with the Maxwell boys, one of whom used afterwards to say, 'It was the butler's sons who made good'.[9] The butler's sons both became distinguished Jesuits, the authors of theological and philosophical works.

A month after restoring the Barony of Herries, the House of Lords recognized Cardinal Giustiniani's niece Cecilia, the widow of Marquess Bandini, as Countess of Newburgh in her own right, the descendants of Lady Mary Eyre, who had mistakenly borne the title since 1814, having become extinct in 1853. No less

Everingham Park, with the Classical church built by William Constable Maxwell, tenth Lord Herries, to the left

William Constable Maxwell, tenth Lord Herries, gives the 'Gone-Away' out hunting with his four brothers. They include Joseph, who was a priest, on his right, and Henry, who later inherited Traquair and took the additional surname of Stuart, on his left

successful in establishing his right to an ancient Scottish title was Lord Lovat, who in 1857 was recognized as the fourteenth Lord Lovat in the Peerage of Scotland as well as the first Lord Lovat in the Peerage of the United Kingdom. But the fourteenth century Earldom of Wiltshire, which the Yorkshire Catholic squire Simon Scrope of Danby claimed in 1859, remained elusive.

Florence and Adela Scrope, Simon's daughters, were friends of Barbara Charlton. In her sweeping way she pronounced them 'far superior in appearance and education to all other Catholic girls'.[10] Barbara, now in her forties and the mother of three sons and three daughters, had been the chatelaine of Hesleyside since 1846 when her father-in-law died; her unfortunate mother-in-law died three years later. She took advantage of her new-found power to make alterations to the house; transforming the stone hall into a drawing room in French Empire taste by the fashionable decorator, Crace; turning the library into a dining room, building a clock tower. Unfortunately she brought in much new furniture and threw out the old, selling it 'by the cart-load on the village green'. One of the best of the new acquisitions, a marble Venus bought by William, was changed by Barbara from 'a thing of beauty into an object of universal reprobation'[11] by being clad in a dress of pink georgette, lest its nudity might have shocked a young convent-bred girl who was coming to stay.

Being mistress of the house also brought the responsibilities of running a large establishment. The footman refused to work under the 'stately-looking idle Catholic butler', as Barbara called him; good Catholic though she may have been, she did not consider that Catholicism made up for idleness in servants. So the stately-looking Catholic was got rid of and replaced by 'a first-class butler', who turned out to be 'a very immoral man'.[12]

As bad as the 'do-nothing Catholic butler' was the 'hopelessly obstinate Presbyterian housemaid' who when smallpox broke out in the house refused to be vaccinated, saying that 'it was wicked and a sin to thwart the Will of God'.[13] Needless to say, she went down with the disease in its most virulent form, and Barbara had to sit with her night and day, having just nursed William through the smallpox. The housemaid was dismissed as soon as she was well enough to go. Barbara was so angry with her that she refused to say goodbye. William, however, saw her off and gave her his plaid to wrap up in.

Though illness and servant trouble were frequent occurrences in Barbara's life at Hesleyside, there were also many large and cheerful house parties. At one of them, a few years earlier, the guests had included the dashing young Teddy Howard and Florence and Adela Scrope. Knowing what keen dancers Teddy and Adela were, Barbara had organized dancing every night. Teddy had danced well even after performing the ritual feat of emptying the goblet known as 'The Standard of Hesleyside', which held a whole bottle of claret, without drawing breath. Since then, Teddy had given up the Life Guards and become a priest.

Another of Barbara's entertainments was a week of theatricals to celebrate the passing of the Border Counties Railway Bill, which William had done much to promote. Lord Camoys' son Tom Stonor wrote a prologue and William 'composed an epilogue with a railway twist to it and spoke it beautifully'.[14] She entertained in London as well as at Hesleyside; she and William would take a London house for the Season and they once did a little season in Paris. For a dinner party which she gave in London in honour of Cardinal Wiseman, she had a cake made specially by Gunter in the shape of a Cardinal's hat.

Barbara and William stayed frequently in other country houses. As well as staying with Catholics such as the Scropes at Danby, they sometimes stayed in great

Isabel Burton

houses where their hosts were not of their persuasion. While they were staying with the Marquess and Marchioness of Westminster at Eaton Hall in December 1860, the conversation at dinner one night happened to be about Chester Assizes and how most of the prisoners being tried were Irish Catholics. 'Gentlemen, a Roman Catholic lady is sitting on my right', said Lord Westminster, trying to be tactful, at which Barbara said, 'Yes, but an English Catholic, not an Irish Catholic, which is all the difference in the world'.[15] The attitude that had caused Daniel O'Connell to be blackballed for the Cisalpine Club was now unfortunately stronger than ever.

A couple of months before Barbara stayed at Eaton, her cousin Sir John Swinburne died aged ninety-eight, without being reconciled to the Catholic Church. In the following year old Sir John's grandson Algernon Charles, now living in London and writing his early lyrics, made friends with Richard Burton. They had convivial evenings together which usually ended with the young red-haired poet being carried home. Burton once put Swinburne under his arm and carried him kicking down a flight of stairs.

In 1861, the year he met Swinburne, Burton was married to Isabel Arundell. A chance encounter in the Botanical Gardens had led within a fortnight to their engagement; but it was several years before they were married, during which time Burton went off on his expedition to find the source of the Nile. The marriage took place without the approval of Isabel's parents and with a dispensation from Cardinal Wiseman, for Burton was not a Catholic. It was generally believed that if he was anything, he was a Muslim; but Isabel, while being far too intelligent to try and convert him, convinced herself that he was a Catholic at heart, since he admired Newman and had attended Mass at one time when he was in India.

Isabel introduced her husband to the Catholic world, taking him to stay with her relations the Arundells at Wardour and the Gerards at Garswood. She also worked hard to obtain a more suitable post for him than the Consulate in the unimportant and unhealthy Spanish island of Fernando Po off the west coast of Africa to which he was appointed soon after their marriage. Her ceaseless lobbyings on his behalf made her something of a bore in fashionable society, even though she looked like a fairy princess with her blue eyes and golden hair. 'We were all charmed with Mrs Burton', one lady recalled. 'But even so, how she did go on! Talking, talking, talking . . . it seemed to me that this beautiful woman came and talked for whole days at a time and it was all about "Dear Richard and the Government."'[16]

Eventually, whether or not through Isabel's efforts, Burton was moved to the Consulate at Santos, the port of São Paolo in Brazil, which was at any rate healthy enough for her to accompany him there. In Brazil, she indulged her taste for grandeur by making friends with the Imperial Family; at the same time she worked hard for the poor and the sick, bullying indolent priests into administering the Sacraments to people in hospital. She served as her husband's secretary and also as his fencing partner; she rode and swam with him and went with him on expeditions into the interior. To one of her Jerningham relations she wrote, 'If you saw the virgin forests of South America in which I am now sitting alone . . . you would own that even the Cossey woods were tame'.[17]

Another devoted wife who followed her husband to a far-off land was Filomena or Mena, daughter of Ambrose March Phillipps de Lisle, as he now was, having taken the name of his medieval ancestors in 1862. In 1859 she had married her cousin Frederick Weld and gone with him to New Zealand where as well as running the sheep enterprise he was now involved in politics, having been elected to the General

Frederick Weld and his wife Filomena, daughter of Ambrose
March Phillipps de Lisle

Assembly of the colony in 1854 and appointed to the Executive Council soon
afterwards. While complaining that the work of government had reduced him 'to
nose and whiskers',[18] he had persevered and in 1864 became Prime Minister. His
cousin and partner Charles Clifford had also entered New Zealand politics and had
served as Speaker of the House of Representatives from 1853 to 1860, when he retired
to England with a knighthood. For the time being Clifford kept his share in the
partnership and eventually his son George went out to manage the two principal
stations, Flaxbourne and Stonyhurst.

When Frederick Weld became Prime Minister of New Zealand, that pioneer
and traveller of an earlier generation, the octogenarian Charles Waterton, was still

alive and well, though troubled by the presence of a 'soap and vitriol works' near Walton which killed many of his trees, polluted his lake and all but ruined the bird sanctuary which he had established in his park. While dressing oddly and shabbily, and indulging in such habits as scratching the back of his head with the big toe of his right foot and pretending to be a dog under the hall table, he was furious at being referred to in the *Ornithological Dictionary* as 'the eccentric Waterton'. He was no less indignant when a fellow-naturalist described the Bahia toad as an 'ugly brute'; that 'a gentleman avowing himself a lover of natural history' should have spoken thus of 'one of God's creation' was, he declared, enough to put him out for a week.[19]

Though cantankerous and argumentative with his fellow-naturalists, Waterton was a benevolent landlord and very kind to the poor of his neighbourhood: he not only gave them food and medicines but paid a doctor to attend on them. He was also generous in allowing the public into his park. Often picnic parties numbering several hundred would be admitted and if Waterton appeared they would serenade him by singing 'The Fine Old English Gentleman' in rousing chorus, accompanied by the band which they had brought with them.

In 1865 Waterton died as a result of a fall when walking in his park not long before his eighty-third birthday. His son Edmund came back from Rome for the funeral, when his coffin was conveyed in a boat from the house to his grave at the far end of the lake. It was preceded by another boat containing the Catholic Bishop of Beverley and fourteen priests chanting the Office for the Dead, and followed by four more boats with mourners who included Frederick Weld's elder brother Charles Weld of Chideock.

The year 1865 saw the death of another and more conventional Yorkshire Catholic squire, Sir Charles Tempest of Broughton, the eldest surviving son of Stephen and Elizabeth Tempest. He had been made a baronet in 1841, but as he never married the title died with him. Broughton Hall had been greatly improved by him; he had added an Ionic portico and a clock tower to the house, as well as a magnificent domed conservatory by William Nesfield who also designed the Italian gardens which he laid out.

Yet another death in 1865 was that of Rudolph Feilding's father the seventh Earl of Denbigh. A few years earlier Lord Denbigh had changed his mind about disinheriting his eldest son for having become a Catholic, so that Rudolph now succeeded not only to the earldom but also to Newnham Paddox, the family seat. Newnham was in Warwickshire, where the other Catholic peer was the Hungarian-born Lord Dormer, a frightening old man in a wheel chair who would wave his stick dangerously when calling for his valet; the valet would refuse to come until the stick was put down.

Lord Dormer and his wife Elizabeth, a daughter of Sir Henry Tichborne, had four sons, three of whom were soldiers; the two eldest, John and Jim, and Henry the youngest. Early in 1866 Henry Dormer, a popular young subaltern who enjoyed life, went to join his battalion in Canada; where something occurred which made him withdraw from the society of his brother officers and devote himself to religious exercises and to the care of the poor and the sick, while carrying on with his military duties. He hoped, when his turn came to go home on leave, to become a Dominican, but died of typhoid in the autumn of 1866 aged only twenty-one. The sick and the poor of the town where he was stationed regarded him as a saint; they tried to get bits of his clothing as relics.

Henry Dormer's far from saintly cousin Sir Alfred Tichborne, younger brother of the ill-fated Roger, also died in 1866. He was twenty-six; he left a widow, Teresa, daughter of the eleventh Lord Arundell of Wardour, and an only son, born posthumously. Such was Alfred's extravagance that only a year after succeeding his father in 1862 he went bankrupt; a second bankruptcy followed and at one stage he was actually imprisoned for debt in Winchester Gaol. There was, however, an excuse for his recklessness; his mother, the tiresome Henriette-Félicité, now the Dowager Lady Tichborne, was convinced that her elder son had not been lost at sea and would one day return. If, as seems likely, Alfred believed this too, he would have been making hay. Even when Alfred was still alive the Dowager Lady Tichborne was advertising in the Australian papers for news of Roger, having been told that Australia was the place to find him; and soon after Alfred's death she had a letter from a butcher in Wagga Wagga claiming to be her long-lost son who after being shipwrecked had been picked up by a vessel bound for Australia where he had lived ever since under an assumed name.

The fact that it was an uneducated letter should have made her suspicious; she should have been more suspicious when her alleged son was reported to be broadly-built and stout, Roger having been slim to the point of being weedy. Nevertheless the Claimant, as the butcher from Wagga Wagga was henceforth known, seemed convincing to Francis Turville, who met him in Australia. Turville had inherited Bosworth, but being unable to afford the life of a country squire was in the Colonial Service and now Secretary to the Governor of New South Wales. 'I went yesterday to see Roger Tichborne' he wrote to his sister. 'What an apparition! And yet I think from his manner, which is the reverse of that of an imposter, that he is the man . . . I noted, though I hardly like to write it, a look about the eyes and mouth which strongly reminded me of his father. His upper front teeth are all missing and he was, I can assure you, dirty enough, both in person and in dress, for even a colonial butcher. His English, too, a little butchery at times'. Turville added that while the Claimant

The funeral procession of Charles Waterton on the lake at Walton Hall

had described Roger's father 'most accurately', his description of his mother had seemed incorrect.[20]

Other statements by the Claimant were obviously wide of the mark, such as that he had been educated at 'High School, Southampton' and his brother at 'Winchester College, Yorkshire'. When she heard about this, the Dowager Lady Tichborne explained it away by saying 'I think my poor dear Roger confuses everything in his head'.[21] With her encouragement, the Claimant sailed for England, accompanied by his wife, the daughter of an Irish bricklayer, and his children. After spending some time in London, he went to Paris to see his reputed mother, who immediately recognized him as her son, even though he knew not a word of French which was Roger's first language.

Most of the other members of the Tichborne family were convinced from the start that the Claimant was an impostor; though Roger's sweetheart Kate, who met him once, was at first not so sure. The twelfth Lord Arundell of Wardour staunchly upheld the interests of his half-sister Teresa and her son the infant Sir Henry Tichborne, for whom the family estates were held in trust. But while the Arundell

The Claimant

and Tichborne cousinhood naturally influenced other prominent Catholics against the Claimant, there were at least two who accepted him; one of them being Roger's friend Talbot Constable, the son of Sir Thomas Constable of Burton Constable. Away from the Catholic world, the Claimant was able to muster a considerable amount of support; among county neighbours of the Tichbornes, among servants and hangers-on of the family, among people who had known Roger in the army. Despite his unprepossessing appearance – he had grown fatter than ever after coming to England – there was something likeable about him; he was a good shot and dry-fly fisherman. Moreover he undoubtedly looked like a Tichborne, albeit a

Tichborne gone woefully to seed; and he was by no means completely ignorant of matters about which Roger would have been expected to know, for example, he was familiar with the house at Tichborne.

The Claimant also won the sympathy of the public at large, which had always tended to be taken in by spurious claims to titles; he became a national figure. Though he suffered a severe reverse in the unexpected death of the Dowager Lady Tichborne in 1868, he raised enough money to start legal proceedings to claim the family estates, which being entailed had not been too seriously affected by Alfred's bankruptcy. As a preliminary to the case, a commission was sent out in the autumn of 1868 to collect evidence in Chile, where Roger had spent some time before his shipwreck. The Claimant went with this commission, but in order to avoid the passage round the Horn he left the ship at Buenos Aires. Here he fell in with Richard Burton, who having no work to do at Santos was playing truant and drinking too much. The young Wilfrid Scawen Blunt, who was then in Buenos Aires at the British Legation, described Burton and the Claimant as 'a strange disreputable couple' but thought that of the two, the Claimant was 'distinctly the less criminal in appearance'.[22]

The sensation over the Tichborne Claimant was equalled by that caused by the conversion of the young Marquis of Bute. Lord Bute was grander than either Lord Denbigh or Lord Gainsborough – as the convert Lord Campden became in 1866; he was of Royal Stuart descent in the male line and had inherited the Earldom of Dumfries through the female line from the Crichtons. He was enormously rich, owning not only large Scottish estates, but also estates in South Wales which had come into his family with an heiress of the Viscounts Windsor. His Welsh property included much of the town of Cardiff, which his father and his trustees had developed into a great seaport. His family seats included two eighteenth century mansions in Scotland, Mount Stuart on the Isle of Bute and Dumfries House in Ayrshire, as well as the medieval Cardiff Castle.

Lord Bute was an undergraduate at Christ Church, Oxford when he decided to become a Catholic. Unlike other young converts, he did not have to worry about upsetting his parents, for his father had died soon after he was born and his mother when he was twelve; his conversion would not prevent his coming into his great inheritance when he reached his majority two years later. Nevertheless, it was a terrible shock to his relations, his guardians and his trustees, as well as to the Oxford dons responsible for the welfare of the young millionaire Marquis. One and all asked the question, who had influenced him?

In fact he had been influenced by nobody. He was a young man of considerable reserve, serious and scholarly; he had few close friends and none of them was a

Catholic. He did not even know that there was a Catholic priest in Oxford. He had come to his own conclusions through reading and thinking and also through his travels, which were not in the Catholic countries of Europe but in the Holy Land and other places in the Levant, where he had got to know the Eastern Churches. With true Scottish tenacity, he resisted all attempts to make him change his mind; agreeing only to wait until he had come of age before taking the great step. He was received into the Catholic Church in December 1868, three months after his twenty-first birthday.

Lord Bute's conversion inspired Disraeli to write his novel *Lothair*, which was published in 1870. But the eponymous hero of the book, a 'romantic, sentimental and somewhat invertebrate youth', in the words of Bute's biographer,[23] only resembles his prototype in being a very wealthy young nobleman attracted to the Church of Rome. He is influenced by various Catholics with whom he makes friends, notably by Lord and Lady St Jerome and by Monsignor Catesby, the 'fascinating prelate who talked fluently on every subject except High Mass'. In writing of Lord St Jerome, Disraeli is thought to have had in mind the Duke of Norfolk's uncle Lord Edward Fitzalan-Howard; St Jerome House in St James's Square can be recognized as Norfolk House and his niece is called Clare Arundel. Lady St Jerome has been variously identified as Lady Edward Fitzalan-Howard – Lord Edward's second wife Winifred, a daughter of Ambrose March Phillipps de Lisle – and as Lady Herbert of Lea, the convert widow of the Secretary of State for War at the time of the Crimea. Monsignor Catesby is a caricature of Monsignor Capel, who actually received Lord Bute into the Catholic Church and became a friend of his, though the two did not meet until after Bute had made up his mind to become a Catholic.

Lothair inevitably falls in love with Clare Arundel, who is beautiful as well as devout. He is, however, enticed away by a fascinating female revolutionary who makes him promise never to enter the Church of Rome: and although the Vatican stages a spurious miracle in a last desperate attempt to get him, he returns to the Anglican fold. Clare Arundel takes the veil and Lothair ends by marrying his first love Lady Corisande, the daughter of a wealthy Anglican duke who is clearly meant to be the Duke of Sutherland. Lady Corisande has strong views on the subject of aristocratic converts. 'I look upon our nobility joining the Church of Rome as the greatest calamity that has ever happened to England. Irrespective of all religious considerations, on which I will not presume to touch, it is an abnegation of patriotism.' This is how many English Protestants in real life felt about the conversion of Lord Bute.

The conversion of the twenty-one-year old Lord Beaumont in 1869 caused no great stir; for one thing he was not particularly rich, for another, he came of a family that was traditionally Catholic. Both he and his brother Miles Stapleton had been brought up in the religion of their Anglican mother, and his late father had turned Anglican during the controversy over the restoration of the hierarchy. Lord Beaumont was afterwards followed into the Catholic Church by his mother and brother.

The number of Catholic peers increased still further in 1869 by the raising of two Catholics to the peerage on Gladstone's recommendation. One was Lord Edward Fitzalan-Howard, who had been a Liberal MP and held minor office and had devoted his life to the cause of Catholic elementary education; he became Lord Howard of Glossop. The other was Johny Acton.

Lord Acton, as Johny became, had not been a success in the House of Commons and his foray into Catholic journalism had ended after his publications had been censured by Rome for their views on the Temporal Power of the Papacy and for the kind of liberalism which Pius IX was to condemn in the *Syllabus Errorum*. But if Acton's journalistic venture brought him into disfavour with the Vatican and also with Cardinal Wiseman, it won him the friendship of Gladstone, who had written to him praising one of his articles, and that friendship was to be the most important thing in his life. Acton had a tremendous regard for the great Liberal statesman but it was Acton who influenced Gladstone, rather than the other way round; he even advised him on the appointment of Anglican bishops. When Gladstone was Prime Minister, Acton was probably closer to the centre of power in Britain than any other Catholic since the seventeenth century. It may seem ironical that someone as un-English as Acton should have attained this position when Catholics were kept out of the corridors of power for the very reason that they were regarded as alien. Yet Acton's un-Englishness could have been to his advantage, in that the ruling class of Victorian England would have found it easier to swallow Catholicism in someone as foreign as he than in a regular John Bull, when it would have seemed to them perverse, even 'an abnegation of patriotism', as Lady Corisande puts it.

While becoming increasingly involved in English affairs, Acton had strengthened his links with the Continent by going to Germany for his bride. She was his second cousin Countess Marie Arco-Valley, daughter of a Bavarian noble house; they were married in 1865. Before his marriage, he had naturally been regarded as an eligible by Catholic mothers like Lady Petre, who had invited him to Thorndon. Lord and Lady Petre had a bevy of good-looking and 'divinely tall' daughters, but one doubts if Acton would have much enjoyed roller-skating with them in the ballroom, which was the chief amusement at Thorndon house-parties. For their part, the Petre girls may have found the learned young baronet a little too

The Gladstone family staying at Tegernsee in Bavaria with Lord Acton, who sits at the extreme right of the group. His old mentor Dr Döllinger sits next to him

earnest and Germanic; he was said to have passed straight from boyhood into middle age. He did, however, possess a sense of humour and he was good-looking, with large eyes, a high domed forehead and a forceful expression; he wore a beard, but no moustache or side whiskers.

It seems that Acton did not feel much at home in the English Catholic world. Having been close to his Throckmorton cousins when young, he had lost touch with them as he grew older. He described a visit to Stonor as 'an unholy Sunday'; he had found the elderly Lord Camoys less intelligent than he had expected. 'Such a sleepy party', he remarked, after staying with the Hornyolds at Blackmore Park in Worcestershire.[24]

When Acton was made a peer he was in Rome for the Vatican Council, which opened in December 1869. He was to remain here for seven months, living in some splendour in the Palazzo Chigi; his wife Marie and their two infant daughters were with him and also his aged grandmother Marianne, known in the family as Nonna, for whom Rome would have brought back memories of when she lived here with her son Cardinal Acton. Rome was full of British during the Council. Lord Bute was here and so were the Denbighs and Lord and Lady Henry Kerr, whose son

Schomberg had left the Navy and was studying to become a Jesuit. Lord Dormer's widower eldest son John and his infant daughter walked with the bishops on the Pincio. Lord and Lady Herries came to see their youngest son Walter Constable Maxwell and their two nephews William and Oswald Vavasour, who were serving with the Zouaves, the international force in the Papal army. Lord Bute became a great supporter of the Zouaves – unlike the fictional Lothair, who actually fights against them in company with his revolutionary *femme fatale*. He liked watching them at rifle practice in the Borghese Gardens; he made friends with many of the officers, visiting them on guard at the Colosseum and giving them a memorable supper. The British Zouaves treated the bishops to a 'theatrical entertainment'.

Dr William Clifford, Bishop of Clifton, arrived safely in time for the opening of the Council – despite reports that he had been killed by an avalanche when crossing the Alps – and his elder brother the eighth Lord Clifford of Chudleigh joined him in the following spring, bringing two of his seven daughters. For the Clifford brothers, Rome was a second home; for they had lived here as children with their parents and their grandfather Cardinal Weld. Bishop Clifford had misgivings about the Definition of Papal Infallibility, which was the main business of the Council. He accepted Infallibility, as orthodox Catholics had done over the centuries, but feared that if it were clumsily defined it would confirm English Protestants in their belief that the Pope was a tyrant. So in the event he voted against the Definition, as did his friend Archbishop George Errington who came of a Northumberland Catholic family. Errington had been Coadjutor to Wiseman and nearly succeeded him when he died in 1865, but had been passed over in favour of the dynamic convert Manning, one of the strongest supporters of the Definition among the assembled bishops. Father Herbert Vaughan, the eldest of the sons of John Vaughan of Courtfield, reported to his friend Lady Herbert of Lea that Manning was 'the most looked-up-to man in Rome after the Pope', and 'all the better' for the good dinner which he was giving him every night at the Hôtel d'Angleterre at Lady Herbert's expense.[25]

Among the laymen present in Rome during the Council, one of the chief opponents of the Definition of Papal Infallibility was Acton. He gave vigorous support to the bishops who opposed it; he enlisted Gladstone's help in an unsuccessful attempt to get the Powers to intervene against the Definition. He offended the Pope, who refused to give his blessing to the Acton children; it was very different from when the newly-elected Pius IX had sent New Year's greetings in verse to Acton's grandmother. Acton retired from Rome in defeat before the Definition was carried by an overwhelming majority. He had none of the feeling for the Eternal City which most English Catholics had; he disliked what he regarded as

Disbanded Papal Zouaves returning home

Roman cunning, he even thought the Jesuits might poison him.

The Council ended abruptly after the Franco-Prussian War broke out on 19 July and the French troops who were helping to guard Rome against the revolutionary and Piedmontese forces were recalled. In September the army of Victor Emmanuel advanced on the city. The night before the attack, Walter Maxwell and his comrades in the Zouaves sipped wine-and-water in the Café Greco and swore undying devotion to Pius IX; but next day the Pope, wishing to avoid unnecessary bloodshed, ordered his troops to surrender after putting up a token resistance; for since the departure of the French they were hopelessly outnumbered. It was the end of Papal Rome; Pius IX became the Prisoner in the Vatican. Through the efforts of Monsignor Edmund Stonor, a Vatican prelate who was a younger son of Lord Camoys, the disbanded British Zouaves were shipped home. They arrived in Liverpool practically penniless, many of them, including Walter Maxwell, still wearing travel-stained Zouave uniforms but a committee headed by Lord Denbigh found them temporary lodgings. Lord Bute came to Liverpool and entertained the Zouave officers to a magnificent dinner, after which they marched through the streets 'singing Papal hymns and soldier-songs'.[26]

CHAPTER 9

Carlists and colonists

Having sunk to a low ebb at Santos, Richard Burton had returned in 1869 to his beloved East as Consul at Damascus; Isabel was with him, enjoying every minute of the life there. When sleeping romantically in a cave outside Jerusalem she had a dream in which Queen Victoria ordered her to set the world to rights; one of her suggestions was that the Queen should take the Koh-i-Noor Diamond out of her crown and sell it cheap to her most powerful rival, the Tsar, in order that the bad luck associated with it should be passed on to him. She wrote a fifty-page account of her dream and sent it to the Press; the *Daily Telegraph* commented drily in its leader, 'We are sure the Tsar will excuse the slight indifference to his personal fate which the proposal implies'.

Isabel's Eastern idyll came to an untimely end in 1871 when Burton fell foul of the British Government and was recalled. He learnt of his recall at a time when Isabel happened to be away from Damascus; he went immediately, leaving a note for her which said, 'Ordered off, pay, pack and follow'. Isabel arrived back in England to find her Arundell cousins greatly involved in the Tichborne Case, which opened in May 1871 having been delayed owing to the Franco-Prussian War which prevented witnesses who had known Roger Tichborne as a boy in Paris from coming over. Serjeant Ballantine was leading Counsel for the Claimant; John Duke Coleridge, a future Lord Chief Justice, led for the Tichborne family. The presiding Judge was the then Lord Chief Justice of the Common Pleas, Sir Henry Bovill, who filled the Bench with his personal friends including a number of ladies with whom he gossiped. Even the Prince and Princess of Wales came and sat on the Bench during the Claimant's cross-examination. Isabel Burton was among those present at various stages of the case; so many of the public wanted to come to what was now the best show in town that the Court had to move into a larger room.

The case dragged on for 103 days and the witnesses were legion; they ranged from a monk to a governess, from a negro servant to an Irish peer, from members of the family to old soldiers, from county neighbours to Roger's schoolfellows at Stonyhurst. The Claimant's ignorance with regard to his old school and anything he might have been taught there – he even said that Caesar was Greek – weighed heavily against him; though when giving evidence on other aspects of Roger's past life and background his ignorance was interlarded with surprising scraps of knowledge. He attributed his ignorance to loss of memory caused by his sufferings in an open boat after being shipwrecked. It was not so easy to explain the absence of the large tattoo mark which Roger was known to have had on his left arm.

There was a sensation when the Claimant stated that he had seduced his cousin and sweetheart Kate Doughty, as she was then, before setting out on his travels. Kate and her husband were in Court when he said this, but owing to an adjournment she had to wait six months before she could deny it on oath. By his pointless defamation of a highly-respected county lady, the Claimant threw away his case; Coleridge had no difficulty in convincing the Court that he was not Sir Roger Tichborne but Arthur Orton, the son of a butcher in Wapping. It was, however, Coleridge's private belief that the Claimant was an illegitimate relation of the Tichbornes, which seems certain in view of his facial resemblance to them.

In March 1872 Ballantine announced that the Claimant did not wish to proceed any further with the case and would pay the costs of both sides. This was an attempt to escape the criminal prosecution that would have resulted from a verdict by the jury that he was an impostor. But although there was no verdict, Chief Justice Bovill ordered the Claimant to be prosecuted on the strength of the evidence. He was charged not only with perjury but with forgery; since in order to raise money he had issued bonds, redeemable if he won his case, which bore a facsimile signature purporting to be that of Sir Roger Tichborne.

There was rejoicing in the Catholic world at the result of the case, and also in the newspapers; *Punch* parodied Lewis Carroll in praising Coleridge for having slain the 'Waggawock'. But there was a wave of sympathy for the Claimant among the public at large. Even the huntsman and whips of the Hampshire Hounds and the tenants of the Tichborne estate cheered him when, having been released on bail while awaiting his trial, he drove about the country near Tichborne in a wagonette decorated with rosettes in the Tichborne colours; people shouted 'Glory to you, Sir Roger!' as he went by. There was the feeling that he had been disowned by his family for preferring to lead the life of a common man; there was also a strong anti-Catholic feeling. The Claimant was held up as a victim of a Jesuit conspiracy. Not only did Coleridge have a Catholic convert brother who was a Jesuit; but the twelfth Lord Arundell of Wardour's younger brother Father Everard Arundell, a half-uncle of

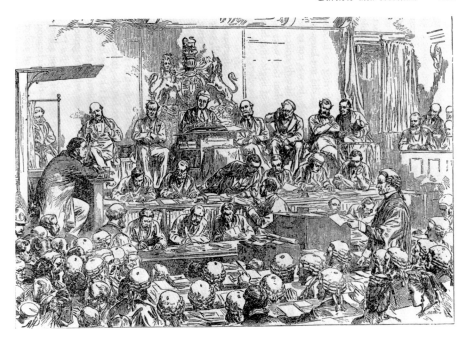

The scene in Court during the Civil Trial of the Tichborne Case. The Claimant is prominent on the left

the six-year-old Sir Henry Tichborne, had been a Jesuit until recently; though he had left the Society of Jesus in 1871 and was now an ordinary secular priest.

The idea, current after the Tichborne Case, that the Tichbornes and their kin were priest-ridden would have gained colour had it been generally known that soon after the case ended, Mary Towneley, a grand-daughter on her mother's side of Roger's uncle Sir Henry Tichborne, entered a convent. In fact Mary's decision to become a nun was entirely her own and surprised her parents, for she was a high-spirited, pleasure-loving girl, tall and good-looking with merry dark eyes. She was popular in Society, danced a lot and was a superb rider; it was said that of the young women who disported themselves on horseback in Hyde Park, the only one who rode better than her was the celebrated courtesan known as Skittles. As Mary and Skittles passed each other at the gallop, Skittles would nod approvingly; Mary became fascinated with her and would pray that she might become a Catholic which, in the fulness of time, she did. One Christmas when Mary and her family

Mary Towneley

were staying at Towneley Hall in Lancashire with her uncle Colonel Charles Towneley, her father's elder brother, there were not enough riding horses to go round; but encouraged by Lord Norreys, the husband of her cousin Caroline Towneley, she mounted a Derby winner – 'Kettledrum', with whom her uncle won the Derby in 1861 – and managed to stay on, even though he bolted.

Mary's father John Towneley, one of the two sons of 'Owd Peregrine', was heir to Towneley Hall, a large Tudor house with a rich eighteenth century interior containing some of the works of art of Charles Towneley the collector. Her uncle Charles had no son; whereas her father, as well as four daughters, had a son, Dick, who was in the Life Guards. Early in 1872 Dick went to Rome with Lord Bute and the future Prime Minister Lord Rosebery; while they were there they quarrelled, with the result that Dick moved into rooms by himself, where he fell ill with typhoid and nearly died. Mary, who was devoted to him, went out with her mother to nurse him; it was on her return from Rome that she decided to become a nun.

whereas Döllinger, as a priest, was required to do so, Acton, as a layman, was not.

In fact Acton was in less danger of excommunication than old Lord Camoys, who published an open letter to Gladstone agreeing with him; but he was to suffer nothing worse than having his name left out of the list of Catholic peers in the 1875 *Catholic Directory*; it was to be put back in the subsequent edition. Henry Petre of Dunkenhalgh in Lancashire, a son of Adela Petre's husband by his first wife, went further and assured Gladstone through the columns of *The Times* that he was 'an Englishman first, a Catholic after' – the opposite to Lord Denbigh who would declare himself to be first a Catholic and then an Englishman. His letter was mistakenly attributed to his cousin and namesake Henry Petre, a brother of the twelfth Lord Petre, who hastened to dissociate himself from the views expressed in it. Lord Petre himself published a resolution of the Catholic Union, of which he was Chairman, that the Catholics of Great Britain 'cordially' accepted the Decrees of the Vatican Council.

Other leading Catholics pointed out that the doctrine of Papal Infallibility was nothing new. John Towneley declared that Papal Infallibility had 'always been held and taught by the Catholic Church' and that Catholic families such as his own 'had always been noted for their loyalty to the Crown' – he chose to forget Francis Towneley of the 'Forty-Five'. 'The Pope', Lord Herries wrote, 'must by nature of the Divine authority committed to him be infallible'.

Lord Herries' son Walter, who served the Pope in the Zouaves, was now ranching in Kansas. His daughters were leaving home one after the other to become nuns; no fewer than seven of them were to go, which was a great sacrifice for their father. However, he still had plenty of sons around. The eldest, the Master of Herries, described by a contemporary as 'a wonderfully good sportsman even for his county',[6] was married in 1875 to Angela Fitzalan-Howard, a sister of Gwendolen Bute. The second, Joey, was married in the previous year to Mary Hope-Scott, daughter of the convert James Hope-Scott by his first wife, Sir Walter Scott's grand-daughter. They took the name of Maxwell-Scott and went to live at Abbotsford in the Scottish Borders, not far from Traquair which in 1875 was inherited by Joey's uncle Henry Constable Maxwell, who in consequence took the additional surname of Stuart. His old cousin Lady Louisa Stuart, the last Lord Traquair's sister, who died that year aged nearly a hundred, had gone round visiting her relations to find a suitable heir; peering into their faces to see which of them appealed to her most.

While the sons of Lord Herries were getting married, their contemporary and Yorkshire neighbour Lord Beaumont was leading a life of celibacy as a Knight of Justice in the Order of Malta. Lord Beaumont was a young romantic who in 1873 went to fight in the last Carlist War as a captain in the Carlist army. This conflict

Marmaduke Constable Maxwell, who became the eleventh Lord Herries, out hunting with his four brothers. He is second from the right between William and Walter, the former Zouave; Joey Maxwell-Scott is at the far left next to Bernard

between the adherents of Don Carlos, head of the Spanish Royal House in the male line, and the government forces, continued even after the short-lived Spanish republic had ended in 1875 and the young Alfonso XII been made King; for Alfonso was regarded by legitimists as a usurper, his claim to the Spanish throne being only through the female line. And Carlism was not just a matter of legitimacy; Don Carlos stood for a traditional Spanish monarchy, Catholic and conservative; whereas Alfonso's kingdom was liberal and secularist. Carlism thus appealed to Lord Beaumont's Catholicism no less than to his romantic temperament. His brother Miles Stapleton, a captain in the British army, also sympathized with the Carlist cause and visited the headquarters of Don Carlos.

While Lord Beaumont's period of service in the Carlist army was brief, his enthusiasm for Carlism lasted longer: he became Carlist representative in England and helped to organize an Order of Malta ambulance team to accompany the Carlist

Henry, ninth Lord Beaumont

forces, buying mules and trying to engage a Spanish-speaking surgeon. But Carlism was not his only enthusiasm; another and far more expensive one was enlarging and remodelling his Yorkshire seat, Carlton Hall, a Jacobean and Georgian house slightly Gothicized by his father. He now called in his father's architect Edward Pugin, who produced designs for transforming the house into a gigantic fantasy of towers, the largest of which would contain a grand staircase leading down to what was described as the Hall of the Barons and up to a chapel of cathedral-like proportions. Lord Beaumont is said to have had plans to receive Don Carlos at Carlton when he became King of Spain. The Most Catholic King would descend the grand staircase in state, to be greeted by the entire European nobility assembled in the Hall of the Barons, before going up to the chapel for a Solemn Mass of Thanksgiving in the presence of all the Catholic bishops of Europe – except, one

Carlton Towers

presumes, the Bishop of Rome – who would somehow be enticed to Carlton for the occasion.

The grand staircase tower, Hall of the Barons and chapel were far beyond Lord Beaumont's means but enough of Pugin's design came into being for Carlton Hall to become Carlton Towers. The work was completed after Pugin's death in 1875 by another Catholic architect, the young John Francis Bentley, who gave the house a series of state rooms richly decorated in colours and gilt and adorned with a multitude of carved heraldic beasts designed specially by York Herald – himself a general in the Carlist army and a Knight of Malta. It was remarkable that so much was achieved and in so short a time; for even in its reduced form the scheme was highly ambitious; it cost more than Lord Beaumont could afford but he carried on with it contrary to the advice of his more practical mother and brother. During the earlier stages of the work, the erratic Pugin was involved in ceaseless litigation while his patron was dashing off on forays to Spain and elsewhere.

In fact Lord Beaumont was a rather unsatisfactory character. His colleagues

The Venetian drawing room at Carlton Towers

complained that he neglected his duties as Carlist representative and that when he should have been in London or in Spain he was in Yorkshire, engrossed in his building works. There were also complaints that he never answered letters. He persisted in writing to the Director of the Carlist ambulance service in English, which the unfortunate Director did not understand, rather than in French. The Director threatened to retaliate by writing to Lord Beaumont in Basque.

The British Carlists seem, on the whole, to have been an ineffectual lot. Lord Beaumont's distant kinsman James Errington, a nephew of the Archbishop – the Stapletons were Erringtons in the male line – managed to get detained by the French authorities in St Jean de Luz, where he had himself photographed in Carlist uniform and grumbled about bad food and worse wine. On one occasion he sallied forth to cross the frontier and visit a Carlist shell factory, but got benighted in a mountain pass on the way back. 'Think what a lot of fun we should have on the march south after a great battle', he wrote wistfully to a Carlist sympathizer in Ireland. 'Let me loose among the Spanish women and you will hear no complaint

James Errington in his Carlist uniform

from me of the hard life or bad living. As for a monastic life, if I wanted it I should not go and look for it there.'[7]

His mention of a monastic life alludes to his becoming a Knight of Justice in the Order of Malta. His brother George Errington was already in the Order; there were now enough Knights in Britain and Ireland for a National Association to be set up. Lord Beaumont took part in the negotiations with the head of the Order in Rome — the Lieutenant, for at that period there was no Grand Master — which led to the setting up of the Association; his British confrères doubted if he was the right person to negotiate with an Italian. And indeed, he ended by displeasing the Lieutenant with a scheme for starting a hospital of the Order in Dover.

If Don Carlos was one of the most romantic figures among the European royalty of his day, the most romantic was undoubtedly the Empress Elisabeth of Austria, who engaged a connection of Lord Beaumont, the young Mary Throckmorton, as governess to her infant daughter Archduchess Valerie. Mary was a daughter of Sir Robert Throckmorton and Elizabeth Acton; she owed her appointment to the Actons' Neapolitan connection, for she was recommended by the Empress's sister Queen Maria Sophia of Naples. Although she won the affection of the little Archduchess, who called her Auntie Minnie, her position at the Austrian Court was not easy. The Empress was remote and unapproachable; her powerful lady-in-waiting Countess Marie Festetics did not care for the young English governess, describing her as 'a dangerous gossipmonger'.[8]

Mary's indiscretion and the enmity of Countess Festetics are both given as reasons for her dismissal, which was ostensibly on account of her passion for fresh air: Valerie got pneumonia and the doctor blamed it on open windows. But although Mary left Vienna in disgrace, she was to enjoy the friendship of the Archduchess Valerie for the rest of her life; while the Emperor Franz Joseph was to show his gratitude to his daughter's former governess by conferring on her the Elisabeth Order, which he founded in memory of the Empress after she was assassinated.

At about the time when Mary Throckmorton was in Vienna, her family's Warwickshire neighbour – and Franz Joseph's putative kinsman – Lord Denbigh was remodelling his ancestral seat Newnham Paddox. He had inherited a property from an uncle which enabled him to pay off the mortgages on the estate with money to spare for building. His wife Mary and their children, who were now almost grown up, were rather sad to see the old house transformed into a French château of bright red brick.

The Denbighs were as active in works of charity here as they had been when living in North Wales. Lord Denbigh would bathe the feet of tramps. Once, in order to cut the corns of an old man, he took him up to his dressing room, much to the fury of the head housemaid. But life at Newnham was far from being all good works; there would be house-parties when the guests would enjoy the creations of the French chef and his two assistants and be waited on by powdered footmen. The Denbighs would also entertain at their London house during the Season; Lord Denbigh was one of the handsomest and best-dressed men in Society.

His good looks made him stand out among the deputation of leading English Catholic laymen who went to Rome in May 1877 for the Pope's episcopal Golden Jubilee; the others, who included the Duke of Norfolk and Lord Gainsborough, were remarked upon as being 'of curiously homely exterior'.[9] There were ladies accompanying the deputation, some of whom 'forgot decorum' and 'mobbed' the Pope, seizing his hand to kiss;[10] Monsignor Stonor tried to fend them off, but the Pope took it good-naturedly.

The ladies of the party had been looked after by Cecil Marchioness of Lothian. 'Oh, isn't it lovely to be in Rome' she had exclaimed on her arrival, seizing the Duke of Norfolk round the waist and dancing about with him; but her duties had exhausted her, for she was no longer young, and she died in her hotel two days before the Papal audience. She died happily in the presence of her son Ralph Kerr, who had arrived unexpectedly from India the day before.

Lady Lothian's death was also attributed to a chill caught when escorting the young Lady Flora Abney-Hastings, a convert like herself, round all the holy places in Rome. Lady Flora's background was Catholic, for her father was a younger son of the one-time Catholic Thomas Clifton of Lytham; her uncle Colonel Talbot Clifton returned to Catholicism. Her father had changed his name to Abney-Hastings after his marriage to a sister of the reprobate last Marquess of Hastings from whom she had inherited the Scottish Earldom of Loudoun. Four months after the Roman visit Lady Flora became engaged to the twenty-nine-year-old Duke of Norfolk. Their wedding was in November at the Brompton Oratory and the crowds stretched back to Hyde Park Corner. The bride wore a pearl necklace which had belonged to Mary Queen of Scots; the clergy officiating at the Nuptial Mass wore the gold vestments given to Father Faber as a thank-offering for the conversion of the Duke's mother. The guests included the Queen's daughter Princess Louise, as well as Disraeli, now Prime Minister again and Earl of Beaconsfield. He happened to walk down the aisle after the ceremony side by side with Monsignor Capel, the original of his Monsignor Catesby, but the two did not know each other.

Ambrose March Phillipps de Lisle saw in the Norfolk wedding 'the dawn of happier, more peaceful days'.[11] His own days were numbered, but his face, now filled out and framed with a Newgate fringe, still had the ebullient expression which it had in the days when Mary Arundell described him as a young saint. Earlier in 1877, he and his wife Laura had suffered a family tragedy when their son-in-law Arthur Strutt, a son of the industrialist Lord Belper, was crushed to death by the great wheel in the Strutt family mill while showing it to a niece. The Strutts were Anglicans and Lord Belper had strongly disapproved of his son's marriage to a Catholic; that it took place may have encouraged Ambrose March Phillipps de Lisle in his hopes for a corporate reunion of the Catholic and Anglican Churches towards which he had been working for some time.

In the same year as the Duke of Norfolk married, his cousin Teddy Howard, by then an archbishop *in partibus*, was made a cardinal; he was the second cardinal in the Norfolk family, the first being the Cardinal Howard of the seventeenth century. As a Prince of the Church, Teddy Howard was still very much the Guards officer, with his great height and powerful build he was the best-looking ecclesiastic in Rome. He departed from precedent by going about Rome on foot, in red and gold hat, red-trimmed overcoat and silver-buckled shoes, followed by a liveried footman carrying his prayer books. He was a genial host at the Villa Negroni where he lived in some state, entertaining guests of all nationalities and conversing with them in a dozen languages. After luncheon he always took his guests to the stables to see his black

Edward, Cardinal Howard

carriage horses of which he was inordinately proud, bringing an apple with him to give to his favourite. Some people thought him vain; when he stayed with the Denbighs at Newnham the family noticed how he would stroke his red stocking and they called it 'the Adoration of the Golden Calf'.[12] But he practised the private austerity of having only one meal a day.

Having acquired a cardinal in his family, the Duke of Norfolk in 1878 helped to persuade the new Pope Leo XIII to make John Henry Newman a cardinal. When Newman returned from Rome after receiving his Red Hat, the Duke and Duchess gave a two-day reception for him at Norfolk House. The eighteenth century mansion in St James's Square had not been the scene of much entertaining when the Duke was single, for he had little taste for Society; now it became the centre of Catholic life in the metropolis.

The Duke and Duchess entertained a great deal at Arundel, where the castle was now lit by electricity. To celebrate their homecoming after their honeymoon a ball was held in the Barons' Hall. The tall and smiling Duchess opened the dancing with the short and stout Mayor of Arundel 'who was literally perspiring with nervousness'; the little bearded Duke danced with the Mayoress, 'a tall, solemn and stately lady, covered with scintillating bugles, from whom even her cheery host failed to extract a smile'.[13] House-parties at Arundel were as much noted for the innocent amusements as for the church-going. Once, when it was not the time of the year for hunting or shooting, the Duke took his male guests on a 'jumping party', a cross-country run with poles for leaping obstacles. In an attempt to jump a ditch, he fell in almost up to his neck and walked back covered with mud through the town of Arundel, 'acknowledging the respectful salutations of the inhabitants with his usual unembarrassed cheerfulness'.[14]

The Duchess of Norfolk's cousin Lady Gerard, the former Harriet Clifton, was prominent among the older Catholic hostesses of this period; she and her husband Lord Gerard dispensed 'stately hospitality of the old-fashioned kind'[15] at Garswood in Lancashire and at their London house. Lord Gerard, an uncle of Isabel Burton, was formerly Sir Robert Gerard; he had succeeded his elder brother Sir John in 1854 and had been one of a batch of High Tory magnates raised to the Peerage on Beaconsfield's recommendation in 1876. The house-parties of Lady Petre, another Catholic hostess of Lady Gerard's generation, ceased abruptly in 1878 when the centre block of Thorndon Hall, the great Palladian mansion of the Petres in Essex, was gutted by fire. Lord and Lady Petre retired to one of the two surviving wings of the house, leaving the centre as a gaunt shell. Most of their 'divinely tall' daughters were by now married, or had become nuns.

If 1878 was a disastrous year for the Petres, it brought triumph to the Stourtons. Alfred, twentieth Lord Stourton, who had succeeded his father in 1872, managed to get the barony of Mowbray called out of abeyance in his favour. He was a co-heir to this title, the premier barony in the Peerage of England, through his descent in the female line from the Dukes of Norfolk. The medieval barony of Segrave, of which he was also a co-heir, was called out of abeyance for him at the same time. He telegraphed the good news to his cousin Charles Langdale of Houghton. 'Have got Mowbray and Segrave, come and dine with me at Prince's Thursday.'[16]

Whether or not in belated celebration of this event, Lord and Lady Mowbray, Segrave and Stourton, as they now were, gave a great ball during the London season of 1881. Richard and Isabel Burton were among the guests, who according to Isabel consisted mainly of the old Catholic families. Unless she exaggerated, this would be an example of how, fifty years after Emancipation, the Catholics were still something of a world apart. Indeed, eighteenth century Catholics like the Jerninghams and

Throckmortons may have moved more freely in fashionable society than their descendants did a century later.

One reason for this is that Catholics were now much more insistent on the children of mixed marriages being brought up in their religion. Another is that even members of the old Catholic families now tended to irritate Protestants by parading their loyalty to the Pope, which their Cisalpine ancestors had played down. Thus at the Mowbrays' ball the Pope's portrait was prominently displayed, 'surrounded with garlands of flowers and lights'.[17] Yet another reason is that the sons of the Catholic aristocracy on the whole did not go to Eton or to any of the other great public schools, but to Catholic schools such as Stonyhurst; in the eighteenth century it had not mattered nearly so much where one went to school. In various minor respects, Catholics were 'different'. For example, they had a habit of making lavatorial jokes, at any rate in all-male company, though even certain Catholic *grandes dames* were not above making them. This was due to the belief that lavatorial or 'dirty' jokes were a preventative against *risqué* or 'improper' jokes, which were taboo on moral grounds.

Catholics of the eighteen-eighties should have been able to make up for not having been to Eton, Harrow or Rugby by going to Oxford or Cambridge, which were now open to them, but the hierarchy, led by Cardinal Manning, as he now was, would not allow Catholics to attend these ancient universities. This was not because they were Anglican, but because they were becoming increasingly irreligious.

There was now, however, one great meeting-ground between British Catholics and their compatriots of other religious denominations which did not exist a century earlier, namely the service of the Crown. Among the innumerable Catholic officers in the navy and army was the forcibly-bearded Major-General Sir Henry Clifford, who having won a VC in the Crimea had been made a KCMG in 1879 when he was Commander-in-Chief Transvaal; he had since returned to England and become Commander-in-Chief Eastern Division. Catholics in the Diplomatic Service included Adela Petre's brother Sir Henry Francis Howard of the Corby family, who was Minister in Munich for many years and his son Henry; as well as Adela's stepson Sir George Glynn Petre, brother of Henry Petre of Dunkenhalgh, who having been Minister to the Argentine and Paraguay was to become Minister to Portugal in 1884. Lord Stafford's cousin Hubert Jerningham, a grandson of Edward Jerningham who worked for Catholic Emancipation, had also been a diplomat but had since left diplomacy and entered Parliament. He was afterwards to go into the Colonial Service and become Governor of Mauritius and then of Trinidad and Tobago, being awarded a KCMG, an honour which Francis

Turville of Bosworth, who was also in the Colonial Service, had received in 1875.

Yet another Catholic with a KCMG was Frederick Weld, who received this honour in 1880, the year in which he became Governor of the Straits Settlements. Having left New Zealand, he had followed a proconsular career since 1869; first as Governor of Western Australia, then as Governor of Tasmania. In Western Australia he had been noted for his energy, travelling 4,000 miles about his territory, mostly on horseback, in less than three years. He had braved public opinion and the Colonial Office by insisting on bringing the son of a leading settler to trial for killing one of the aborigines.

As a Governor, Frederick Weld always had one or two relations on his staff. His brother-in-law Frank de Lisle, a brother of his wife Mena, was his ADC in Western Australia; his cousin Henry Weld-Blundell was his Private Secretary both in Western Australia and Tasmania; while in the Straits Settlements his Private Secretary was Mena's brother Edwin de Lisle. In the Straits Settlements, where he was to achieve immortality by having Port Weld named after him, one of his junior officials was his and Mena's young cousin Hugh Clifford, a son of the VC who was beginning a career in the Colonial Service.

Frederick Weld's old partner Charles Clifford was to be made a baronet in 1887 for his services to New Zealand, where his son George, who in 1880 had married Mary, daughter of Sir John Lawson of Brough, was managing the family sheep stations. Mary's uncle Henry Lawson had settled in New Zealand a generation earlier and was drowned trying to save the life of his shepherd. Other Cliffords in New Zealand at this time were Lewis, who in 1880 succeeded his father as the ninth Lord Clifford of Chudleigh, and his brother William, or Silly Willie as he was known in the family. Silly Willie bought a sheep station of his own and built a house there with his own hands which he named Ugbrooke after the family seat but in other respects he did not do so well. He quickly ran through his capital and had to be given more by Lewis, who returned to England in 1883. He insisted on marrying the seventeen-year-old Catherine Bassett, daughter of a small local farmer, though his family regarded her as unsuitable and predicted that the marriage would be a disaster which indeed it was. Having a plague of rabbits on his land, he decided to can them and export them to Europe but knowing nothing about canning he succeeded in killing half-a-dozen people with ptomaine poisoning. This eventually caused him to move to Tasmania.

There was one daughter of a Catholic family much closer to the centre of Imperial power than Frederick Weld and that was the former Ethel Errington, who was married to Sir Evelyn Baring, Finance Member of the Viceroy of India's Executive Council until 1883 and after that the virtual ruler of Egypt. Her marriage was,

A group at Government House, Singapore, in 1882, when Prince Eddy and Prince George, the two sons of the Prince of Wales, were paying a visit; they stand on either side of the Maharaja of Johore, with the bewhiskered Sir Frederick Weld, as he now was, on Prince Eddy's right. Sir Frederick's wife Filomena sits in the middle, flanked by their four daughters

however, without the blessing of the Catholic Church, for she had agreed to bring up her children as Anglicans. Lady Baring was the daughter of the last of the Catholic Stanley baronets, who changed his name on inheriting the estate of an Errington cousin; he was a great-grandson of Maria Fitzherbert's mother who was by birth an Errington. Baring was to take Viscount Errington as his second title on being made Earl of Cromer, though there were various actual Erringtons then living, notably the Knight of Malta George Errington, an MP who was eventually given a baronetcy which died with him. In the early eighteen-eighties he was sent by the British Government on several unofficial missions to the Vatican to try and prevent the Irish clergy from taking part in the land agitation.

Errington was one of the very few English Catholics with a property in Ireland; another was John Vaughan of Courtfield, who bought an estate in County Mayo some years before his death in 1880, only to become embroiled in agrarian troubles. Though politically opposed to the Irish Nationalists from 1881 onwards, Errington was in a better position to understand the Irish than Vaughan, being himself half Irish; his mother came of a distinguished Irish landowning family. Aristocratic British Catholics might have felt greater sympathy for their Irish co-religionists if more of them had married into Ireland. Surprisingly few did, considering how many suitable Irish Catholic families there were, of ancient lineage and undoubted loyalty to Queen Victoria, with high-spirited daughters and sons who went to Stonyhurst and into the army or navy, diplomacy or the Colonial Service.

Lord Mowbray, Segrave and Stourton was one of the few leading English Catholics of this period with an Irish spouse; others included Viscount Campden, Henry Petre of Dunkenhalgh and Mary Denbigh's brother Robert Berkeley of Spetchley as well as various Jerninghams. The Duke of Norfolk's niece Minna Hope – a daughter of James Hope-Scott by his second wife Lady Victoria Fitzalan-Howard – was to marry the brilliant diplomatist Nicholas O'Conor, a descendant of ancient Irish High Kings. Alice Towneley, a cousin of Mary Towneley the nun, had married the widower Lord O'Hagan, a Catholic lawyer from Belfast who became Lord Chancellor of Ireland. And then there was Lord Petre's daughter Frances who had married the convert Earl of Granard; her uncle Arthur Petre had married the convert daughter of another Irish earl.

Marmion Ferrers, squire of Baddesley Clinton in Warwickshire, had also married a convert from the Irish Protestant Ascendancy, the much younger Rebecca Dulcibella Orpen, known as Pysie. At the time of their marriage in 1867, it had seemed that Baddesley Clinton would soon have to be sold. As far back as the eighteen-thirties, Marmion's widowed mother, Lady Harriet Ferrers, had come near to being imprisoned for debt. Marmion himself, a man of great kindness and charity – he once found an old woman stealing his wood, and instead of scolding her merely said, 'That load of wood is a great deal too heavy for you, you must let me carry it home for you' – was not the sort of man who could have rescued a heavily mortgaged estate.

The situation was saved by Pysie's aunt Georgiana Lady Chatterton and her second husband Captain Edward Dering, who was much younger than her and well-off; they came to live with the Ferrers at Baddesley. For the nine years that followed, these two childless couples lived together in their moated grange in an atmosphere of Catholic piety, romantic affection and nostalgia for the past. They read the works of Tennyson to each other; Pysie painted and Georgiana wrote novels, as did Edward Dering, who was also musical. The two bearded gentlemen and the two ladies dressed in a way that was as much Elizabethan as Victorian. Then, in 1876, Georgiana died and in 1884 Marmion Ferrers followed her to the grave. A year later came the inevitable conclusion to the romance: Edward Dering married Pysie, whom he had clearly long admired.

Less fortunate than Baddesley Clinton among Catholic houses where there was no money was Nevill Holt; it had been sold in 1868 following a disastrous investment in ironstone quarries by Cosmo George Nevill which did for the family

The great hall at Baddesley Clinton, with Marmion Ferrers on the left, Edward Dering and his wife, Georgiana Lady Chatterton, sitting on either side of the fire, and Pysie Ferrers standing

fortunes, already undermined by his father's extravagance. Another old Catholic house which passed from its family at about this time was Walton; Charles Waterton's spendthrift son Edmund sold it to the family of the industrialist who had caused his father so much distress. He gave his father's natural history collection to Ushaw, the Catholic seminary and school in County Durham; it afterwards went to Stonyhurst.

Three months after Barbara Charlton's husband William died in 1880, leaving innumerable debts, the entire contents of Hesleyside were sold, even the gas brackets from the walls. The house was let, but this did not solve the financial problems of Barbara's diplomat son William Oswald and a few years later the house and estate were put up for auction. However, in that time of severe agricultural depression the bidding failed to reach the reserve and Hesleyside was saved for the Charltons, while continuing to be let.

The hall at Mount Stuart

The banqueting hall at Cardiff Castle. Lord Bute, wearing his cloak which resembled a monk's habit, stands talking to another gentleman

One Catholic landowner unaffected by the agricultural slump of the eighteen-eighties was Lord Bute. During these years he was constantly building. After Mount Stuart was burnt down in 1877 he rebuilt it as a palace in Italian Gothic, its lofty hall inlaid with rare marbles. He rebuilt much of Cardiff Castle, employing as his architect the talented if eccentric William Burges, who gave the old castle an interior aglow with wall paintings and emblazoned heraldry. He restored some of his minor seats, such as Old Place of Mochrum and the Welsh Castell Coch. Amidst all the rather exotic splendour which he was creating, he and Gwendolen lived quietly with their children, who eventually numbered three sons and a daughter. Bute cared little for Society, preferring the company of a few close friends such as his fellow-Scot and convert the Ayrshire baronet's son David Hunter Blair who became a Benedictine monk, rather to Bute's disapproval; which is surprising, since monasticism was one of his many interests. His idea of enjoyment was to have Hunter Blair to stay with him alone at Old Place of Mochrum, two separate towers on a wild Wigtownshire moor. They would go for long walks together in the bleak country and in the evenings Bute would read aloud from French novels or work on his translation of the Roman Breviary, wearing a cloak like a monk's habit which with his full beard gave him something of the air of an archimandrite.

Another of his pleasures was excavating old buildings; he would stand by, wrapped in his cloak and smoking innumerable cigarettes, while a band of workmen dug out the foundations of a medieval lady chapel. He restored old churches and a friary, as well as the old royal palace of Falkland. His other interests ranged from astrology and the occult to little-known Scottish saints. 'Isn't it perfectly monstrous' he once asked a lady in a London drawing room, for no apparent reason, 'that St Magnus hasn't got an octave?'.[18] He also loved animals, introducing beavers and wallabies into the woods around Mount Stuart.

When not restoring old buildings or working on his translation of the Breviary — for which he studied Hebrew with a rabbi — Bute travelled in the East or made protracted visits to Rome. Yet he also found time for public duties, not only in Scotland but also in Wales, where he became less of a Scot and learnt Welsh. He was a public figure no less than an authority on Premonstratensians and Pedro de Luna; he was made a Knight of the Thistle and was to become Lord Rector of St Andrews University.

However respected a position Bute may have come to occupy in the Catholic life of Scotland, the first Catholic layman in the Highlands was undoubtedly Lord Lovat. An impressive figure, bearded like Bute with 'a sense of power and reserve',[19] he was, to his fingertips, a great Highland chief. His interests were military and sporting, his favourite amusement salmon fishing; he would stand for hours in icy water with no waders, his kilt floating round him, wielding a twenty-foot rod.

He had succeeded his father in 1875. Five years later a Welsh miner came forward, claiming the Lovat title and estates on the grounds that he was descended from a younger son of a sixteenth century Lovat who had fled to Wales after murdering a piper and had married at the age of eighty. His story was fantastic enough but, like the Tichborne Claimant, he managed to find people to back him. At the last minute a document was found proving that his reputed ancestor had died in Scotland without issue and the case was decided in Lovat's favour. There were celebrations on the Lovat lands; bonfires blazed and the claimant was burnt in effigy.

The case put Lovat to a great deal of expense at a time when he was already spending heavily on building a new family seat, something which his father had hoped to do. Agricultural and sporting rents were still high in 1880, when the work started; but the building of Beaufort Castle, as the great Scottish Baronial pile above

John Patrick, third Marquis of Bute, wearing his
robes as Lord Rector of St Andrews University

the River Beauly was called, dragged on into the depression, so that in the event it
was never completely decorated or furnished. Lovat also built a church. He and his
wife Alice were both deeply religious and took a great interest in the Benedictine
monastery at Fort Augustus at the head of Lough Ness for the founding of which
Lovat had given the monks some land as well as the eighteenth century fort. Alice
Lovat was a Weld-Blundell, which made her a cousin of the first prior of the
monastery, Father Jerome Vaughan. Lovat used to say that he had been unable to
find a Catholic girl in Scotland so had to go south and find a Weld-Blundell; he had
gone south once before in search of a bride and been an unsuccessful suitor for the
hand of Roger Tichborne's sweetheart Kate Doughty.

The new Beaufort Castle in the course of construction. The eighteenth century house, built after the old castle was burnt in the 'Forty-Five', can be seen on the right

Alice Lovat's father, Thomas Weld-Blundell, had carried out many improvements to Ince Blundell since he inherited it more than forty years earlier, building a
wing to join the original block to Henry Blundell's Pantheon sculpture gallery and
adding a large new chapel. Thomas and his wife Teresa had a family of five sons and
seven daughters. Though sons went away, like Henry, who was Private Secretary to
Frederick Weld in Western Australia and Tasmania, and daughters married or
became nuns, the house always seemed to be full of Weld-Blundells of the younger
generation, all talking at the tops of their voices while their mother made vestments
and their father sat at his desk answering begging letters. Having become rich so
unexpectedly through inheriting the Ince Blundell estate from his cousin, Thomas
felt a particular obligation to give money to those less fortunate, while Teresa and
their daughters were even more assiduous than most Victorian county ladies in
visiting the poor. The second daughter Teresa, who neither married nor became a
nun, took a three-year course in nursing in order to be able to care for the sick.

Ince Blundell was a second home to the Vaughans; not only was its chatelaine a
sister of John Vaughan of Courtfield, known as the Old Colonel since he
commanded the Monmouthshire Militia after returning from the Crimea, but the

latter had married Thomas Weld-Blundell's sister Mary as his second wife. In August 1883 the Old Colonel's second son Roger, now Archbishop of Sydney, arrived at Ince looking yellow and weak, having, as he said, left Australia only just in time to save his life by a good rest. He had not left soon enough, for he died that night in his sleep.

As well as Herbert, the eldest, now Bishop of Salford, Roger and Jerome the Prior of Fort Augustus, three more out of the eight sons of the Old Colonel and his first wife Eliza had become priests: Kenelm, a missionary in South America; Bernard, a Jesuit; and John, a future Bishop Auxiliary of Salford. Four out of the five Vaughan daughters had become nuns. Herbert, on inheriting Courtfield, had made it over to his brother Francis, who was married to an American, in return for an annuity of £1,000 which he spent entirely on charity.

While in appearance Herbert Vaughan was everyone's idea of the handsome *grand seigneur* prelate, in fact he lived a life of great austerity. Having paid him to feed Archbishop Manning in Rome, his friend Lady Herbert of Lea would go to great lengths to ensure that he himself did not go hungry, sending him hampers of food and on one occasion confronting him with a doctor who ordered him to eat more. Herbert Vaughan retaliated by making Lady Herbert eat meat on Fridays for the sake of her health.

Another eldest son in the priesthood was the twelfth Lord Petre's eldest son William, who started a school in Surrey in an attempt to provide the sons of the Catholic upper class with a more civilized education than that offered by existing Catholic schools. The boys at his school, who included the future colonial administrator Hugh Clifford, were put on their honour as gentlemen and governed themselves with an elected body modelled on the House of Commons. The standard of comfort was very much higher than in other schools of the day; there was unlimited hot water so that cleanliness and tidiness were at a premium; the boys dressed for dinner every night. Unfortunately Monsignor Petre's health gave way; he was cheated by his manager and two of his most promising boys died on his hands, one being his young cousin Vincent Petre. Then in 1884, Lord Petre, on his deathbed, made his son promise to give the school up, since he thought it degrading for the next Lord Petre to be a schoolmaster.

CHAPTER 10

'Father Vaughan will entertain the Pope'

THE fifteenth Duke of Norfolk surpassed his father as a church builder. He built churches all over the country, mostly Gothic, like the Cathedral at Arundel which he built to celebrate his coming-of-age and the great church at Norwich which he began in 1884 as a thank-offering for his happy marriage; but he also contributed £20,000 towards the building of the new baroque church of the Brompton Oratory, as well as giving an altar of richly-coloured marble. The young Duchess also gave an altar to the Oratory, but hers was black and dedicated to the Mother of Sorrows. She and her husband knew what sorrow meant, for all that their marriage was happy: their only child, a son, had been born blind and mentally defective. They prayed hard for a miracle and took the little boy every year to Lourdes where on one occasion the chanting of the words 'Divites dimisit inanes' – the rich He hath sent empty away – in the Magnificat caused the Duchess to say tearfully, '*We* shall get nothing'.[1]

In 1887 the Duchess, whose health had long been delicate, died aged only thirty-four. Her bereaved husband devoted himself to the care of his handicapped son, whom he adored, and found solace in architecture. He built more churches and went on with the remodelling of Arundel Castle which he had started in 1875, gradually replacing Jockey's Regency Gothic with something larger and more convincingly medieval; his architect being Charles Alban Buckler, the convert son of Chessell Buckler who had worked for the Staffords at Cossey and for the Bedingfelds at Oxburgh. Architecture was the only one of the arts in which the Duke was at all interested, nor had he any interest in literature or science. Yet he was no ignoramus and could converse intelligently on a wide variety of subjects.

As a further distraction from his personal sorrows, the Duke was active in public life; he was by now the undoubted leader of the English Catholics, who would speak with affection of 'our little Duke'. He acted as a link between the British

The young Sir Humphrey de Trafford and his wife Violet entertaining royalty at
Trafford Park in 1887. Sir Humphrey leads the party down the staircase with Princess
Mary, Duchess of Teck, on his arm. Her daughter, Princess May, the future Queen
Mary, follows immediately behind her; behind again is Lady de Trafford – known as
Vi – with the Duke of Teck

Prince George, the future King George V, with
Julia Stonor

Government and the Vatican, where Britain still had no diplomatic representative;
it was through his good offices that Pope Leo XIII was able to send a special envoy
to congratulate Queen Victoria on her Golden Jubilee in 1887. The Duke made
history when the Queen sent him to convey her thanks to the Pope; he was the first
official envoy from a British Sovereign to the Vatican since the time of James II.

When he lost his wife, the Duke had already lost his mother and also his eldest
sister Victoria who had married the widower James Hope-Scott and died in 1870.
Of the five other sisters of the Duke, Minna was a nun, having stuck to her
childhood resolve, and so was Etheldreda; while Mary remained single without
taking the veil and worked among the poor of the East End of London. Anne was
suitably married to Lord Ralph Kerr, one of Cecil Lady Lothian's Catholic sons.
Philippa was married in 1888 to Edward Stewart, a Protestant doctor who was
regarded as less than suitable, even though he had promised to bring up their
children as Catholics. 'You will be shocked to hear that Lady Philippa Howard is

going to marry a young Protestant doctor who attended her professionally', Bishop Herbert Vaughan wrote earlier that year to Lady Herbert of Lea. 'It is a great humiliation and pain to the poor Duke. How he is tried with crosses!'[2]

The Duke's brother Lord Edmund, who had taken the surname of Talbot having inherited some property from the last Catholic Earl of Shrewsbury, had married Mary Bertie, daughter of the convert Lord Norreys, in 1879. Soon afterwards she ran away to France with another man, but her husband fetched her back and the marriage was repaired. Lady Edmund's mother, who had died in 1873, was Caroline Towneley, a sister of Lady O'Hagan and a cousin of Mary Towneley the nun. Since the death in 1877 of Mary's brother Dick, the Towneleys of Towneley had become extinct in the male line; the family estates, said to be worth more than £50,000 a year, were now owned jointly by Lady O'Hagan and Mary and their respective sisters.

Even richer than the Towneleys among Lancashire families were the de Traffords; and the hard-headed foxhunting Lady Annette de Trafford, a sister of the last Catholic Earl of Shrewsbury, had arranged a settlement of the family fortunes to ensure that they would not be dissipated. In 1887 her son, the young Sir Humphrey de Trafford, and his wife Violet entertained royalty at Trafford Park; the fat Princess Mary and her husband the Duke of Teck, together with their daughter Princess May, the future Queen Mary. Another prominent Lancashire Catholic who entertained royalty was Henry Petre of Dunkenhalgh, 'that prince of English gastronomes', as Sir Hubert Jerningham's man-about-town brother Charles called him. The royals came to 'charming little feasts' at his house in Berkeley Square.[3]

Closer than any other English Catholic family to the late-Victorian Court were the Stonors. Old Lord Camoys' son Francis, who died a week before him in 1881, had married the Prime Minister Sir Robert Peel's daughter Elise, a favourite of Queen Victoria and Woman of the Bedchamber to the Princess of Wales, the future Queen Alexandra. Elise Stonor's eldest son, the fourth Lord Camoys, became a Lord-in-Waiting to Queen Victoria and her second son Harry Stonor a Gentleman Usher.

After Elise's death in 1883, her three sons and her daughter Julia were virtually adopted by the Prince and Princess of Wales. They spent a great deal of time at Sandringham and the young Prince George fell in love with Julia, who was both pretty and sympathetic. At that time the future George V was not yet the eventual heir to the Throne, for his elder brother Prince Eddy was still alive; but for even the younger son of the Prince of Wales to have married a Catholic would have been difficult enough. Whatever hopes Prince George may have had were ended in 1891, a few months before Prince Eddy's death, when Julia married the French Marquis d'Hautpoul. While the younger Stonors were enjoying the friendship of the British Royal Family, their uncle Monsignor Edmund Stonor was consorting with the Pope. He was made an archbishop *in partibus* in 1888 and became the chief resident English prelate in Rome after Cardinal Howard had been stricken with an illness which gradually deprived him of the power of speech and eventually proved fatal.

Cardinal Howard's old dancing partner Isabel Burton had been living since 1872 in Trieste, where Richard Burton was Consul. It was a dull posting after Damascus: Isabel's lobbying, redoubled over the years, had failed to get him transferred to somewhere more congenial, though there had been the consolation of a KCMG. And Burton had made good use of the ample spare time which Trieste afforded him; when he and Isabel were not travelling – they went as far afield as India – he was busy with his translation of the *Arabian Nights* and other literary work. Isabel saw his books through the press and arranged the lucrative sale of the unexpurgated *Arabian Nights* to private subscribers, while producing her own 'household' edition which was not a financial success.

When not acting as her husband's secretary, literary agent and nurse, Isabel wrote books of her own and campaigned against cruelty to animals. Unlike Burton, she grew fond of Trieste where, since it was then Austrian, she could claim the rank of *Gräfin* as a descendant of the first Lord Arundell of Wardour who had been made an hereditary Count of the Holy Roman Empire. She 'still bore great traces of beauty', though her Oriental habit, shared with her husband, of putting *kohl* round her eyes, combined with 'a towering golden wig',[4] must have made her look a thought bizarre.

Burton died in Trieste in 1890. Having convinced herself that he had long been a secret Catholic, Isabel managed to persuade a priest to give him Extreme Unction – though by then he had almost certainly breathed his last – and she infuriated his Protestant relations by giving him a Catholic funeral. She also infuriated public opinion by burning the manuscript of Burton's translation of the *Scented Garden*, a celebrated treatise of Oriental erotica, together with his journals. Her holocaust has been misrepresented as prudery. In fact it was a rather heroic sacrifice on the altar of her husband's reputation, for the proceeds from the *Scented Garden* would have made all the difference to the comfort of her few remaining years, when she was not only poor but stricken with cancer. She endured these years of poverty and mortal illness with her habitual courage, living mainly in a cottage near the Catholic cemetery at Mortlake where Burton lay in the tomb which she had made for him and for herself in the form of an Arab tent. She lived for his memory, writing his biography to convince posterity that he was the greatest Englishman of his time. Her strength was failing, but she could still fight for her Richard; just as she could still give a cabbie a

The tomb made by Isabel Burton for her husband
and herself in the form of an Arab tent

painful prod with her umbrella if he so much as flicked his whip at the horse.

Isabel's love of animals involved her in a long controversy on the subject of
vivisection with Herbert Vaughan, who had succeeded Manning as Archbishop of
Westminster in 1892, becoming a cardinal in the following year. In his new and
exalted position he continued to lead a life of austerity, refusing Lady Herbert of
Lea's offer of a carriage and horses suitable to his dignity as a Prince of the Church.
He devoted much of his energy to raising money for the building of Westminster
Cathedral; the Duke of Norfolk gave £10,000. The architect selected for the great
work was John Francis Bentley, who had completed Carlton Towers for Lord
Beaumont.

Like the Nevills of Nevill Holt, Lord Beaumont had been ruined by a

Cardinal Vaughan

combination of building and unwise investments; his spending spree at Carlton had been followed by some disastrous speculations by his man-of-business in 1879, while he himself was away fighting in Zululand. In a time of falling land values, his estate was saddled with a debt of more than a quarter of a million. He had, however, managed to save the situation for the time being by having himself released from his vows as a Knight of Justice in the Order of Malta and marrying a rich wife. His bride was not, as might have been expected, the daughter of a Grandee of Spain, but a jolly English hunting girl named Violet Wootton Isaacson whose fortune of £120,000 came from a fashionable departmental store in Regent Street. He was to enjoy less than four years of married life, dying of pneumonia in 1892 at the age of forty-three.

Having no children, he was succeeded by his sensible brother Miles Stapleton, a regular soldier who had served in various parts of the world and was now a colonel commanding the 20th Hussars. A year after succeeding, Miles saved the Carlton estate, which would otherwise have had to be sold, by marrying an heiress. She was Mary, only surviving child of Sir Charles Tempest who had been made a baronet like his uncle and who leased Broughton from the trustees of his younger brother Arthur. While Arthur Tempest was to have Broughton, Sir Charles had a valuable

Mona, Baroness Beaumont, and her sister Ivy
Stapleton

estate of his own which he was able to leave to his daughter. Mary was the daughter of his first wife, a cousin of the Tichbornes who had died tragically of burns in 1865. Sir Charles had remarried and then divorced his second wife; thereby causing something of a scandal in Catholic circles, though he had not married again.

He died at Broughton in 1894, on the same night as his daughter Lady Beaumont, who was staying in the house, gave birth to her elder daughter Mona; the doctor had to keep hurrying up and down stairs between the dying man and the mother in labour. Miles Lord Beaumont survived his daughter's birth by only a year, for he was killed in a shooting accident in 1895. His second child, who was posthumous, was also a daughter; so the infant Mona inherited Carlton and the Beaumont barony was called out of abeyance for her.

Another sporting casualty of about this time was the twelfth Lord Dormer's soldier brother Jim, who had risen to being General Sir James Charlemagne Dormer, Commander-in-Chief of the Madras Army and before that commander of the troops in Egypt. He was mauled by a tiger which he was stalking on foot; when the doctor told him that his leg would have to be amputated or he would die, he said 'Damn it, I'd rather die!' And die he did. 'I have never seen a more elastic, I might say "cocky" fellow on service than Jim Dormer' a friend wrote.[5] General Jim had a glass eye; when serving in the Sudan in the days of the Mahdi he had impressed some sheikhs by tossing it into the air, catching it and putting it back again.

One of General Jim's daughters, Gwendeline Dormer, had married the widower Earl of Abingdon, as the convert Lord Norreys now was; he was of her father's generation and they had children of the same age as his grandchildren by his first wife Caroline Towneley. Caroline's sister Alice, the widowed Lady O'Hagan, caused a sensation in the 'Nineties by leaving the Catholic Church. She is said to have done so under the influence of her former chaplain, a Jesuit who became a Unitarian and then a Positivist; and who, in 1897, married one of her daughters. At the time, Lady O'Hagan and her family were living at Towneley Hall, now beleaguered by industry and soon to be sold to Burnley Corporation as a museum and art gallery.

Lady O'Hagan's cousin the fourth Lord Camoys was again a Lord-in-Waiting from 1892 to 1895 along with Acton, who when his friend Gladstone came back into power in 1892 had hoped for something better, a seat in the Cabinet or the Berlin Embassy. Nevertheless, Acton had been a success with the old Queen, able to converse knowledgeably with her on the genealogies of her German relations. And then in 1895, Rosebery, who had succeeded Gladstone as Prime Minister, gave him an appointment which really suited him: the Regius Chair of History at Cambridge.

Having retired from politics and given up trying to reconcile the Catholic Church – of which he remained a devoted, if critical, son – with nineteenth century liberalism, Acton at last found his true vocation as an academic. He had, over the years, devoted himself ever-increasingly to scholarship, working long hours in his great iron-galleried library at Aldenham and in libraries at his villa at Cannes and at the villa on the Tegernsee in Bavaria belonging to his wife's family, the Arcos. He could read, annotate and more or less memorize a large German octavo every day. All this work was for the great *History of Liberty* which he planned but never wrote, and which, had it been written, might well have been unreadable.

A few essays and his oft-quoted saw 'Power tends to corrupt and absolute power corrupts absolutely' are all he left as a monument to his prodigious learning. He also left his library, some 60,000 volumes, which went to Cambridge after his death thanks to the generosity of the American Andrew Carnegie who, at Gladstone's suggestion, bought it from him anonymously and allowed him to keep it for his lifetime. The financial crisis which had made him put his library up for sale had also

Left: General Sir James Charlemagne Dormer
Right: Lord Acton in later life

obliged him to sell the Dalberg schloss inherited from his mother.

Acton was happy at Cambridge as Regius Professor. With his beard, formerly sparse, now grown into a luxuriant hearthrug, he looked the typical late-nineteenth century Cambridge historian; he fitted in well on High Table being a brilliant conversationalist with a sense of humour for all his pedantry. He was also a good judge of wine. And his bachelor rooms in Trinity suited him, for he and his wife Marie had parted; she now lived mostly in her native Bavaria. The cause of the rift is uncertain; a letter to him from Marie, which speaks of 'the loneliness of being deserted' by him and begs for 'a word of pity' would suggest that it was of his making.[6] He never answered this letter. There seems to have been a harsh streak in him which shows also in his attitude to the memory of his grandmother Marianne or Nonna. After her death at the age of eighty-nine in 1875, he had refused to put up a tablet to her in the Aldenham chapel; perhaps because he knew that at some period during her long widowhood she had taken a lover, by whom she had a son.

Another Victorian intellectual, the novelist and social reformer Mrs Humphry Ward, turned to Acton for advice and encouragement when she was working on her novel about a Catholic family, *Helbeck of Bannisdale*, which was published in 1898. Mrs Ward was not a Catholic herself, though her father, a son of Dr Arnold of Rugby and a brother of Matthew Arnold the poet, was a Catholic convert who later returned to Anglicanism. The novel treats of the hopeless love affair of Alan

Sizergh Castle

Helbeck, a pious and impecunious Westmorland Catholic squire of ancient lineage, and the pretty young freethinker Laura Fountain, daughter of a Cambridge don.

The inspiration for *Helbeck*, as Mrs Ward herself recalls, came from the plight of a Westmorland Catholic squire of the time, Walter Strickland, who was being forced by 'mortgages and lack of pence' to give up Sizergh Castle, which his family had held 'unbrokenly, from father to son, through many generations'.[7] After she had decided to write the book, she and her husband rented Levens Hall, a famous Elizabethan house close to Sizergh; it is on Levens, rather than on Sizergh itself, that Bannisdale is based. Yet Levens is not all that different from Sizergh, an old peel tower with sixteenth century wings.

Walter Strickland, like Helbeck, was a lonely and unhappy character and just as Helbeck has sold most of the treasures out of Bannisdale, so was Walter Strickland forced to sell pictures and silver from Sizergh as well as the best of the Elizabethan panelling for which the house was famous. Again, just as Bannisdale eventually passes to a rich cousin – Helbeck having gone to become a Jesuit after the tragic end of his romance – so was Sizergh eventually saved by being made over to Walter's distant cousin Gerald Strickland, who could afford to maintain it. Walter had in fact left Sizergh by the end of 1896, three months before Mrs Ward came to Levans, so it is doubtful if she actually met him. And in any case he differed from Helbeck in some important respects. Whereas Helbeck is thirty-seven and single, Walter Strickland was over seventy when Mrs Ward first heard of him; he had married a Belgian and had an only son named Roger with whom he was not on good terms.

Gerald Strickland, Sizergh's new squire, was of an age with Helbeck but certainly did not resemble him except in belonging to an ancient Westmorland Catholic family. He was the son of another Walter Strickland, the naval officer who married the Maltese heiress Donna Louisa Bonici; his father had died when he was a child but his mother was still alive and disapproved of money being taken out of Malta to pay for Sizergh. His loyalties were both British and Maltese; he had been to school in England and was at Cambridge in the days when Catholics were not supposed to go there. He was married to Lady Edeline Sackville, the convert daughter of Earl de la Warr. On the other hand he was making his career in Malta where he owned extensive property including the palatial Villa Bologna. He had become Chief Secretary to the Maltese Government in 1889 at the age of twenty-eight; he was clever and energetic if somewhat aggressive and was awarded a KCMG in 1897. As Sir Gerald Strickland, he dropped the Maltese title of Count della Catena which he had inherited from his mother's family.

As a young man Gerald Strickland had wanted to marry Lady Clare Feilding, who preferred to remain single and devoted herself to the Third Order of St Francis until her death in 1895. Clare was one of the children of the convert Rudolph, Lord Denbigh, who had died in 1892, and of his second wife Mary Berkeley. Of the others, the younger Rudolph, now the ninth Earl of Denbigh, was a soldier and married to Cissy Clifford, sister of the ninth Lord Clifford of Chudleigh and of Silly Willie. Everard Feilding, the second son, was still single and without a profession; he suffered from religious difficulties and was attracted to spiritualism. The third son Basil was ordained priest in 1898. Of the three other daughters, Winefride and Agnes were married respectively to the handsome Gervase Elwes, son of a convert Northamptonshire squire, and to the Leicestershire cricketer Charles de Trafford, brother of Sir Humphrey; while Edith was in China as a Sister of Charity.

The newly-ordained Father Basil Feilding went out to the South African War as a chaplain. Herbert Weld-Blundell went out as war correspondent for the *Morning Post*. Lord Stafford's nephew Francis Fitzherbert of Swynnerton went out with the Staffordshire Imperial Yeomanry, was mentioned in dispatches and awarded the DSO; two of his younger brothers also served in South Africa. Their cousin Henry Bedingfeld, eldest son of the then baronet of Oxburgh, went out as a major in the

Militia; his younger brother Frank was already out there, growing timber in the Eastern Transvaal. Before the war Henry had ranched in Wyoming, along with some of his other brothers, one of whom was known as 'Whisky Dick' and rode with Wild Bill Hickok.

Ambrose March Phillipps de Lisle's grandson Edward Strutt was, like Francis Fitzherbert, mentioned in dispatches. Joseph Petre, youngest of the three brothers of Monsignor Lord Petre, who had died in 1893, was killed at Spion Kop. Lady O'Hagan's son the young Lord O'Hagan fell ill and died on active service; a report that he had died a Catholic was publicly contradicted by his mother. Among others who served in South Africa were three Stourtons, a Dormer, a Kerr and two Cliffords, Joey Maxwell-Scott's son Walter, Courtenay Throckmorton, nephew of the reigning Throckmorton baronet, and Cardinal Vaughan's nephew Charles.

Charles Vaughan's cousin Simon, the young Lord Lovat, who had succeeded his father in 1887 when still a schoolboy, was to achieve greater fame in South Africa than any other British Catholic. Lord Lovat was a born soldier, a man of splendid physique and boundless energy. After leaving Oxford – where he had gone with the blessing of a Scottish bishop – he had served in the Life Guards, a somewhat unlikely regiment for a Scot; he had later transferred to the more suitable Cameron Highlanders. He had travelled in Abyssinia and gambled at Monte Carlo for higher stakes than he could afford; he had made friends with all manner of people, from the Prince of Wales and the Duke of York to racing touts. He enjoyed low company, but did not allow himself to be influenced by his more dubious acquaintances.

Having already visited South Africa in the course of his travels, Lovat was convinced that many of the worst disasters of the early months of the war were due to lack of reconnaissance. He accordingly set about raising the Lovat Scouts, with the Highlands as his recruiting ground. The regiment was trained at Beaufort; the Home Farm served as a barracks and the officers were put up in the Castle. Lovat's brother Hugh Fraser, a crack rifle-shot in the Scots Guards, gave musketry instruction. A generous clansman who was a distiller provided the regiment with whisky. Khaki cloth for the uniforms at first seemed impossible to come by; and was only obtained after arrangements had been made to use the tweed known as Lovat Mixture as a substitute.

The Scouts left for South Africa in March 1900. Lovat was among the officers, but having not yet seen active service he did not consider himself qualified to command the regiment. Instead, he had secured the appointment of a veteran of the Sudan campaign, who was to be killed in a surprise attack in September 1901. This was the Scouts' only disaster; their record was otherwise one of unbroken success.

Lovat was not the only Catholic aristocrat with Scouts named after him. Captain

Lord Lovat (in profile, sitting on the steps in the centre) with the officers of the original contingent of Lovat Scouts, at Beaufort before leaving for South Africa

Roger Tempest, son of Arthur Tempest of Broughton, who went out to South Africa with the Scots Guards, was given command of his own unit, known officially as The Tempest Scouts, though he was only twenty-four. He was mentioned in dispatches by both Roberts and Kitchener.

While Tempest had his own command, the Duke of Norfolk's kinsman Esmé Howard served as a humble trooper in the Yeomanry. He had interrupted his diplomatic career to enlist, feeling it his duty to do so since he knew South Africa and could speak Afrikaans. His knowledge of the language was to stand him in good stead when he was taken prisoner by the Boers; he eventually managed to escape under cover of a dust-storm.

A year before the outbreak of war, Esmé Howard, whose brother was the squire of Greystoke in Cumberland, had been married to Donna Isabella, daughter of Prince Giustianini-Bandini who held the Scottish Earldom of Newburgh. Donna Isabella's family were very much of the Black Nobility of Rome; her religion meant everything to her and she had consented to marry him only if he became a Catholic; for he was then still an Anglican, although no longer a practising one. This at first had seemed to him an impossible condition; however, the future Cardinal and Secretary of State Monsignor Merry del Val had managed to convince him of the

Esmé Howard at the South African War, with a beard which he did not have in civilian life; he stands at the right of the group, marked by a cross

truth of Catholicism and he had returned to the Faith which his grandfather, 'Naughty Henry' of Greystoke, had abandoned. A more distant kinsman of the Duke of Norfolk, Francis Howard of the Corby family, son of the diplomatist Sir Henry Francis Howard, commanded a brigade at Ladysmith and was given a KCB.

The Duke of Norfolk himself, now in his fifties, gave up being Postmaster-General in Lord Salisbury's Government in order to go out to South Africa with the Yeomanry. On the voyage out he spent his time getting up deck games to amuse the other passengers; he even organized a fancy dress ball, to which he came as an Australian miner. 'Perhaps there never was a man who looked less like a duke than the Duke of Norfolk dressed in khaki' remarked the artist Mortimer Menpes, who painted him in South Africa.[8] The Duke's war service did not last very long, for he hurt himself falling off his horse soon after he arrived and was invalided home. His younger brother Lord Edmund Talbot achieved greater distinction in South Africa as a colonel in the Hussars; he was mentioned in dispatches and awarded a DSO. He also helped to direct the war from Westminster as Assistant Secretary of State for

War, having been an MP since 1894 and held various junior Government posts.

After the war was over, the Duke of Norfolk's nephew Philip Kerr went out to South Africa and worked for the High Commissioner Lord Milner as one of his so-called 'Kindergarten'. A son of Lord Ralph Kerr, now a major-general, and of Lady Anne Fitzalan-Howard, young Philip was clever and good-looking and took life seriously while being more than a little arrogant. Having grown up in the intensely Catholic atmosphere of his home in the Scottish Borders under the influence of a devout if rather frightening father and a saintly mother, he had, as a schoolboy, considered becoming a priest. But at Oxford – which, like Cambridge, was now no longer subject to any episcopal ban – he began to suffer religious doubts. Surprisingly, in view of his considerable intellect, they were caused by reading the works of Shaw and Wells.

Henry, fifteenth Duke of Norfolk dressed in khaki, painted in South Africa by Mortimer Menpes

Soon after returning to England, the Duke of Norfolk, as Earl Marshal, was hard at work organizing the funeral of Queen Victoria and the coronation of Edward VII. The postponement of the Coronation on account of the King's illness was, for the Duke, a blessing in disguise, for it gave him time for an extra rehearsal without which, as he admitted, 'only a miracle could have averted a fiasco'.[9] On the night of the Coronation, the town and castle hill at Arundel were illuminated, but the great pile of the castle itself was in darkness because the Duke was mourning the death of his handicapped son.

In the following year Edward VII made history by being the first reigning English Sovereign since medieval times to visit the Pope. The visit was on the King's initiative, but as it would have offended Protestant opinion had he himself asked Leo XIII to receive him, his wishes had to be expressed indirectly through the Duke of Norfolk. Since the Duke could not be contacted in time, Esmé Howard, who was then in Rome, spoke for his kinsman. The arrangements at the Vatican were made by Monsignor Stonor. The British Ambassador to Italy, Sir Francis Bertie – brother of the convert Lord Abingdon – was not satisfied with the smiling assurances of this courtly old prelate that all would be well on the day. But all did go well. Stonor understood the Roman mind, while remaining incorrigibly English; so English that when, a few years later, he was asked if he were going to the Beatification of Joan of Arc, he answered with some surprise, 'Why should I go? She was a Frenchwoman'.[10]

The Monsignor's nephew Harry Stonor, a courtier, a friend of the Royal Family, a popular bachelor and a legendary shot, was a frequent guest at Windsor, Sandringham and Balmoral. But with a few notable exceptions such as he, the Catholics did not really fit into the King's circle, for all his well-known sympathy for Catholicism. It was not so much that they were too unworldly for fashionable Edwardian society as that their code of proprieties was too strict. The Duke of Norfolk was one of the very few people who refused to have the King's mistress Mrs Keppel to stay.

Mrs Keppel was also barred by the Anglican Marquess and Marchioness of Salisbury. It is perhaps significant that the Salisburys and the Duke of Norfolk were close friends; when, after his son's death, the Duke decided to marry again, he first thought of Lord Salisbury's sister Lady Gwendolen Cecil. But there was the religious problem and he eventually settled for a younger and Catholic Gwendolen, the eleventh Lord Herries' daughter Gwendolen Constable Maxwell; they were married in 1904.

Perhaps the most typical Edwardian in the Edwardian Catholic world was Lady de Trafford, known to her family and friends as Vi, who belonged to the Catholic

The invitation to the coming-of-age of Humphrey de Trafford, with portraits of the young man and his parents, Sir Humphrey and Vi de Trafford

world only through marriage; for she was born Violet Franklin, daughter of a family connected with the West Indies. She had beauty, charm and vitality: she was a great friend of Mrs Keppel and her cavaliers included the Marquess of Londonderry. Her husband, the sportsman and horse-breeder Sir Humphrey de Trafford, had sold Trafford Park to the Manchester Ship Canal Company in 1896 for a vast sum, but this did not prevent him from getting into financial difficulties a few years later so that there had to be a private Act of Parliament in 1904 to pay his debts out of capital in trust. In the year of her husband's trouble, Vi was at a bridge and poker party at the Wilfred Ashleys; her neighbour at dinner thought her 'singularly unspoilt', with 'a gentleness, a sympathy and a joyousness about her outlook'.[11] To an impecunious young cousin of Winston Churchill who told her that he planned to be an electrical engineer, she seemed less sympathetic. 'An electrical engineer? But how *very* curious', she said. 'Do you mean you could come and mend my electric bells? My butler has been complaining.'[12]

Vi de Trafford's hostess Mrs Ashley was the daughter of Edward VII's friend the Jewish financier Sir Ernest Cassel, who was received into the Catholic Church by

Father Bernard Vaughan. Father Bernard's association with Cassel, who was known as 'the Pope', is commemorated in the envoi of a ballade on Edwardian high life by Belloc:

> Prince, Father Vaughan will entertain the Pope,
> And you will entertain the Jews at Tring,
> And I will entertain the higher hope,
> And Mrs James will entertain the King.

The Jesuit brother of Cardinal Vaughan, who had died in 1903 just as his great cathedral in Westminster was completed — when it was first opened for public worship he was there before the high altar in his coffin — Father Bernard divided his time between the poor of the East End and the pulpit of the fashionable Jesuit church in Farm Street, Mayfair. His sermons on the sins of what he called the 'Smart Set', delivered in stentorian tones and generally beginning with some resounding phrase such as 'Watchman, what of the night?' won him the admiration of the very people whose sins he denounced; the King himself is said to have gone to hear him. He owed much of his success to his mordant wit, which was by no means reserved for the pulpit. Once, on a train journey, when a fellow-passenger got out at a station, he called after him, 'Hey you, you've left something behind'. The man came hurrying back, to be told by Father Bernard, 'You've left behind *a very bad impression*'.[13]

In 1906, the year when Father Bernard Vaughan was preaching on 'The Sins of Society', the twelfth Lord Arundell of Wardour died; a martyr, it was said, to his devotion to Catholic interests, for he insisted on going up to London to vote for an amendment to the Education Bill and the journey proved fatal to him. He was succeeded by his brother the one-time Jesuit Father Everard Arundell. Despite his illustrious birth and fine presence, Father Everard had kept away from fashionable pulpits, preferring to work as an obscure parish priest, devoted to his flock and giving generously to the poor. 'I have had to spend on the presbytery which was awfully uninhabitable', he had written to his brother on taking over a parish in North Wales. 'I should like to see you making your way to the wc which I have transferred to *close vicinity* with the house, but still outside.'[14] Father Everard was not Lord Arundell of Wardour for very long; he died in 1907, before taking his seat in the House of Lords. The title passed to a cousin, while his childless sister-in-law Anne Lucy Lady Arundell continued to live at Wardour having been left a life interest in the estate.

Another peer's son in the priesthood, Father Basil Feilding, had lost his life in 1906. Like the young Lord Montagu more than a century before, he was drowned in

Father Bernard Vaughan

the Rhine. His brother-in-law Gervase Elwes, husband of his sister Lady Winefride, was now a professional singer. It was an unusual way for the elder son of an Edwardian country squire of old family, the heir to estates in Northamptonshire and Lincolnshire, to earn a living; but there was not much money and he had been unhappy in his original career of diplomacy. He had a tenor voice of rare quality and could hold audiences with his good looks and his charm of manner; within a few years he was famous.

He now gave performances all over the country, he toured in Germany, he had sung twice before the Royal Family. When not performing or rehearsing, he led the life of a country gentleman; shooting in the winter, playing cricket in summer. Once, when he sang the *Dream of Gerontius* in the Barons' Hall at Arundel, a charity performance arranged by the young Duchess of Norfolk with the Sheffield Choir and part of the Queen's Hall Orchestra conducted by Henry Wood, his appearance

The inner court of Arundel Castle, as remodelled by the fifteenth Duke of Norfolk

was somewhat marred by a swollen lip, the result of wicket-keeping in a village cricket match while staying the previous weekend with the Duke's nephew James Hope.

The Barons' Hall usually echoed to more homely sounds as the Duke romped there with his children. The Duchess, known to her family and friends as Gwendy, gave him three daughters and a son, Bernard, who was born in 1908. Surrounded by his young family, the Duke, now in his sixties, was happier than at any other period of his life. He was also happy to have at last completed his great rebuilding of the castle, which had gone on for more than thirty years. 'Yes,' he said, with a twinkle in his eye, as he showed his guests the last bit of masonry being built into the curtain wall, 'it will be finished this week; and after that the castle will be absolutely impregnable – against bows and arrows'.[15] The gregarious Benedictine abbot Sir David Hunter Blair was not alone in thinking that the castle had been more comfortable before it was transformed, but the simple friendliness of the Duke in his shabby suit made up for the chill of his baronial halls.

The Duchess of Norfolk's father Lord Herries died in 1908. Having no brother, she now became Lady Herries in her own right and inherited Everingham. While Lord Herries had only two daughters, his brother Bernard Constable Maxwell already had five sons and five daughters by his second wife, the beautiful Alice Fraser, a sister of Lord Lovat, and she was yet to present him with another daughter and son. They had married in 1890 when she was twenty and he a widower of forty-two.

Of Lord Herries' two other brothers, Walter, the Zouave, was now back in England having failed to make a success of his ranch in Texas. Joey Maxwell-Scott had four sons and three daughters by his wife Mary Hope-Scott, the heiress of Abbotsford. Living at Abbotsford had cost more than they could afford, on account of too much entertaining; they had taken up the carpets in some of the bedrooms in an attempt to reduce the number of guests, but the beds were still there and the guests had continued to come. So Abbotsford was let and the family moved to London where Joey worked in insurance.

While Mary Maxwell-Scott and her family were living modestly in Wimbledon, her half-sister Minna, whose maiden name was not Hope-Scott but Hope, held court in a vast Italianate palace in Constantinople, where her husband, Sir Nicholas O'Conor, was British Ambassador. He was there for a good ten years, being more

Bernard Constable Maxwell and his wife Alice Fraser in 1912, with ten of their twelve children; ranging from Ian, who was born in 1891, to Ursula, who was born in 1911. Their second son Ronald was not present, and their youngest son Michael was not yet born

successful than other British diplomatists in dealing with the troublesome Sultan Abdul Hamid. Unfortunately he died in office in 1908; he was buried in Constantinople and his widow returned home. A year later she felt a desire to look again on her husband's dead features, so she and a woman friend travelled out to Constantinople where his corpse was exhumed for her benefit. As she gazed down into the open coffin, she said sadly, 'Oh dear, how thin he looks!' 'What do you expect, my dear,' said her friend. 'He hasn't eaten for a year.'[16]

Just as a generation earlier the English Catholics had been divided over Papal Infallibility, so now did their opinions differ over the movement in the Catholic Church known as Modernism. The Duke of Norfolk considered the publication in England of Pope Pius X's Encyclical against Modernism to be ill-timed; his father-in-law Lord Herries had accused a leading English Modernist of intellectual pride. More in sympathy with the Modernist movement than any other English Catholic of aristocratic birth was Maude Petre, who, except that she disapproved of foxhunting, could have been taken for a very ordinary middle-aged county lady, red-faced, dog-

Walter Constable Maxwell, the former Zouave and rancher in Texas, shooting in Scotland

Maude Petre

loving, rather shy and full of good works. In fact, she was a woman of powerful intellect and the author of books and articles on many different subjects.

She was a daughter of the twelfth Lord Petre's half-brother Arthur Petre by his wife Lady Katharine, the convert daughter of the Earl of Wicklow, an Irish Protestant. Monsignor Lord Petre, at whose school her favourite brother Vincent had died as a pupil, was her cousin. She had grown up in the depths of rural Essex in an atmosphere intensely Catholic; though her father, unlike his two elder half-brothers, had adhered to the old Cisalpine tradition of the Petres which gave her what has been described as 'a fierce style of independence towards ecclesiastical power'.

At the age of twenty-two she went to Rome to study scholastic philosophy, which had been recommended as a remedy for the religious doubts which were to plague her throughout her life. 'Maude has gone to Rome to study for the priesthood', said an aunt.[17] After hovering between marriage and taking the veil, she had chosen a middle course by joining a religious community living in the world of which she became a provincial superior at the age of thirty.

The publication in 1907 of her book *Catholicism and Independence* probably had something to do with her leaving the community, as did her friendship with Father George Tyrrell, the Jesuit theologian who was dismissed from the Society of Jesus in 1906 and afterwards excommunicated for refusing to retract the Modernist views expressed in some of his writings. Maude Petre's friendship with Tyrrell was the greatest thing in her life; it certainly had in it an element of human love, though she herself regarded it as a spiritual vocation and would never have dreamt of taking advantage of his rift with the Church to allow it to grow into anything different. In fact she loved him more as a priest than as a man. 'To me,' she afterwards wrote, 'the continuance of his life as a Catholic priest mattered more than anything else, and I would certainly have died to secure his spiritual safety.'[18] She not only wanted him to remain a priest, she wanted him to remain a Jesuit. After his dismissal from the Society of Jesus and his excommunication, she protected him and gave him material support, providing him with an annuity and a cottage in the garden of her house in Sussex. For his part, he accepted her devotion but gave little in return. She was frequently hurt by his coldness, which may well have been due to his being more aware than she was of the dangers of their friendship. He poked fun at her attitude to Church authority in a poem which he wrote:

> Lo, in the rear an Amazon who shoves
> And murmurs to herself: 'I feel it moves'.
> Herself immobile, nothing can defeat her;
> Rock versus Rock and Petre versus Peter.[19]

In 1909 Tyrrell died after a brief illness. On his deathbed he relaxed his defences. 'A first kiss!' poor Maude wrote pathetically in her diary. Four days later she wrote, 'He put his arm round me so lovingly, he drew my face down and kissed me on each cheek and on the mouth'.[20] He died without retracting his Modernism, but was given Extreme Unction. Maude saw fit to publish these facts in a letter to *The Times*, which brought down the wrath of the local bishop, the redoubtable Gibraltarian Dr Amigo, whose displeasure she had already incurred by harbouring Tyrrell. Not only did Bishop Amigo deny Tyrrell Catholic burial, but he would not allow Maude to be given Holy Communion unless she publicly abjured Modernism. This she refused to do, as much out of loyalty to Tyrrell's memory as on account of her own beliefs. Bishop Amigo's ban caused her much distress, frequent Holy Communion being of great importance to her in fighting her doubts. However, it did not extend beyond his own diocese of Southwark; so while deprived of the Sacrament at her Sussex home, she received Holy Communion whenever she went to London.

CHAPTER 11

'Your only monument'

THE young fourth Marquis of Bute, who had succeeded his father in 1900, had his father's retiring disposition but was interested in shooting rather than in Scottish saints and ancient buildings. His wife Augusta, daughter of the convert Irish baronet Sir Henry Bellingham and a grand-daughter of the convert Earl of Gainsborough, was more sociable. She gave balls during the London Season at St John's Lodge, the mansion in Regent's Park which her father-in-law had bought towards the end of his life. Like her father-in-law, Lady Bute became suitably Welsh when in residence at Cardiff Castle, entertaining the Cymodorion in the castle grounds and appearing as Dame Wales in a pageant.

Lord Bute's brother Lord Ninian Crichton-Stuart, who lived at Falkland Palace, also went to Ireland for his bride; she was Ismay Preston, daughter of Viscount Gormanston; her family had always been Catholic and held the premier Irish Viscountcy. In the first General Election of 1910, Lord Ninian stood for Cardiff as a Unionist; on polling day his two-year-old son Ringan was driven through the streets in a motor car with a banner bearing the legend 'Vote for Daddy'. Sadly he caught a chill from which he died a few days later; his death was to no purpose, for his father was defeated. However, Lord Ninian won the seat in the second election of that year.

That same autumn, Lord Lovat married at the age of nearly forty. Like his father, he had gone south to find a bride; the girl of his choice, the cultured eighteen-year-old Laura Lister, was not a Catholic when he first met her; though she became one before their wedding. She was, however, half Scottish; her mother, Lady Ribblesdale, was one of the Tennant sisters, prominent in the coterie known as the Souls. Her father, Lord Ribblesdale, was called 'The Ancestor' on account of his old-fashioned good looks immortalized by Sargent.

Up till then, Lovat had been too busy to think of marriage. He had kept the

The wounded Viceroy of India Lord Hardinge of Penshurst being taken away in a motor-car, having been lifted down from his elephant by his ADC, Hugh Fraser. The elephant's trunk can be seen on the right

Lovat Scouts in existence as two regiments of yeomanry which he raised after the end of the South African War. He was active in the House of Lords, speaking frequently on defence, as well as on forestry, housing and land settlement. He helped to launch a successful scheme for growing cotton in the Sudan.

Lovat's brother Hugh Fraser went out to India in 1910 as ADC to the Viceroy, Lord Hardinge of Penshurst. When Lord Hardinge was injured by a bomb during his State Entry into Delhi in December 1912, Hugh Fraser managed to get him down from his elephant, which was too frightened to kneel. Climbing up on to an erection of packing cases which he had brought from a nearby shop, he reached the Viceroy, who was now unconscious through loss of blood, and lifted him down like a child.

Whereas Hugh Fraser was a mere ADC, Sir Gerald Strickland and Sir Hugh Clifford, though not so very much older, were both Governors. Strickland was Governor of Western Australia, having previously governed Tasmania and before that again, the Leeward Islands. Tired of Maltese politics, he had embarked with gratitude on a proconsular career. Clifford was Governor of the Gold Coast. A son of Sir Henry Clifford, the VC, and an old boy of Monsignor Petre's school, he had been for many years in Malaya, where he served under his cousin Sir Frederick Weld. He was a friend of Kipling, of Joseph Conrad, and of Thomas Hardy. Both he and his wife Elizabeth, whom he had married as a widower in 1910, were authors. He wrote books with titles such as *Studies in Brown Humanity*, *Bush-Whacking* and *Malayan Monochromes*, as well as adventure stories for *Blackwood's Magazine*. She wrote novels, plays and poems.

She also published a humorous account of a day in their life at Christiansborg Castle, the old Danish fort which served as the Government House at Accra. The day starts with a tornado which blows the roof off His Excellency's bedroom and bathroom. The Governor nearly treads on a large puff-adder; a crocodile is found elsewhere in the house; a flight of bats takes refuge in Lady Clifford's boudoir. A bridge party is interrupted by a rat hunt in the drawing room. At dinner time the dining room ceiling, ravaged by white ants, collapses on to the dinner table. 'Luckily no dinner party.' So the Cliffords and their ADC dine on the veranda. 'Perfect moonlight night. Hot, not a breath. Sit silently enjoying the scene on the small balcony overlooking the sea.' They go happily to bed; and after Lady Clifford has summoned the ADC to remove a toad which is troubling her, she manages to go to sleep; only to be woken by an earthquake. She claims that all the episodes in her account actually happened, though not on the same day.

Sir Hugh Clifford's cousin Lewis, the ninth Lord Clifford of Chudleigh, who as a young man had travelled adventurously in North America and joined General Custer's expedition against the Indians, as well as farming in New Zealand with his brother Silly Willie, was married to Mabel Towneley, a sister of Mary the nun and a cousin of Lady O'Hagan. A large, domineering, eccentric woman, Mabel Lady Clifford liked amateur theatricals; her husband built her a theatre at Ugbrooke. Another of her passions was swimming. Once, on her way to open a fête in Devon, she passed a beach and fancied a swim. She saw a convenient hut which she used but, as she was drying herself, an irate man came pounding on the door and said that it was his hut. 'I am Lady Clifford of Chudleigh!' she called out haughtily from inside. She was, however, obliging enough to put her clothes on over her wet bathing-dress so as not to keep the man waiting and opened the fête dripping with sea water.

Since Mabel was childless, her husband's heir was Silly Willie, who was still in Tasmania, farming unsuccessfully. As the future Lord Clifford, Willie's eldest son Charles had been brought back from Tasmania at the age of eleven and sent to a preparatory school in Belgium before going to Downside, the Benedictine school

A visit to Ugbrooke by the Duke and Duchess of York, afterwards King George V and Queen Mary. Lewis, ninth Lord Clifford of Chudleigh, is the bearded figure standing behind the Duchess; his wife Mabel is sitting third from the right. The clean shaven man in a boater standing behind her is Lord Clifford's cousin Hugh Clifford, who became Sir Hugh and a distinguished proconsul

near Bath which was becoming more fashionable than Stonyhurst. During his holidays, he was only allowed to visit his uncle at Ugbrooke when his Aunt Mabel was away, owing to her jealousy at having no children of her own. Willie's two other sons, young Lewis and Bede, were educated in Australia and worked on their father's various farms; they felled trees, chopped wood and fought bush fires. By now Willie was separated from his wife Catherine, the small farmer's daughter from New Zealand. She had become mentally unstable and taken to drink, so he had sent her back to her parents. Eighteen months after leaving him she had given birth to a son whom she registered as Leopold Clifford. With the Tichborne Case still fresh in their memory, the Cliffords carefully preserved all the legal correspondence to do with this affair, lest a claimant to the title and estates should appear at some future date.

There was an echo of the Tichborne Case in 1913, when the young Sir Joseph

Mabel Towneley, wife of Lewis, ninth Lord
Clifford of Chudleigh

Tichborne, son of the Sir Henry whose interests had been successfully defended
against the Claimant, got married to Denise Greville, a cousin of the Earl of
Warwick. The Claimant's daughter, who had been sent money by Sir Joseph's
father and wanted more, threatened to shoot him at the church; which landed her in
Holloway. Another fashionable Catholic wedding of 1913 was that of Lionel,
sixteenth Lord Petre, a nephew of the Monsignor. Two of the Monsignor's brothers
had held the title after him in succession, the younger being Lionel's father. Lionel's
bride was Catherine Boscawen, a niece of Viscount Falmouth. 'She is so *rayonnante*

and attractive that one wishes the best for her', wrote one of the guests at the wedding in Westminster Cathedral.[1]

In the same month as Lord Petre married, another Catholic peer died: the octogenarian eleventh Lord Stafford, son of Edward Jerningham who took part in the Eglinton Tournament and of Marianne Smythe who might have been Maria Fitzherbert's daughter by George IV. As he had no children, the Stafford peerage and estates passed to his sister's son Colonel Francis Fitzherbert, who had won a DSO in South Africa. The new Lord Stafford was the elder son of another octogenarian, Basil Fitzherbert of Swynnerton; he was thus descended from the brother of Maria Fitzherbert's second husband and also perhaps from Maria herself. On the death of the eleventh Lord Stafford, the Jerningham baronetcy passed to Henry Jerningham, a great-grandson of William Jerningham who served in the Austrian army at the time of the French Revolution.

Feelings ran high in 1913 over the Irish question; the Home Rule Bill had passed its third reading, the Ulster Protestants were drilling and ready to fight to keep Ulster out of an Ireland with Home Rule. Though they had few Irish connections, the aristocratic Catholics of Britain felt as strongly about Ireland as everybody else. Having formerly tended to be Liberals, following the old Whig tradition which went back to before the time of Emancipation, they had mostly gone over to the Conservative and Unionist camp on account of Gladstone's Home Rule policy. Among those who changed sides in this way were the Duke of Norfolk, the ninth Lord Clifford and Lord Lovat's father. In 1913 the Duke of Norfolk attended a great Unionist rally at Blenheim and presented a sword to the Ulster Unionist leader, Sir Edward Carson. Lord Lovat suffered heart-searchings as to which side he would fight on should the Irish situation lead to civil war, torn between his sympathy for the loyal Ulstermen and his distaste for Orangeism; he eventually decided that he would fight for the Ulstermen.

A year later, the threat of civil war in Ireland was forgotten as war engulfed all Europe. The Duke of Norfolk organized the reception of Belgian refugees. Lord Lovat spent the fortnight before war was declared in the corridors of Whitehall; he used to say that those two weeks were the most interesting in his whole life. After some trouble with Kitchener, he was given the command of the Highland Mounted Brigade which included his Scouts; he looked forward to leaving for the front in three months' time when training was completed. He assured his wife Laura that by then the war would be 'in German territory, with the first-line troops exhausted'.[2] Once again there were officers billeted at Beaufort, where Willy the Moon, the old Fraser clansman who trimmed and polished the lamps, now had the additional task of cleaning their field-boots.

Roger Tempest went to the front as a major in the Scots Guards. Maude Petre went to France to nurse, but hurried back to England when she heard that her dog was gravely ill. Major-General Sir Francis Howard of the Corby family became Inspector-General of Infantry; his diplomatist brother Sir Henry was British Envoy to the Pope. Lord Stafford's naval brother Edward Fitzherbert commanded HMS *Colossus* in the Grand Fleet and soon became an admiral. Lord Denbigh commanded the Royal Horse Artillery and Lady Denbigh turned Newnham into a hospital, their brother-in-law Gervase Elwes sang for war charities and to cheer the wounded. Of the three young Clifford brothers from Tasmania, Bede, who during the weeks leading up to the war was staying at Ugbrooke, which, as he afterwards recalled, 'had never seemed so beautiful and so peaceful',[3] enlisted as a private. Lewis tried to join up but failed his medical owing to a bad hip. Charles joined the Royal Naval Brigade and after giving himself blisters rowing on the Thames was sent with his unit to Antwerp, only to be caught in Holland and interned there for the duration.

The sister of his Aunt Mabel Clifford, Mary Towneley, who was now not far off seventy and had been English Provincial of the Notre Dame Nuns since 1886, was at the Mother House of her Order at Namur when the Germans invaded Belgium. When a German officer came searching for arms, she held open a bag containing her knitting and asked him coldly if he wished to search it. The officer clicked his heels, saluted, bowed and withdrew. After allowing Mary to work for a few months nursing the wounded, the Germans sent her back to England, no doubt glad to be rid of her. As her steamer approached Tilbury, having safely negotiated the minefields, her voice was heard on the night air singing God Save the King and her own version of Rule Britannia, 'Britons never, never, never shall be *German* slaves'.[4]

The war took its toll of the Catholic families. Hugh Fraser and the Duke of Norfolk's nephew David Kerr, Philip Kerr's devoutly Catholic brother, were killed in October 1914. In the following year Lord Ninian Crichton-Stuart was killed and the young Lord Petre died of wounds. He was the first of three Petres among the victims of the war, who also included two Welds and two Weld-Blundells and their cousin Kenelm Vaughan, two Stonors and no fewer than four de Traffords, cousins of Sir Humphrey, and four Maxwell-Stuart brothers, nephews of the laird of Traquair.

On the day in 1916 when the Boer War veteran Colonel Courtenay Throckmorton was killed in Mesopotamia, the family arms fell from the gatehouse tower at Coughton. Also killed in 1916 were Sir Hugh Clifford's son Hugh and his brother Brigadier-General Henry Clifford; their cousin Walter Clifford of the New Zealand branch had been killed in the previous year. The Cliffords and their

Colonel Courtenay Throckmorton

relations suffered badly; Lord Clifford's sister Cissy, Lady Denbigh, lost two of her sons which broke her heart so that she herself barely survived the war. Sir Hugh Clifford's sister Blanche, the wife of Lord Stafford's cousin William Fitzherbert-Brockholes of Claughton in Lancashire, was so devastated by the death of her eldest son and the wounding of her youngest that she shot herself. Another relation of the Cliffords to be killed was Alexander de Lisle. Crathorne Anne, who was recommended for a VC, was drowned on active service in 1917; he was a grandson of Barbara Charlton, whose second son had taken the name of Anne on inheriting Burghwallis. Francis Plowden, the young squire of Plowden, died of wounds in

Mary Towneley as English Provincial of the Notre
Dame Nuns

1918, his younger brother Godfrey having died on active service in the previous year.

People who had gone into the war cheerfully soon realized its horrors and frustrations. Lord Lovat went to Gallipoli with his brigade, only to fall seriously ill with dysentery. Bede Clifford wrote in his diary during the Battle of the Somme, 'On all sides the sickly stench of dead men and beasts assails the nostrils. Everywhere the cries of wounded men pleading in vain to be evacuated.'[5] By now he had a commission, a year later he felt sufficiently sure of himself to have a row with his general about the question of overworking one's men. 'He gave me a hell of a dressing down, which as one only has to be bad enough at one's job or disliked enough by one's superiors to get a good fat job, I listened to with a vacant smile.'[6]

In 1916 Bede Clifford's father Silly Willie became the tenth Lord Clifford of Chudleigh on his brother's death. At the time he was working as a builder, since he was making nothing from farming; it is said that he jumped down from the roof of a chicken house which he was building to be told he was a peer. He set off for England with his belongings in a sack on his back. His first stop was Sydney, where he turned up at Government House, being vaguely connected to Sir Gerald Strickland who was now Governor of New South Wales. The young footman who opened the door thought he was a tramp, but admitted him after being told off for not being at the front. He stayed at Government House until his ship sailed; Strickland described him as 'just off a genius'.[7] Silly Willie did not come into the family estates, which went straight to his eldest son Charles, who provided for him.

Sir Hugh Clifford continued as Governor of the Gold Coast throughout the war years. His wife published a poem in thirty-five stanzas entitled *To the Colonial Civil Servant in West Africa*:

> The wife you love leads restless days,
> Her heart is always torn,
> Between her babes in strangers' hands
> Or husband left forlorn.

Bede Clifford in the front lines at Festubert in 1915; he is second from the right

'Silly Willie', the tenth Lord Clifford of Chudleigh.
He holds a microscope, having embarked late in life
on a new career as a scientist and inventor

Her letters come to cheer you, but
Your bungalow seems bare,
And loneliness descends on you
Whene'er you enter there.
They told you once, they told you twice,
They had to be severe,
That if you'd help your country, you
Must carry on out here.

At last he gets leave to go and fight in the war; but on his way home, his ship is
torpedoed.

A bubble on the water shows
That your last breath is spent,
And with its passing vanishes
Your only monument.

Early in 1917 the Duke of Norfolk died and was succeeded by his eight-year-old son Bernard. While the new Duke was a minor, his position as the leading English Catholic was taken by his uncle Lord Edmund Talbot, who was still an MP and held minor Government office. In 1918 Lord Edmund joined with Lord Walter Kerr – Cecil Lady Lothian's sailor son, now an Admiral of the Fleet – and other members of the Catholic Union, in a resolution condemning the Irish Catholic bishops for resisting the introduction of conscription in Ireland. The resolution was passed with the best of intentions at a critical moment of the war; but it caused ill-feeling. A few months earlier Lord Bute's surviving brother Lord Colum Crichton-Stuart had suggested that the Irish should be conscripted to fight in Italy on the plea of the Pope being in danger.

Lord Walter Kerr's nephew Philip Kerr played a part in the Peace Conference, as a member of Lloyd George's secretariat, which he had joined on Milner's recommendation. He had left the Catholic Church in 1915 and was now attracted to Christian Science, to which he had been introduced by his American friend Viscountess Astor. It had been a fearful blow to his mother and sisters; his unmarried sister Cecil was making herself ill by fasting and doing penance to bring him back.

The grandson of another leading nineteenth century convert also played a part on the European scene during the months of confusion following the end of the war. Ambrose March Phillipps de Lisle's grandson Colonel Edward Strutt was sent in 1919 by King George V to ensure the safety of the young Austrian Emperor Karl and his family, lest they should suffer a fate similar to that suffered by the Tsar and his family in the previous year. The Emperor refused to abdicate but was willing to go into exile in Switzerland; Karl Renner, the socialist Chancellor of the new Austrian Republic, demanded that the Emperor should abdicate before leaving the country.

Strutt wrote out a telegram instructing the British Government to blockade Austria if the Emperor were not allowed to leave without abdicating and showed it to Renner. It was a wild bluff; the British Government would certainly not have taken orders from a mere colonel and there were the other *Entente* powers to be considered. But the bluff worked. Renner, having looked at Strutt's telegram, threw up his hands and exclaimed 'Grosser Gott!' The Emperor was able to leave, as he himself put it, 'as Emperor and not as a thief in the night'.[8]

Philip Kerr at the Peace Conference in 1919

The end of the war was followed by the Irish troubles. In the spring of 1921, as a conciliatory move, the British Government decided to send a Catholic Viceroy to Ireland and chose Lord Edmund Talbot who was at first reluctant to take on the appointment but was persuaded to go by the King. Before he could be appointed, a special Act of Parliament had to be passed; for the Irish Viceroyalty was one of the few offices which Catholics still could not hold. He was raised to the peerage as Viscount FitzAlan of Derwent and reverted to his original surname of Fitzalan-Howard.

For the first time since the reign of James II, the Sovereign's representative attended Mass in Dublin. Lord FitzAlan also had Family Rosary every day and prayed aloud when driving in his car, no matter who was with him. But what was more important to the Irish – who set less store by the new Viceroy's religion than the British did – was that he seemed to have come as an emissary of peace. After he had been in Ireland a month he publicly admitted that the notorious British force known as the Black and Tans had committed 'crimes, horrible crimes'[9]. Having started in an atmosphere of mutual distrust, FitzAlan and Nationalist Ireland soon came to respect each other. He stayed on for a year after the Anglo-Irish Treaty of December 1921, reigning over the infant Free State as well as over Northern Ireland.

Whereas FitzAlan's predecessor Viscount French had left his family in England, Lady FitzAlan was in Ireland throughout her husband's Viceroyalty; despite the continuing Anglo-Irish conflict during its earlier months and the Civil War afterwards. The FitzAlans' son and daughter came with them, both fortyish and single. The son, Henry, known as Boydie, had been wounded in the war and taken prisoner; he had come back with a German girl-friend, much to his father's annoyance. However, he would soon be safely married to Joyce Langdale who was not only very attractive and a Catholic of impeccable birth, but heiress to the Houghton estate in Yorkshire. The FitzAlans' daughter, Magdalen, was rather sad. Her Catholicism had kept her on the shelf; for even now, Protestant eligibles were reluctant to marry Catholics.

There was plenty of entertaining at Viceregal Lodge when the FitzAlans were there. One of their dinner parties, however, was spoilt because Lord FitzAlan's motor car had been stolen that day at the races; his Free State guards having failed to protect it against the Irregulars. He was so furious that he never uttered a word at dinner; and since if the Viceroy remained silent it was not etiquette for anybody else to speak, the whole large party of smart and talkative Irish had to sit in silence.

When Lord FitzAlan was Viceroy, a cousin of his late sister-in-law Flora Duchess of Norfolk was also living in Ireland: Talbot Clifton, the squire of Lytham in Lancashire, a tall man in his middle fifties with vague blue eyes and a nautical beard. Having become rich and independent at the age of sixteen, when he inherited the family estates – which included part of Blackpool – from his grandfather and namesake Colonel Talbot Clifton, he had indulged his wanderlust ever since. He had been twice round the world before he was twenty; he had travelled and explored in Africa, Siberia and Tibet; he had ranched in Wyoming and lived among the Eskimos. In Mexico City he had been converted to Catholicism, having been brought up an Anglican, despite his grandfather's return to the Faith which his great-grandfather Thomas Clifton had abandoned in 1831. 'It was like finding an orchid on a dung-heap', he wrote in his diary.[10] His wife Violet Beauclerk, a descendant of Charles II whom he had met on a ledge of rock in the Andes when her father was British Minister in Peru, was also a convert.

In 1917 he had bought a house in Connemara, where he was then stationed as an officer in the RNVR, watching for German submarines from his yacht. In this house, as a friend recalled, 'a quarterdeck atmosphere prevailed'. He had installed a loudspeaker system, so that 'at any moment one of the Galway wenches would receive barking commands from the walls'.[11] His neighbour, the writer and wit Oliver St John Gogarty, nicknamed him 'Lookey-heah', which was how he prefaced everything he said.

At about the same time as Lord FitzAlan lost his car, Talbot Clifton's motor was likewise 'commandeered' by Irregulars. He offered them his Ford, but they took the great glittering Lanchester which was the apple of his eye. A few days later, on hearing that the Lanchester would be passing his way, he set out with his gun under his arm to ambush it; Violet went with him, wearing her diamonds under her dress and bringing ropes to tie up the captives. Talbot's ambush miscarried; he did not get his car back, and he shot and wounded one of the men; which meant that he had to leave Ireland without delay. Violet followed with the children, bringing his favourite billiard cue, a Japanese figure and a stuffed head of the *bos anoa* which he had shot during their recent journey through Celebes. Everything else, pictures, family silver, she abandoned; though in the event their possessions were restored to them and even the Lanchester was recovered, albeit in a battered state. After the Civil War ended, the leader of the Irregulars wrote Talbot a friendly letter asking him to return; but by then he had bought the castle and estate of Kildalton on the Isle of Islay.

Having looked after Talbot's *bos anoa* at his Dublin house, Oliver St John Gogarty was invited to Lytham with his family for a long stay. This caused Talbot to be immortalized in *Sackville Street*, which is dedicated to Violet. Gogarty depicts him as a man of boundless generosity and hospitality, but with a rather childish desire always to be one-up that is reminiscent of his contemporary Sir George Sitwell whom he resembled physically. On the night of the Gogartys' arrival at Lytham, the Clifton gold plate is out in their honour as they dine in a room hung with old-rose velvet, their host resplendent in scarlet at the head of the table; it is not a hunt coat but 'a uniform which he had designed for the President of the Lytham Golf Club over which he presided'.

They are only allowed to enjoy Lytham for a few days before they are whisked off to Kildalton in the now-refurbished Lanchester. 'What the devil were you doing on that hill? You had no gun', Talbot once asked Gogarty; but only now is it fully apparent what sport means to him. The first day is grouse-shooting, when Talbot orders off Gogarty's schoolboy son for shooting a greyhen and then accidentally shoots one himself. The second day is deer-stalking, when Gogarty's shot goes a few inches too high, giving Talbot the satisfaction of telling him so. That night at dinner, after the piper has retired, Gogarty remarks, 'without any suggestion . . . of

Talbot Clifton

relief', that the day's sport is over.

His host overhears him. 'Nonsense! Flighting begins at eleven.'

Next day they go stalking again and Talbot is greatly put out when Gogarty kills a stag. Dinner that night is decidedly sticky until Gogarty, by way of making conversation, happens to mention that Imperial Tokay has been unobtainable since the war. He is instantly taken down to the cellar by his host, who opens one of 'ten or twelve squat flasks'.

'My cousin Esterhazy kept some for me. Here's your very good health.'

To Gogarty, Talbot seemed 'a figure unhorsed in our humdrum days from Roncesvalles or Fontarrabia'. His wife Violet, in the biography of him which she wrote after his death in 1928, reveals that the infant Talbot Clifton 'sucked his mother so fiercely that she had a wound in her breast'. The book is dedicated 'To God for Talbot'.[12]

Talbot Clifton's cousin and exact contemporary Cuthbert Riddell of Swinburne in Northumberland was also a law unto himself. His complete disregard for his personal appearance caused him to be known as 'Dirty Bertie'; he was also nicknamed 'The Preface' from his habit of arriving much too early. Once, when invited to luncheon with Lady Swinburne at Capheaton, he arrived at twelve to find that his hostess was out. When twelve-thirty came and still she had not returned, he demanded his lunch, since he himself always lunched at that hour. He had finished his lunch and departed by the time Lady Swinburne returned home at one o'clock.[13]

Dirty Bertie was equalled for sartorial untidiness among the Catholic aristocracy by Silly Willie; who, having become the tenth Lord Clifford and returned to England, had embarked on a new career as a scientist and inventor. In 1922 he discovered what he called the 'Clifford Colour Rays', which were supposed to cure various ailments. A journalist who interviewed him at about this time found him in his workshop in morning dress covered in wood shavings, holding his latest invention which he claimed would 'save half a ton of coal per year per grate'.[14]

While Silly Willie carried out his experiments in a suburban house in Ealing, his eldest son Charles lived at Ugbrooke. Charles Clifford was already a widower, his wife Dorothy, who came of the Worcestershire Catholic family of Hornyold, having succumbed to the so-called Spanish 'flu leaving him with an only child, a daughter. Another house where there was now no chatelaine was Newnham, Charles Clifford's Aunt Cissy Lady Denbigh having died in 1919, heartbroken at losing two of her sons in the war and worn out by running her hospital. The Denbigh family suffered a further bereavement in 1921, when Lord Denbigh's brother-in-law Gervase Elwes was fatally injured through falling under a train while on a singing tour of the United States and Canada.

The Denbighs' Warwickshire neighbours the Throckmortons had also suffered through the war; Colonel Courtenay Throckmorton, who would have been the heir, having been killed in 1916. His widow lived at Coughton with her schoolboy son Robert and her two daughters. The house had been modernized by her husband's uncle Sir William Throckmorton after selling Buckland in Berkshire, the other Throckmorton seat, in 1908. Even the family ghost, the Pink Lady, had been got rid of, though this was done without Sir William's consent by the over-pious wife of his agent, who officiously brought in a priest to exorcize her while he was away; Sir William never forgave the agent's wife for doing him out of his ghost.

For all of Sir William's modernizations, Coughton in the nineteen-twenties was run very much in the old manner. Milk was brought to the house by a man with two pails hanging from a wooden bar over his shoulder. Meals had to be carried across the courtyard from the kitchen, which was in the northern range, to the dining room on the first floor of the range opposite; in wet weather they had to go round all three sides of the house. Yet somehow the food kept hot.

The war, which robbed the Throckmortons of an heir, deprived their cousins the Actons of the Dalberg estates in Germany which were confiscated in 1914. The second Lord Acton had been a Lord-in-Waiting under the Liberals like his father and also a diplomat; but had been removed from his post as Minister to Finland in 1920 for an injudicious remark about 'the light coming from the East'.[15] After that he joined the Labour Party and hoped for office when Labour came to power in 1924. But he died suddenly in June of that year, leaving a young family of two sons and seven daughters. The two sons were the only surviving descendants in the male line of the great Sir John Acton. There were, however, Actons descended from Sir John's younger brother Joseph, most of whom had become Neapolitan. Joseph's great-grandson Alfredo Acton was an admiral in the Italian navy and Chief of the Italian Naval Staff; he was made a baron in the Kingdom of Italy as well as an honorary KCB.

Two of Joseph Acton's grandsons had, however, gone to England after the fall of the Bourbons of Naples in 1860. One of them was the father of Arthur Acton, who worked in the United States as an interior designer and married a rich American, enabling him to buy and restore the magnificent Villa La Pietra near Florence and to fill it with works of art. Having grown up in such surroundings, it is not surprising that Arthur's elder son Harold should have been an aesthete from an early age. As a schoolboy at Eton immediately after the war, he had produced an arts magazine called the *Eton Candle*. At Oxford, where his contemporaries included Robert Byron, Cyril Connolly, Anthony Powell and Evelyn Waugh, he influenced his generation more than any other undergraduate of the time.

But while Harold Acton did actually read from *The Waste Land* through a megaphone from the window of his rooms in Meadow Buildings, which were painted lemon-yellow and filled with Victorian bric-à-brac, he was not, as is often supposed, the original of Anthony Blanche in *Brideshead Revisited*. Blanche is based on another of Waugh's Oxford contemporaries, the affected, effeminate and rather sinister Brian Howard, who was incidentally no relation of the Norfolk family. The tall and powerfully-built Harold Acton was not, like Howard, a poseur, but genuinely devoted to the arts.

The Oxford contemporaries of Evelyn Waugh included Francis Turville-Petre, whose father, a grandson of Adela Petre and a half-nephew of Henry Petre of Dunkenhalgh, had inherited Bosworth from Sir Francis Turville to whom he was related through the Talbots. Then there was young Esmé Howard, whose father, now Sir Esmé, became British Ambassador in Washington in 1924 having before that been Ambassador in Madrid. Esmetto, as he was known to his family, was a young man of great promise with the warmth and charm of his Italian blood, inherited from his mother along with the blood of the Scottish Earls of Newburgh. He was also Italian in some of his tastes; staying at Greystoke with his aunt Lady Mabel Howard he asked for pasta, and was disappointed when the cook sent up a minute dish of macaroni cheese. Towards the end of his time at Oxford he contracted an illness which eventually proved fatal; though suffering agonies, he insisted on taking his degree so as not to disappoint his father.

Lord Abingdon, the brother of Sir Esmé Howard's former chief in Rome, died in 1928 aged ninety-one. By then, the eldest daughter of his first marriage, Lady FitzAlan, was nearly seventy; but the children of his second marriage were a generation younger. One of them, the lively Lady Gwendoline, known as Goonie, was married to Winston Churchill's brother Jack. Lord Abingdon's youngest son, the sailor James Bertie, was married in 1928 to Lady Jean Crichton-Stuart, the younger daughter of Lord and Lady Bute. It was a great occasion at Mount Stuart with Nuptial Mass in the chapel and a gathering in the marble hall when the bridegroom's naval sword got stuck in the cake, 'Lucky there's no war on, Jimmy, you'll never get it out', one of his brothers-in-law shouted. The Butes' eldest son, the Earl of Dumfries, came of age that same year; the festivities lasted a week, with presentations, addresses, dinner parties and a garden party for seven thousand.

The young Butes were brought up to go barefoot on the hill, as were the young Master of Lovat — known as Shimi, the Gaelic for Simon — and his brother and sisters. Lord Lovat's energy had not diminished with the ending of the war. Since then he had been Chairman of the Royal Commission on Forestry and of the Overseas Settlement Committee; as well as Under-Secretary of State for the Dominions. He had gone to Canada for the Empire Forestry Conference and been idolized. It was generally believed that he would have been made Governor-General of Canada had not the Government been afraid of offending the powerful Canadian Orange Lodges by appointing a Catholic.

Beaufort during these years was full of guests; with the stylish intellectual leavening of Lady Lovat's friends, who included three writers, the cosmopolitan Princess Marthe Bibesco, the convert priest Ronald Knox and Maurice Baring, a convert scion of the banking family. Maurice Baring had Catholic connections; his aunt was the Catholic Lady Cromer, his sister was married to the Earl of Kenmare.

In his novel *Cat's Cradle*, published in 1925, he describes Alton-Leigh, home of the recusant family of Lacy, which is almost certainly inspired by Baddesley Clinton:

> The warm walls, the flaming creeper on the square tower, the large mullioned windows with the sun glinting on the square panes, the still moat full of water-lilies, in which one swan was proudly swimming.

In the years immediately after the war, Maurice Baring used to join Lord Lovat for bachelor weekend parties at the Royal York Hotel in Brighton, when he would entertain the company after dinner by balancing a glass of port on his bald head. The parties were for all ages and included retired generals as well as young Shimi and one or two other boys. They also included Maurice Baring's friend Raymond de Trafford, youngest of the three sons of Sir Humphrey and the irresistible Vi. Raymond de Trafford was a handsome young man with a lively mind and plenty of charm; he was genuinely literary, hence his friendship with Maurice Baring, while being a good polo player. But he was also a daredevil who had been obliged to leave both Downside and the Coldstream Guards. Evelyn Waugh, who later became a friend of his, calls him a 'fine desperado' and recounts an evening with him in Kenya, 'He got very drunk and brought a sluttish girl back to the house. He woke me up later to tell me he had just rogered her and her mama, too.'[16]

Raymond de Trafford went to Kenya in 1926 and almost immediately fell in love with Alice de Janzé, a young American man-eater who played with lion cubs and was said to look like a 'wicked madonna'.[17] He wanted to marry her, but could not do so according to the teachings of the Catholic Church, for she was already married to a French count. When he returned home in the following year his family succeeded in talking him out of the marriage; he went to Paris, where Alice de Janzé was then staying, and told her so. Alice came to see him off at the Gare du Nord; she entered his compartment and having kissed him, shot him and then shot herself. Both were badly wounded, though they recovered; he was to marry her in the end, but they parted after three months.

Raymond's eldest brother Humphrey de Trafford was a highly-respected figure on the Turf; he had acquired a fine Georgian house and estate in Hertfordshire, not far from Newmarket where he was to become one of the most effective Stewards of the Jockey Club. He had married grandly, though outside the Catholic world; his wife Cynthia was a daughter of the eldest son of the fifth Earl Cadogan; one of her sisters was married to the elder son of the Duke of Marlborough, another to the elder son of the Earl of Derby. Vi de Trafford lived to see her son Humphrey's successful marriage; but she was spared Raymond's near-fatal romance, for she died in 1925.

Raymond de Trafford with Alice de Janzé in
Kenya in 1926

Her husband Sir Humphrey now lived rather sadly in Eastbourne with a mistress.

The de Traffords were not the only wealthy Lancashire Catholic family now
established in Hertfordshire. The third Lord Gerard had married a cousin who was
the heiress to an estate near Ware; they had abandoned Garswood, the great
Classical house of the Gerards in Lancashire, which had been pulled down in 1921
after standing for less than a century. Other Catholic houses given up between the
wars included Cossey, the Norfolk seat of the Jerninghams, Blackmore, the
Worcestershire seat of the Hornyolds, and Glossop Hall in Derbyshire, seat of the
branch of the Howards from which sprang the twelfth and subsequent Dukes of
Norfolk. The thirteenth Duke gave Glossop to his second son who was later made
Lord Howard of Glossop; but the third Lord Howard of Glossop, who was
married to Mona, Baroness Beaumont in her own right, preferred to live at Carlton
Towers, his wife's family seat in Yorkshire. While the post-war period saw the
destruction of many country houses, it also saw the return of the Charlton family to
Hesleyside, which had been let for nearly forty years. Barbara Charlton's grandson
William took advantage of the buoyant land market in 1919 and sold part of the
estate to clear the mortgages, which enabled him and his wife and children to live at
their ancestral home.

Mona, Baroness Beaumont and her sister Ivy Stapleton (second and third from the left) at a hunt meet at Carlton Towers in 1924

The most important Catholic house lost during the nineteen-twenties was Lulworth Castle. On the death of the bachelor Humphrey Weld in 1928, Lulworth passed to his cousin Herbert Weld-Blundell, who consequently dropped the name of Blundell. Herbert was an explorer, an antiquary, an Oriental scholar and a linguist whose work on the Amharic language had won him an honorary fellowship at Oxford. He was also an inventor, though his inventions, which included the folding camera, had brought him little money; and like his grandfather Joseph Weld he was a great yachtsman, winning the King's Cup at Cowes with his cutter *Lulworth*.

In 1923, as a seventy-one-year-old bachelor, he married a wife very much younger than himself. The marriage, though childless, was a great success; but in 1928 his wife died, leaving him heartbroken. Then in August 1929 he had the further tragedy of seeing Lulworth Castle burn to the ground. At the height of the fire, the bust of Cardinal Weld in the hall was seen to turn one way and then the other, as though surveying the devastation; it then fell down into the flames.

In the year Lulworth was burnt, Herbert Weld's cousin Sir Hugh Clifford resigned from being Governor of the Straits Settlements. He had held this post since 1927, following in the footsteps of his cousin Sir Frederick Weld and ending his career in Malaya where it had begun. Before that, since leaving the Gold Coast, he had been successively Governor of Nigeria and of Ceylon.

That other Catholic proconsul Sir Gerald Strickland had returned to Maltese politics in 1917 and since 1927 had been Prime Minister of Malta. When he first became Prime Minister, he was also MP for Lancaster; but this anomaly ended in 1928 when he was raised to the peerage. Throughout his premiership – during which there was an attempt on his life – Lord Strickland, as he had become, fought hard to resist the influence of Mussolini. He also engaged in a battle with the Church, which began when the ecclesiastical senators, who held the balance of power in the Senate, refused to pass his Government's first budget. The conflict, aggravated by Strickland's inflammatory language, reached its height on the eve of a

Lulworth Castle in flames

Sir Hugh Clifford as Governor of the Straits
Settlements

general election in 1930 when the bishops of Malta and Gozo proclaimed it a grave
sin for Catholics to vote for Strickland or for any of his candidates. The Vatican
supported the bishops and diplomatic relations between Great Britain and the Holy
See were temporarily strained.

Eventually, through the good offices of Sir Esmé Howard, now back from
Washington and raised to the peerage as Lord Howard of Penrith, Strickland made
his peace with the Vatican. He was persuaded to be more conciliatory towards the
bishops by Everard Feilding, a brother of his old love Lady Clare, to whom he was
now connected by marriage; for his daughter Cecilia was the wife of Feilding's

Lord Strickland

nephew Hubert de Trafford. Strickland was greatly helped during the crisis by his unmarried daughter Mabel, who also assisted him with the *Times of Malta*, the newspaper which he had founded to combat Italian influence. He had three other daughters living, but both his sons had died in infancy. Having lost his first wife Lady Edeline in 1918, he had remarried in 1926. His second wife Margaret, a daughter of the wealthy Manchester newspaper proprietor Edward Hulton, was to build that great landmark of modern Valletta, the Phoenicia Hotel.

In 1930 Sir Joseph Tichborne died young. The Claimant's daughter had continued to plague Sir Joseph after she came out of prison; selling matches and flowers on the pavement outside his London flat with her name in large letters on her basket. Sir Joseph left an only son, Sir Anthony, who was still at Eton, where another Catholic boy of the same age, the young seventeenth Lord Petre, was following the progress of his cousin Mildred as she flew solo from London to Tokyo.

Mildred was the daughter of Maude Petre's brother Laurence and had grown up at Maude's old home in Essex. She was as strong-willed as her aunt but much more

Mildred Bruce with the aircraft in which she flew solo from London to Tokyo

George Eyston in *Thunderbolt*, the car with which he established the world speed record on land

Sir Bede and Lady Clifford (centre), aboard a yacht with President Roosevelt

decorative, petite and elegant; she always insisted on wearing a skirt and blouse and a string of pearls whether at the wheel of a racing car or in the cockpit of an aircraft or speedboat. In 1927 she and her husband Victor Bruce, a son of Lord Aberdare, had driven further north into Lapland than anybody else had until then. She had crossed the Channel twice by motor boat, she had broken many speed records as a motorist. In the summer of 1930 she saw a small aircraft in the window of a London shop and bought it on the spur of the moment, even though she had never been up in the air. She took a few flying lessons and in September set off for Tokyo on her own. In spite of getting lost in Turkey and crashing in Persia and nearly running out of petrol over the mountains of Indo-China, she managed to reach Tokyo by the end of November. She continued on round the world, though she and her plane had to cross the Pacific and Atlantic by ship. The flight made her name as an airwoman and she would henceforth devote her life to flying. It was left to her cousin George Eyston of the Hendred family, whose grandmother was a Petre, to hold the world speed record on land.

As epic a journey as Mildred's flight was Bede Clifford's crossing of the Kalahari Desert in 1928. The youngest of the three sons of Silly Willie was then Secretary to the Governor-General of South Africa; in 1931 he became Governor of the Bahamas, at forty-one the youngest Governor in the Colonial Service. He looked the archetypal proconsul of the time: tall and erect, with a trim moustache. His wife Alice was American. He immediately set about making the Bahamas into a fashionable tourist resort; encouraging well-known people, royalty as well as film stars, to come. He and his wife paid many visits to the United States and stayed with the Roosevelts at the White House.

Lord Lovat, who but for his religion might have been governing Canada while his cousin Sir Bede Clifford governed the Bahamas, dropped dead at an Oxford point-to-point meeting in 1933, after seeing his son Shimi win a race. Two years later Beaufort Castle was badly damaged by fire. A son of the old retainer Willy the Moon braved smoke and flames to rescue a forty-eight-pound salmon from the billiard room, leaving the family portraits in the picture gallery to perish.

CHAPTER 12

'Mowbray is here'

LORD and Lady FitzAlan and their spinster daughter Magdalen now lived at Cumberland Lodge in Windsor Park, where they had many people to stay. To one of their younger guests, Lord FitzAlan 'with his stocky figure and drooping moustache resembled the walrus' and Lady FitzAlan 'with her sharp, tormented features, the carpenter'. The same guest made up for this irreverence by describing Lord FitzAlan as 'an extremely patrician and saintly old man, whom it was impossible not to revere and love'.[1]

A frequent guest at Cumberland Lodge was the Prime Minister, Stanley Baldwin, who was a close friend of Lord FitzAlan. Two other political figures who stayed often were Lord FitzAlan's nephew the eleventh Marquis of Lothian, as Philip Kerr had become on the death of his cousin in 1930, and his friend Lady Astor who had introduced him to Christian Science. The FitzAlans were very worried about Lord Lothian's immortal soul. Lord Lothian, who was briefly in the Government, was not the only political nephew of Lord FitzAlan; there was also James Hope, now Lord Rankeillour, who was an MP for many years and held several junior Government posts before being raised to the peerage in 1932. While Lord FitzAlan's two nephews were influential in politics, Lady FitzAlan's niece Priscilla – whose mother was another daughter of Lord Abingdon – was married to the most powerful man in the City of London, the legendary Governor of the Bank of England, Montagu Norman.

King George V and Queen Mary would sometimes come over from Windsor Castle to Cumberland Lodge. Lord FitzAlan once took them into the chapel and showed the King the prayer for the Royal Family. 'May, come and see this prayer which they say for us every day', the King called out to the Queen.[2] 'Of course, the King hasn't got his father's brains', Lord FitzAlan said of George V. 'On the other hand, he hasn't got his father's *dreadful morals*.'[3]

Viscount and Viscountess FitzAlan of Derwent

Lord FitzAlan's sister Lady Philippa Stewart was still alive in the nineteen-thirties. Her 'Protestant doctor' had made good and was now Sir Edward Stewart, KBE. Though she was the sister of two nuns and as devout a Catholic as the rest of her generation of Fitzalan-Howards, Lady Philippa had no use for religious orders; she had shared this prejudice with her elder brother the fifteenth Duke, whose benefactions had all been to the secular clergy, or to the Oratorians who are in fact secular priests living in community. 'Those Franciscans who live near us – *what do they do?*', Lady Philippa would ask. And when there was talk of the Dominican Father Bede Jarrett being canonized, she said, 'An excellent good man, my dear, I've no doubt an excellent good man. *But a saint?*'[4]

When, following the Abdication – in which Lord FitzAlan stiffened Baldwin's resolve – King George VI was crowned, the ceremony was well organized by Lord

The young Bernard, sixteenth Duke of Norfolk, in a family party of his Constable Maxwell relations in 1926. He stands third from the left in the second row, in front of his great-uncle and aunt Bernard and Alice Constable Maxwell. Bernard and Alice's third son Gerald and his American wife Carrie are to the left of, and in the front of, the young Duke; they were to have a daughter who would one day be the wife of the subsequent Duke of Norfolk. David, the next younger of the Constable Maxwell sons, who sits in the front row between the youngest son Michael and Ursula, the youngest of the daughters, was to marry Alethea Turville-Petre, the heiress of Bosworth. At the back of the group on the left is the Benedictine abbot Sir David Hunter Blair

FitzAlan's twenty-eight-year-old nephew Bernard, the sixteenth Duke of Norfolk; who was made a Knight of the Garter on the previous day. Many of the meetings to do with the Coronation were held at Norfolk House where, during the previous London Season, the Duke's mother gave a ball. Four footmen stood in the hall wearing the scarlet Norfolk livery with knee breeches and powdered hair. The guests were received by the Duchess at the top of the stairs and passed into the rooms of gilded rococo. It was a warm evening and people went out on to the balcony

Norfolk House

overlooking St James's Square; passers-by could see the tiaras glittering. Nobody knew that within two years the house would be sold and demolished.

A few months before the Coronation, the Duke married Lord Belper's daughter Lavinia Strutt, an Anglican cousin of Colonel Edward Strutt who helped the Emperor Karl. Lord Belper was no relation of Lord Rayleigh, whose surname was also Strutt, and whose daughter Daphne was married to the third Lord Acton. Evelyn Waugh has described Lord Acton as 'a light-hearted, sweet-tempered, old-fashioned horsey young man' and his wife as 'a tall, elegant beauty'.[5] She was also an intellectual, as might be expected since her father and grandfather were both eminent scientists – her grandfather, the third Lord Rayleigh, discovered argon.

Lady Acton's father was an agnostic and like the rest of his family had been dismayed when his daughter married a Catholic. There had been no question of her converting at the time of her marriage; but her interest in Catholicism was subsequently aroused by her husband's sister Mia, wife of the Catholic journalist

The staircase, Norfolk House

Douglas Woodruff, and she became a Catholic in 1937. She was given her first Holy Communion by Ronald Knox, with whom she had made friends after deciding to convert. The ceremony took place in the chapel at Aldenham which the mother of the first Lord Acton had built. Mass had not been said there for fifteen years, for the Actons were away a great deal; owing to the loss of the Dalberg lands Lord Acton was not well off and had to work as a stockbroker in Birmingham.

Lord Acton's friend and contemporary John Arundell, only son of the fifteenth Lord Arundell of Wardour, was also a stockbroker. John Arundell had grown up with his parents and sisters in the east wing of Wardour Castle, the centre block of the house being occupied by the twelfth Lord Arundell's widow Anne Lucy, whose husband had not only left her a life interest in the estate but had bequeathed much of the contents of the house to her outright. Having no children of her own had embittered Anne Lucy and made her totally uninterested in the future of the family and estate. She had let the place go to rack and ruin; she had sold land for next to

The fifteenth Lord Arundell of Wardour and his
wife at Wardour Castle, with their son John and
their daughter Mary Isabella

nothing, as well as a great deal of the furniture. Apart from giving John an
allowance to enable him to go to Oxford, she had done nothing for the fifteenth Lord
Arundell and his family. She had even refused to see them when she was dying at the
age of ninety-one in 1934. And although they were living in the wing, they were so
much strangers to the main part of the house while she was alive that they did not
realize until after her death that the great dome of the rotunda was on the point of
collapse and the saloon floor was sagging.

Inheriting a property so run down, with the burden of mortgages and succession
duty, might have proved too much for the elderly Lord Arundell had it not been for
his son. But John Arundell was devoted to Wardour; it was, for the time being, his
wife, for he was still unmarried; it was his vocation. He was a first-rate manager, an
expert on forestry; he was doing well on the Stock Exchange. By the time his father
died in March 1939 – when the white owl, harbinger of death in the Arundell
family, was seen – he had paid off most of the succession duty; he was fortunately
spared a second lot by his father's foresight in making over the property to him in

Daphne Strutt, wife of the third Lord Acton,
in her Coronation robes in 1937

good time. He had put the estate into order and restored the house, helped by the generosity of a family friend.

John took his seat in the House of Lords as the sixteenth Lord Arundell of Wardour in June 1939, with Lord Acton as one of his sponsors. A few months later, he went off to the war. He wrote an affectionate farewell message to his tenants and to his other friends around Wardour, who loved him as much as he loved them.

When the war started, Lord Lothian had just arrived in Washington as British Ambassador, while another of the Duke of Norfolk's relations, his uncle by marriage the Earl of Perth, was appointed Chief Adviser on Foreign Publicity to the Ministry of Information, having just retired from being Ambassador to Italy. Lord Perth, who as Sir Eric Drummond had been the first Secretary-General of the League of Nations, was a convert and married to the Dowager Duchess of Norfolk's sister, Angela Constable Maxwell. He came of a Protestant branch of the Drummonds to which the Earldom of Perth had passed after the senior Catholic and Jacobite line became extinct.

Sir Eric Drummond, sixteenth Earl of Perth

Four out of the five surviving sons of Lady Perth's uncle Bernard Constable Maxwell – who had died at the age of ninety in 1938 – served in the Second World War. Gerald and Michael, who fought in the Battle of Britain, were in the RAF. David, whose wife Alethea, a daughter of Oswald Turville-Petre, eventually inherited Bosworth, was a Gunner. Andrew was in the Scots Guards, in which his cousin Lord Lovat had served before transferring to the Lovat Scouts. He had four other first cousins in the Scots Guards, the four sons of his mother's sister Margaret Fraser who had married the convert Perthshire laird Archibald Stirling of Keir. The Scots Guards was a regiment favoured by Catholics from south of the Border as well as from Scotland. Its officers during the Second World War included the fifteenth Lord Dormer's brother Joseph as well as Michael Fitzalan-Howard, a son of the third Lord Howard of Glossop and of Mona, Baroness Beaumont in her own right, and his cousin Stephen Tempest.

Raymond de Trafford started the war in prison, where he had been sent for manslaughter, having killed a pedestrian with his car while drunk. When his sister came to visit him, he said to her, 'You must meet my friend the Governor – charming chap'. After his release he served in the Pioneer Corps. He wrote to his sister from North Africa asking her to send him a dozen red silk handkerchiefs, 'the girls will keep them as souvenirs'.[6]

Mildred Bruce spent the opening months of the war operating an air ferry service to France; she afterwards ran a factory in Cardiff repairing crashed RAF planes. Her aunt Maude Petre, though not far off eighty, did fire watching during the Blitz; going around at night complete with helmet and uniform trousers, carrying sand buckets. Maude Petre now lived permanently in London and went to daily Communion. She could not have done so had she remained in Sussex, where her old adversary Dr Amigo was still the local bishop. Over the past thirty years she had continued to write books, including a biography of Father Tyrrell and her autobiography, *My Way of Faith*, which was published in 1937. She had mellowed but had certainly not recanted and was now the last surviving Modernist within the Catholic fold.

Another Catholic who had been in trouble with the Church authorities, Lord Strickland, went out on to his terrace at Villa Bologna and 'silently pointed a gnarled finger' at Mussolini's planes as they dropped their bombs on Malta.[7] He died soon afterwards so did not live to see the ultimate victory. Sir Hugh Clifford died at the end of 1941 and so did not live to see his beloved Malaya invaded by the Japanese. His cousin Silly Willie died in 1943, 'gaunt, bearded, odd and probably more than half mad'.[8] In his later years, having founded a Mystical Evolution Society, he had, as his sons put it, imagined himself a Messiah. Silly Willie's youngest son Sir Bede Clifford continued his proconsular career during the war years, first as Governor of Mauritius and then as Governor of Trinidad and Tobago. He was not the only Catholic among British proconsuls of the time; Lord Rankeillour's son Sir Arthur Hope was Governor of Madras and Sir John Herbert of the Llanarth family was Governor of Bengal.

On the outbreak of war Lord Acton, who held a commission in the Yeomanry, let Aldenham for the duration to the Assumption nuns and their school from Kensington Square. Ronald Knox, who was coming here as chaplain to the family on his retirement from the Catholic Chaplaincy at Oxford, came instead as chaplain to the nuns and the girls. Lord Acton's cousin Harold Acton joined the RAF, having lived in China before the war he tried to get himself sent there to do intelligence work, but without success. As he himself puts it, 'It was easy to believe that an Oxford aesthete of ephemeral fame had settled in China for the purpose of wallowing in vice. The rumour of my moral decline had assumed such concrete shape as to become a stumbling-block.'[9]

Sir Anthony Tichborne acted as Liaison Officer with the Free French Forces. It was a post which called for diplomacy and tact, and never so much as when he had to try and smooth down an elderly peer who had just seen his favourite cedar tree take off into the air and disintegrate. The Free French encamped in his park had returned from an exercise with some explosive to spare and had not wanted to waste it. Sir

Shimi, seventeenth Lord Lovat

Anthony's cousin Dolores Lees, known as Dodo, a great-grand-daughter of Roger Tichborne's sweetheart Kate Doughty as well as of Sir Frederick Weld, served gallantly as the only British nurse in the Free French army. As a young journalist in Germany before the war, she had attracted Hitler, who admired her long legs and her oratorical gifts.

Lord Lovat achieved fame as a commando leader. His cousin David Stirling, known as the Phantom Major, personally raised and commanded the SAS. Both had valuable rewards put on their heads by Hitler. Gustavus March Phillipps, a cousin of the de Lisles and a Catholic though not actually descended from the convert Ambrose, was one of an intrepid band who took part in small-scale raids on the enemy coast. Like most of his comrades he was eventually killed, one of the few survivors being Esmé Howard's son the second Lord Howard of Penrith, who was wounded and lost an arm.

Lord Dormer's young cousin Hugh Dormer, whose uncle Sir Cecil Dormer was British Minister to Norway at the time of the German invasion, volunteered to be dropped by parachute in enemy-occupied country to attack special targets. In the plane on his way to be dropped over France in April 1943 he read *Henry V*. His target was a shale oil mine; but the alarm was given and he and his companions escaped over the Pyrenees into Spain, eventually returning to England by way of Lisbon. After a second abortive attempt in June he led a third attempt in August and succeeded in blowing up the mine.

This time it seemed that he and his companions would be captured, for the Germans chased them with bloodhounds in a wood. 'It only behoved us to die with dignity', he wrote in his diary. When a picture of St Theresa of Lisieux accidentally fell out of his pocket, he told his companions 'that we were in such a hole that only she could get us out of it'. They managed to reach Paris, but only just succeeded in finding shelter for the night before the curfew. 'In our desperation,' Hugh Dormer wrote, 'I promised silently that should we ever escape, I would never refuse shelter to a beggar for the rest of my life.'

Once again he crossed the Pyrenees. 'The effects of the moonlight on the stony scene had all the apocalyptic unearthliness of an El Greco painting', he wrote. 'Near to the limits of human endurance, I thought of the words of that Indian mystic, "If there is a Hell on earth, it is here, it is here".' Having arrived safely in England by way of Gibraltar and been awarded a DSO, he decided to return to his regiment, the Irish Guards; not wishing to lead 'armed bands of hungry, desperate men' behind the enemy lines. 'I have never spilt human blood yet and if I must, then I will do it impersonally and in obedience of orders and not in cold murder . . . Death now seemed inevitable and I preferred to meet it in uniform.'

Before setting off for D-Day in the summer of 1944, he sat talking one evening in the Sussex Downs with his friend Father Julian Stonor, a Benedictine monk now an army chaplain. 'We talked of the unique mellowness and richness of the English countryside, of how the whole art and achievement of life was to learn how to appreciate the myriad beauty of humanity and the Universe as the creation of God.' He was killed in Normandy two months later. 'Once again at Mass this morning in the village church I offered my life to God to do with it entirely as He chooses', he had written in his last diary entry. 'All men must die sometime, and for a long time I have felt a stranger on this earth.'[10]

Hugh Dormer and Gustavus March Phillipps were not the only two Second World War victims from the Catholic families; though the toll was, of course, far less than it had been in the Great War. Thomas More Eyston of Hendred died of wounds in May 1940. Two Petres were killed, as well as an Anne, a Charlton and a

Hugh Dormer

Clifford of the New Zealand branch. Philip Kerr, a son of Admiral of the Fleet Lord Walter Kerr, died on active service in February 1941, two months after his cousin and namesake Lord Lothian died in Washington of an illness from which he might have recovered had he not, as an adherent of Christian Science, refused normal medical treatment. Lord Lovat's cousin Hugh Stirling was killed in Libya in 1941 and his brother-in-law Alan Phipps, the husband of his sister Veronica, was killed at Leros in 1943. Athelstan Stourton, whose mother was an heiress of the Swinburnes, was killed in Burma in 1942. His cousin Charles Stourton, only son of Lord Mowbray, Segrave and Stourton, lost an eye when fighting in France in 1944; as he lay wounded, his brother officers sent for a doctor while he himself called for a priest.

John, Lord Arundell of Wardour, was wounded near Douai in May 1940 and taken prisoner. In June 1943, having tried to escape from one camp in Germany, he

John, Lord Arundell of Wardour, as a
prisoner-of-war

was sent to Colditz. Here he kept himself occupied by making notes on Italian painting as well as about such matters of topical interest as the Beveridge Plan; he cheered his companions with his humour and sustained them with his faith. He wrote elaborate menus in French for the dinners which he and his fellow-prisoners gave for each other with delicacies such as tinned salmon and sardines from food parcels. He looked after the prisoners' library, which inspired one of them to sing of him:

> When Arundell discusses the Pictorial
> His manner is urbane, though grand seignorial.
> But acting as Librarian
> Makes him quite totalitarian,
> The Old Noblesse becomes New Dictatorial.[11]

In the cramped conditions of the fortress, his health broke down; he developed tuberculosis and in June he was moved to a sanatorium. In September it was heard that he was to be repatriated. There were great rejoicings at Wardour; the tenants started putting up triumphal arches for his return. But when he arrived at Liverpool he was gravely ill and had to be carried ashore; he was taken to hospital in Chester and his mother and sisters travelled through the night to be at his bedside. He was able to recognize them, but soon became unconscious and died after being back in England for just a week.

Some time before writing *Brideshead Revisited*, which he completed in the spring of 1944, Evelyn Waugh went to Wardour. He clearly had Wardour in mind when describing Brideshead, the Palladian house of a Catholic family in the same part of the country with a chapel in one of its wings; though the fictional Brideshead differs from Wardour in several respects. Its dome can be seen from outside, whereas the dome at Wardour is only internal; its chapel is Arts-and-Crafts, dating from the turn of the century and easily recognizable as the chapel of Waugh's Anglican friends the Lygons – whose father Lord Beauchamp went into exile as Lord Marchmain in *Brideshead* does – whereas the Wardour chapel is of course eighteenth century. Then the lakes at Brideshead are reminiscent not of Wardour but of another great domain in the neighbourhood: Stourhead, originally belonging to the Stourtons but in its present form the creation of the banking family of Hoare. Stourhead obviously helped to inspire the name of the novel, which may also have been suggested to Waugh by 'Bridehead', the name of a character in a novel by Thomas Hardy.

While *Brideshead Revisited* is a great novel, with a strongly Catholic theme, and features a house with certain resemblances to Wardour, it is not really a picture of an old Catholic family as it is popularly supposed to be. The only member of an old Catholic family among the characters is Lady Marchmain, whose marriage has made her husband and her children Catholic; and she is rather too self-conscious in her Catholicism to be a convincing portrait of one of the Old Catholics, whose religion generally tends to be more natural and down-to-earth. Sir Edmund Bedingfeld, the present baronet of Oxburgh, sees a certain resemblance between Lady Marchmain and his mother, Sybil Lady Bedingfeld, wife of Sir Henry who ranched in Wyoming; like the fictional Lady Marchmain, Lady Bedingfeld would say, when not prepared to discuss something, 'We are very tired now, let's go to bed'. But even if Waugh knew Lady Bedingfeld, Lady Marchmain is, in Sir Edmund's words, 'a gross exaggeration' of her.

In fact Waugh's knowledge of the Catholic world came not so much from old Catholic families as from families recently converted to Catholicism, such as that of his wife. Among 'old' Catholics, as well as the 'fine desperado' Raymond de Trafford, as he called him, he knew Francis Turville-Petre, an Oxford contemporary who died unmarried in 1942 and to whom the character of Sebastian may owe something; while being largely based on Alastair Graham, another Oxford contemporary who was not a Catholic. He had stayed at Carlton with

Lord Howard of Glossop and Baroness Beaumont and their large family; 'I never discovered exactly how many' he wrote in his diary, 'seven or eight of them, each with a Christian name beginning with M'. He knew Lord Lovat, with whom he had a notable dispute when he was in the army, and he knew some of the Actons. While the Lovats and Actons can be counted as 'old' Catholics, even though their Catholicism does not really go back to recusant times, it is perhaps significant that of the Actons whom he knew best, Lady Acton was herself a convert and Harold Acton too cosmopolitan to be typical of the English Catholic world.

When he was working on *Brideshead*, Waugh wrote to Ronald Knox at Aldenham to ask his help in describing the closing of a chapel. Knox replied, 'If, which Heaven forbid, I should ever have to close the chapel here, I suppose I should . . .'[12] What he went on to say was put into the mouth of Cordelia:

> They've closed the chapel at Brideshead, Bridey and the Bishop; Mummy's Requiem was the last Mass said there. After she was buried the priest came in – I was there alone. I don't think he saw me – and took out the altar stone and put it in his bag; then he burned the wads of wool with the holy oil on them and threw the ash outside; he emptied the holy water stoop and blew out the lamp in the sanctuary and left the tabernacle open and empty . . . then, suddenly, there wasn't any chapel there any more, just an oddly decorated room.

Three years after telling Waugh what he should do if he had to close the Aldenham chapel, Knox found himself in the melancholy position of having to do it. The convent school had left the house after the war ended and Lord and Lady Acton and their children had returned; but they soon found the problems of farming and managing a large country house in post-war England too much for them. So they sold up and emigrated to Southern Rhodesia.

Lord Acton's cousin Arthur Acton and his American wife Hortense, the parents of Harold, had no difficulty in returning to the old life at La Pietra, even though the house had been occupied by the Germans. Apart from broken and chipped statues and neglected hedges in the garden, there had been not much damage. But the elderly Arthur Acton was now a sad figure; he had not got over the death of his artist son William in 1945. He had lost his faith many years before, so lacked the comforts of religion; 'surrounded by religious art, he remained an agnostic'.[13] When he was dying, his son Harold fetched a priest; but by then he was only half-conscious. His head dropped down onto his chest when he received Extreme Unction; he made no last-minute Sign of the Cross as Lord Marchmain does in a scene inspired by the death of Evelyn Waugh's friend Hubert Duggan, the

AET:SUAE 91.

David Hawkinson
74

Sybil, the Dowager Lady Bedingfeld, aged ninety-one

charming but wayward Irish-Argentinian stepson of Lord Curzon.

Whereas the fictional Lady Marchmain has a destructive effect on her family, albeit unintentionally – '*She sucks their blood*', Anthony Blanche says of her – Sybil Lady Bedingfeld was a loveable character and the saviour of the family home. When in 1951 her son Sir Edmund was forced by taxation to put Oxburgh up for sale, she courageously bought it; having like Hugh Dormer enlisted the help of St Theresa of Lisieux to whom she had a special devotion. Had she not bought the house, it might very likely have been pulled down. Once Oxburgh was hers, she made it over to the National Trust, reserving the right for herself and her descendants to live there. Lady Bedingfeld was to live at Oxburgh until shortly before her death in 1985 at the age of nearly 102. Until the late nineteen-seventies, she maintained a priest to say Mass in the chapel across the moat. One priest fell into the moat on his way to say Midnight Mass at Christmas and was never quite the same afterwards.

Matilda Bedingfeld, an aunt of Sybil Lady Bedingfeld's husband, married

Blundell Hall, which he has given to Augustinian nuns for use as a convalescent home. The burnt-out ruin of Lulworth Castle has been very extensively repaired by Sir Joseph, who has also restored the church built by Thomas Weld in the eighteenth century which continues to be used for Catholic worship. Sir Joseph's cousins Mr and Mrs Charles Weld still live at Chideock. Among other cousins of the Welds, the Vaughans still own Courtfield and occupy a house on the estate; but the big house was sold after the war to the Mill Hill Fathers, a missionary society founded by Cardinal Vaughan. Mr Antony Hornyold has bought back part of the Blackmore estate, sold in 1919, and lives here in a house built after the big house was demolished.

Of the convert families, the present sixth Marquis of Bute still lives at Mount Stuart and at Dumfries House; though Cardiff Castle was given to the city of Cardiff after the death of his grandfather. His cousin Viscount Campden, son of the present Earl of Gainsborough, still lives at Exton Park, the family seat in Rutland. Though the eleventh Marquis of Lothian gave away Newbattle Abbey, the present twelfth Marquis still lives at Monteviot and at Melbourne Hall in Derbyshire which came from his grandmother. The two daughters of Major-General Sir Walter Maxwell-Scott, who was given a baronetcy which died with him, still live at Abbotsford.

Among the houses of the converts, the chief casualty is Newnham Paddox, seat of the Denbighs, which was demolished in 1952. And of the houses of other Catholic families, the two most important to be sold since the war, apart from Aldenham, were Everingham and Lytham. Everingham, together with the Herries barony, was inherited by Lady Anne Fitzalan-Howard – now the wife of Sir Colin Cowdrey the cricketer – eldest daughter of the sixteenth Duke of Norfolk, who had no son; but in 1982 she sold the house and estate while remaining a trustee of her ancestor's splendid Classical church which continues to serve the Catholics of the neighbourhood. The 16,000 acre Lytham estate was sold piecemeal from 1937 onwards by Henry de Vere Clifton, son of Talbot Clifton and his wife Violet who in her widowhood became a nun. Lytham Hall itself was sold in 1963. Henry de Vere Clifton wrote poetry and took out French citizenship. He kept a suite at the Ritz in London and another at the Dorchester; when asked why he needed the latter he replied: 'If I'm passing down Park Lane and feel tired, then I've got somewhere to go'.[14] He also followed his father's example and lived for a time in Ireland, though not in Connemara but at the Royal Hibernian Hotel in Dublin. Here he would invite people to dinner, receive them in bed and then send them down to dine without him but at his expense in the hotel restaurant.

Following the extinction of the Jerningham baronetcy in 1935, two other old

Catholic baronetcies have died out. Sir Edward Smythe, the ninth baronet, who died in 1942, was the last male heir of Maria Fitzherbert's family. And Sir Anthony Tichborne, who died in 1968, was the last male heir of the Tichbornes. Another historic baronetcy likely to become extinct in the near future is that of Throckmorton. Sir Anthony Throckmorton, the present baronet, who lives in the United States, was formerly a priest in Northampton Diocese and then in the Archdiocese of Seattle; he eventually married but has no children so there is no heir to the title. Sir Anthony's elder brother Nicholas, who would have succeeded his cousin Sir Robert Throckmorton had he not predeceased him, is remembered for his reply when someone asked him if the Throckmortons had been implicated in the Gunpowder Plot. 'No' he said laconically. 'We had a plot of our own'. He alluded, of course, to the Throckmorton Plot.

Catholic landowners in the years since the Second World War have mostly been too busy with their estates to play much part on the national or international scene; though many of them are active in the affairs of their own counties, like Sir Joseph Weld or Mr John Riddell of Swinburne who is known affectionately as 'Squire Riddell' throughout Northumberland. A few, however, have achieved a wider prominence. The sixteenth Duke of Norfolk was famous as the organizer of great State occasions, carrying out his duties with imperturbable efficiency; in answer to the inevitable question 'What will you do if its rains?' he would reply: 'We shall get wet'. He was also well-known on the Turf and as a cricketer. Though personally a devout, traditional Catholic, he did not play as great a part in Catholic affairs as his father had done, or as the present Duke does now. The present Duke of Norfolk also resembles the fifteenth Duke in having married a Constable Maxwell. His Duchess is Anne, daughter of Gerald Constable Maxwell; she is well-known for her work to provide hospices for the terminally ill. The Duke was a regular soldier and rose to the rank of Major-General, as did his brother Lord Michael Fitzalan-Howard who was afterwards Marshal of the Diplomatic Corps. As well as being Premier Duke, he has the distinction of being the chief male heir of a saint; for his Elizabethan ancestor Philip Howard, Earl of Arundel, was canonized in 1970. A later Howard, the Popish Plot victim William Howard, Viscount Stafford, has been beatified; Blessed William's senior representative is his descendant in the female line, Lord Stafford.

Lord Lovat, as well as distinguishing himself in the war, was a member of the Government in 1945 as Joint Parliamentary Secretary of State at the Foreign Office. His brother the late Sir Hugh Fraser was also in the Government – eventually becoming Secretary of State for Air and Minister of Defence for the RAF – as was his brother-in-law Sir Fitzroy Maclean, the second husband of his war-widow sister

Miles, seventeenth Duke of Norfolk, and Anne his Duchess, formerly Constable
Maxwell. By June Mendoza

Veronica. At the Lancaster election of 1951, Sir Fitzroy was nearly unseated by the
Labour candidate, the former French army nurse Dolores Lees, who was a cousin of
his wife through the Welds. The Marquis of Lothian has been a member of the
Government, as well as a Delegate to the Council of Europe, to the European
Parliament and to the United Nations. His son the Earl of Ancram – a son-in-law
of the sixteenth Duke of Norfolk – has been an MP, a junior Minister and
Chairman of the Conservative party in Scotland.

Members of the Catholic families who have achieved distinction in other fields
include Sir Edwin Plowden, a cousin of the present squire of Plowden, who was
Chairman of the Atomic Energy Authority from 1954 to 1959 when he was made a
life peer as Lord Plowden. His wife is well-known as an exponent of progressive
theories of education and also in the world of broadcasting. Sir Harold Acton – he
was knighted in 1974 – has achieved international fame not only as an aesthete but as
a writer, as the historian of the Bourbons of Naples and as a delightful host at La

Fra' Andrew Bertie, after his election as Prince and Grand Master of the Sovereign Military Hospitaller Order of Malta in 1988

Pietra, where he points out the wonders of the garden to his guests in a voice that sounds almost as if he is singing. Simon Elwes the portrait painter was a son of Gervase and Lady Winefride Elwes and a grandson of the convert Earl of Denbigh. Lord Strickland's daughter Mabel Strickland was famous as the forceful editor of the *Times of Malta*. Dame Ann Parker Bowles, a daughter of Sir Humphrey de Trafford and a niece of the wayward Raymond, was Chief Commissioner of Girl Guides for the Commonwealth. Dame Jean Maxwell-Scott, one of the two sisters who live at Abbotsford, has been for many years Lady-in-Waiting to Princess Alice, Duchess of Gloucester. Edward Turville-Petre, whose sister Mrs David Constable-Maxwell inherited Bosworth, was Professor of Ancient Icelandic Literature and Antiquities at Oxford. The present Marquis of Bute is Chairman of the Trustees of the National Museums of Scotland and Vice-President of the

Charles, Lord Mowbray, Segrave and Stourton

Scottish National Trust; his son, the Earl of Dumfries, is a racing driver. Major Rupert Gerard, who at the time of his death in 1978 was heir to his bachelor cousin the present Lord Gerard, made his career as a Hollywood actor.

The journalist Sir Peregrine Worsthorne is a great-grandson of the convert Earl of Abingdon and his first wife Caroline Towneley. His mother – who married Montagu Norman as her second husband – inherited the Worsthorne part of the Towneley estate and his father consequently took the name of Worsthorne. The property now belongs to his elder brother Mr Simon Towneley, Lord-Lieutenant of Lancashire and a former Lecturer in the History of Music at Oxford, who took the name of Towneley in 1955.

A cousin of Sir Peregrine Worsthorne and Mr Towneley, Fra' Andrew Bertie, who became a Knight of Justice in the Order of Malta in 1981, was elected Prince and Grand Master of the Order in 1988. Fra' Andrew is either the first Briton to lead this ancient Order, or the first since the thirteenth century, when one Grand Master might possibly have been English. As Prince and Grand Master, he is acknowledged as a Sovereign Head of State by the fifty or so countries of the world with which the Order maintains diplomatic relations; and which include Austria, Italy, Spain and Portugal as well as countries in Latin America, Africa and Asia. In the Catholic Church, he ranks as a cardinal.

Since he can thus be said to have risen higher than any other son of the Catholic families, it is fitting that Fra' Andrew Bertie is himself descended from so many of them. On his father's side he is a grandson of the convert Earl of Abingdon and his second wife Gwendeline Dormer, through whom he also descends from Tichbornes and Plowdens. Through his mother, a daughter of the fourth Marquis of Bute, he is descended from Dukes of Norfolk, Catholic Earls of Shrewsbury and the convert Earl of Gainsborough. Like so many sons of the Catholic families, he has been an officer in the Scots Guards and still has a soldierly bearing. He is young for his sixty-odd years and since his election has travelled a great deal, visiting charitable and hospitaller works of the Order all over the world. He has also paid official visits to various capitals, including Washington, where he gave an award to President Reagan.

An active member of the Order of Malta in Britain is Lord Mowbray, Segrave and Stourton, a genial and erudite figure who lost an eye in the war when serving with the Grenadiers and has since worn a patch. He has also been active in politics and has been a Conservative Whip in the House of Lords and a Lord-in-Waiting. A fellow-peer, speaking in the Lords, once repeated the well-known quotation from Lord Chief Justice Crewe, 'Where is Bohun, where's Mowbray, where's Mortimer ...' He was interrupted by a cheerful voice from one of the other benches. 'Mowbray is here, and very well thank you.' The same could be said for most of the Catholic families.

Source References

Chapter 1 Grandeur and frustration

1 Quoted M.D. Petre, *The Ninth Lord Petre*, London 1928.
2 Ibid.
3 Ibid.
4 Ibid.
5 Charles Butler, quoted Denis Gwynn, *The Struggle for Catholic Emancipation 1750–1829*, London 1928.
6 Quoted Alistair Rowan, 'Wardour Castle Chapel, Wiltshire', in *Country Life*, 7 October 1968.
7 *Dictionary of National Biography*.
8 Hubert Chadwick S.J., *St Omers to Stonyhurst*, London 1961.
9 M.E. Lancaster, *The Tempests of Broughton*, Broughton Hall, near Skipton, North Yorkshire, 1987.
10 Information given to the author by Major David Trappes-Lomax.
11 Sir Nathaniel Wraxall, *Historical and Posthumous Memoirs*, vol I, London 1884.
12 Namier and Brooke, *History of Parliament, The Commons 1754–1790*, vol II, London 1964.
13 *Oxford Dictionary of Quotations*, New Edition, 1979.

Chapter 2 'Mrs Fitzherbert makes a great deal of talk'

1 Robert Julian Stonor O.S.B., *Stonor*, Newport Mon. 1951.
2 Jerningham Letters, ed Egerton Castle, 2 vols London 1896.
3 Ibid.

4 Quoted D.B. Wyndham Lewis and Charles Lee, *The Stuffed Owl*, London 1930.

5 Jerningham Letters.

6 Ibid.

7 Ibid.

8 Ibid.

9 Hon. Charles Langdale, *Memoirs of Mrs Fitzherbert*, London 1856.

10 Ibid.

11 Ibid.

12 Constable Maxwell papers.

13 Ibid.

14 Ibid.

15 Ibid.

16 Catholic Record Society 50, Mawhood Diary.

17 Ibid.

18 Ibid.

19 Ibid.

20 Constable Maxwell papers.

21 Ibid.

22 Ibid.

23 Ibid.

24 Ibid.

25 Quoted Stonor, op cit.

26 Quoted ibid.

Chapter 3 Relief and Revolution

1 David Mathew, *Catholicism in England*, Third Edition, London 1955.

2 Catholic Record Society 50, Mawhood Diary.

3 Dr George Oliver, quoted Hugh Clifford, *The House of Clifford*, Chichester, Sussex ND (1987).

4 Catholic Record Society 50, Mawhood Diary.

5 Constable Maxwell papers.

6 Quoted F.C. Husenbeth, *The Life of the Rt Rev John Milner, D.D.*, Dublin 1862.

7 Petre, op cit.

8 Father Charles Plowden, quoted Joan Berkeley, *Lulworth and the Welds*, Gillingham, Dorset ND (1971).

9 Quoted Berkeley, op cit.
10 Quoted Husenbeth, op cit.
11 Robert Huish, *The Public and Private Life of George the Third*, London 1821.
12 Thomas Weld to Lord Arundell of Wardour, quoted Berkeley, op cit.
13 Quoted ibid.
14 Quoted Peter Gunn, *The Actons*, London ND (1978).
15 Ibid.
16 Jerningham Letters.
17 Ibid.
18 Catholic Record Society 17.
19 Jerningham Letters.
20 Catholic Record Society 17.
21 Constable Maxwell papers.
22 Ibid.
23 Quoted John Martin Robinson, *The Dukes of Norfolk*, Oxford and New York 1982.

Chapter 4 Trying to serve King George

1 Jerningham Letters.
2 Ibid.
3 Ibid.
4 Ibid.
5 Ibid.
6 Ibid.
7 Ibid.
8 Ibid.
9 Ibid.
10 Ibid.
11 Ibid.
12 Quoted Richard Aldington, *The Strange Life of Charles Waterton*, London ND (1949).
13 Stonor, op cit.
14 Jerningham Letters.
15 Ibid.
16 Quoted Christopher Hussey, 'Ince Blundell Hall', in *Country Life*, 24 April 1958.
17 Clifford papers.

18 Archives of Ontario, John Graves Simcoe papers.
19 Quoted Gunn, op cit.
20 Quoted ibid.
21 Quoted ibid.
22 Quoted ibid.
23 Langdale, op cit.
24 Ibid.
25 Quoted Anita Leslie, *Mrs Fitzherbert*, London 1960.
26 Lord Howard of Penrith, *Theatre of Life*, vol I, London 1935.
27 Clifford papers.
28 Ibid.
29 Ibid.
30 Berkeley, op cit.
31 Langdale, op cit.

Chapter 5 'It is really become fashionable to be a Catholic'

 1 Jerningham Letters.
 2 Ibid.
 3 Ibid.
 4 Ibid.
 5 Ibid.
 6 Ibid.
 7 Quoted Gwynn, op cit.
 8 Husenbeth, op cit.
 9 The Recollections of a Northumbrian Lady, ed L.E.O. Charlton, London
    ND (1949).
10 Jerningham Letters.
11 Clifford papers.
12 The Creevey Papers, ed John Gore, London 1970.
13 Aldington, op cit.
14 Ibid.
15 Ibid.
16 Stonor, op cit.
17 Ibid.
18 Northumbrian Lady.
19 Ibid.
20 Jerningham Letters.

21 Ibid.
22 Ibid.
23 Husenbeth, op cit.
24 Jerningham Letters.
25 Ibid.
26 Ibid.
27 Ibid.
28 Charles Lines, *Coughton Court and the Throckmorton Story*, Manchester ND.
29 Leslie, op cit.
30 Ibid.
31 Richard Buckle, *The Prettiest Girl in England*, London ND (1958).
32 Leslie, op cit.
33 Very Rev. Joseph Hirst, *Memoir and Letters of Lady Mary Arundell*, Ratcliffe College, Leicester 1894.

Chapter 6 Red Hats and Coronets

1 Hirst, op cit.
2 Ibid.
3 Ibid.
4 Ibid.
5 Constable Maxwell papers.
6 Ibid.
7 Ibid.
8 Ibid.
9 Hirst, op cit.
10 Cardinal Wiseman, *Recollections of the Last Four Popes*, London 1858.
11 Langdale, op cit.
12 Ibid.
13 Ibid.
14 Katherine Bedingfeld, *The Bedingfelds of Oxburgh*, privately printed 1915.
15 Jerningham Letters.
16 Henry Bedingfeld, *Oxburgh Hall*, National Trust 1987.
17 Katherine Bedingfeld, op cit.
18 Ibid.
19 Diary of Edward Jerningham in the possession of Major Trappes-Lomax.
20 Ibid.
21 Constable Maxwell papers.

22 Quoted Mark Girouard, 'Lytham Hall', in *Country Life* 28 July 1960.
23 Hirst, op cit.
24 Ibid.
25 Quoted Edmund Sheridan Purcell, *Life and Letters of Ambrose Phillipps de Lisle*, vol I, London 1900.
26 Hirst, op cit.
27 Letters in the possession of Mr Michael Dormer.
28 Ibid.
29 Ibid.
30 Ibid.
31 Ibid.
32 'A Mill Hill Father', *Remembered in Blessing*, London 1955.
33 Northumbrian Lady.
34 Ibid.
35 Ibid.
36 Ian Anstruther, *The Knight and the Umbrella*, London 1963.
37 Stonor, op cit.

Chapter 7 The Good Earl John and the Converts

1 Northumbrian Lady.
2 Ibid.
3 Ibid.
4 Ibid.
5 Ibid.
6 Hirst, op cit.
7 Quoted Purcell, op cit.
8 Quoted Denis Gwynn, *Lord Shrewsbury, Pugin and the Catholic Revival*, London 1946.
9 Ibid.
10 Ibid.
11 Quoted Martin Robinson, op cit.
12 The Creevey Papers.
13 Martin Robinson, op cit.
14 Ibid.
15 Hirst, op cit.
16 Quoted Martin Robinson, op cit.
17 Quoted Alice Lady Lovat, *The Life of Sir Frederick Weld*, London 1914.

18 Quoted Jeanine Graham, *Frederick Weld*, Auckland N.Z. ND (1983).
19 Ibid.
20 Ibid.
21 Quoted Denis Gwynn, *A Hundred Years of Catholic Emancipation 1829–1929*, London 1929.
22 Quoted Elizabeth Longford, *Victoria R.I.*, London 1964.
23 Quoted Denis Gwynn, *Cardinal Wiseman*, London 1929.
24 Quoted Purcell, op cit.
25 *Remembered in Blessing*, op cit.
26 Quoted Purcell, op cit.
27 Faber, Poet and Priest: Selected Letters by Frederick William Faber, ed Raleigh Addington, Cowbridge and Bridgend 1974.
28 Ibid.
29 Ibid.
30 Ibid.
31 Quoted Winefride Elwes, *The Feilding Album*, London 1950.
32 Ibid.
33 Ibid.
34 Ibid.
35 Anne Pollen, *John Hungerford Pollen 1820–1902*, London 1912.
36 Cecil Marchioness of Lothian, ed Cecil Kerr, London ND (1922).
37 Ibid.
38 Rt. Rev. Sir David Hunter Blair, *A Medley of Memories*, London 1919.
39 Wilfrid Scawen Blunt, *My Diaries*, London 1919, 1920.
40 Quoted Lesley Blanch, *The Wilder Shores of Love*, London 1954.
41 Ibid.
42 *Complete Peerage*.
43 J.G. Snead-Cox, *The Life of Cardinal Vaughan*, 2 vols, London 1910.
44 Constable Maxwell papers.
45 Clifford papers.
46 Ibid.

Chapter 8 'Papal Hymns and Soldier-Songs'

1 Quoted Mark Girouard, 'Scarisbrick Hall', in *Country Life*, 20 March 1958.
2 Cecil Marchioness of Lothian.
3 Ibid.
4 Elwes, op cit.

5 David Mathew, *Lord Acton and his Times*, London 1968.
6 Martin Robinson, op cit.
7 Quoted ibid.
8 Quoted Oliver Hill, 'Traquair House', in *Country Life*, 26 August 1949.
9 Alice Constable Maxwell, *Avenue of Ancestors*, Dumfries 1965.
10 Northumbrian Lady.
11 Ibid.
12 Ibid.
13 Ibid.
14 Ibid.
15 Ibid.
16 Laura Hain Myall, *In the Sixties and Seventies*, London 1905.
17 Quoted Jean Burton, *Sir Richard Burton's Wife*, London 1942.
18 Graham, op cit.
19 Aldington, op cit.
20 Quoted Douglas Woodruff, *The Tichborne Claimant*, London 1957.
21 Ibid.
22 Blunt, op cit.
23 Rt. Rev. Sir David Hunter Blair, *John Patrick, Third Marquis of Bute*, London 1921.
24 Quoted Mathew, *Acton*, op cit.
25 Letters of Herbert Cardinal Vaughan to Lady Herbert of Lea 1867–1903, ed Shane Leslie, London 1942.
26 Rt. Rev. Sir David Hunter Blair, *In Victorian Days*, London ND (1939).

Chapter 9 Carlists and Colonists

1 Hornyold papers.
2 Ibid.
3 Quoted Violet Powell, *Margaret Countess of Jersey*, London 1978.
4 Quoted Hunter Blair, *Bute*, op cit.
5 W.H. Mallock, *Memoirs of Life and Literature*, London 1920.
6 Hornyold papers.
7 de la Poer papers.
8 Joan Haslip, *The Lonely Empress*, London 1965.
9 Hunter Blair, *Medley of Memories*, op cit.
10 Hornyold papers.
11 Purcell, op cit.

12 Elwes, op cit.
13 Rt. Rev. Sir David Hunter Blair, *More Musings and Memories*, London 1931.
14 Ibid.
15 Hunter Blair, *Medley of Memories*, op cit.
16 Told to the author by Lord Mowbray and Stourton.
17 Quoted Burton, op cit.
18 Hunter Blair, *Bute*, op cit.
19 Sir Francis Lindley, *Lord Lovat*, London 1935.

Chapter 10 'Father Vaughan will entertain the Pope'

1 Martin Robinson, op cit.
2 Letters of Herbert Cardinal Vaughan.
3 Charles Edward Jerningham, *Piccadilly to Pall Mall*, London 1908.
4 Walburga Lady Paget, *Embassies of Other Days*, 2 vols, London 1923.
5 Papers in the possession of Mr Michael Dormer.
6 Quoted Gunn, op cit.
7 Mrs Humphry Ward, *A Writer's Recollections*, London 1918.
8 Mortimer Menpes, *War Impressions*, London 1901.
9 Martin Robinson, op cit.
10 Blunt, op cit.
11 Almeric FitzRoy, *Memoirs*, 2 vols, New York ND.
12 Seymour Leslie, *The Jerome Connection*, London 1964.
13 Told to the author by Mr Patrick Vaughan.
14 Arundell of Wardour papers.
15 Hunter Blair. *More Memories and Musings*, London 1931.
16 Told to the author by one of the family.
17 Clyde F. Crews, *English Catholic Modernism, Maude Petre's Way of Faith*, Notre Dame, Indiana 1984.
18 Maude Petre, *My Way of Faith*, London 1937.
19 Quoted Crews, op cit.
20 Ibid.

Chapter 11 'Your only Monument'

1 FitzRoy, op cit.
2 Quoted Lindley, op cit.

3 Sir Bede Clifford, *Proconsul*, London 1964.

4 *Mary Elizabeth Towneley, A Memoir*, London 1924.

5 Bede Clifford, op cit.

6 Ibid.

7 Quoted Hugh Clifford, op cit.

8 Quoted Gordon Brook-Shepherd, *The Last Habsburg*, London 1968.

9 Quoted Anne Marreco, *The Rebel Countess*, London 1967.

10 Quoted Violet Clifton, *The Book of Talbot*, London 1933.

11 Seymour Leslie, op cit.

12 Clifton, op cit.

13 Information provided by Fra' Matthew Festing.

14 Quoted Hugh Clifford, op cit.

15 Quoted Gunn, op cit.

16 The Diaries of Evelyn Waugh, ed Michael Davie, London ND [1976].

17 James Fox, *White Mischief*, London 1982.

Chapter 12 'Mowbray is here'

1 James Lees-Milne, *Another Self*, London 1970.

2 Information given to the author by Monsignor A.N. Gilbey.

3 Told to the author by the person to whom Lord FitzAlan said this.

4 Information given to the author by Monsignor A.N. Gilbey.

5 Evelyn Waugh, *Ronald Knox*, London 1959.

6 Information given to the author by Sir Dermot de Trafford, Bt.

7 Harrison Smith, *Lord Strickland, Servant of the Crown*, Amsterdam 1983.

8 Hugh Clifford, op cit.

9 Harold Acton, *More Memoirs of an Aesthete*, London 1970.

10 Hugh Dormer's Diaries, London 1947.

11 By A.L. Munby, Arundell of Wardour papers.

12 Quoted Waugh, *Knox*, op cit.

13 Harold Acton, op cit.

14 Quoted John Martin Robinson, *A Guide to the Country Houses of the North-West*, London 1991.

Select Bibliography

MANUSCRIPT AND OTHER UNPUBLISHED SOURCES

Arundell of Wardour papers, in the possession of Lord Talbot of Malahide.
Clifford papers, in the possession of Lord Clifford of Chudleigh.
Constable Maxwell papers, in the possession of Mr Robert Turville‑Constable‑
Maxwell and in Leicester Record Office
de la Poer papers, in the possession of Count de la Poer.
Papers in the possession of Mr Michael Dormer.
Hornyold Papers, in the possession of Mr Antony Hornyold.
Diary of Edward Jerningham, in the possession of Major Trappes‑Lomax.
Papers in the possession of Lord Mowbray and Stourton.
John Graves Simcoe papers, Archives of Ontario.

PRINTED SOURCES

ACTON, HAROLD: *More Memoirs of an Aesthete*, London 1970.
Letters of Lord Acton to Mary Gladstone (ed Herbert Paul), London 1904.
ALDINGTON, RICHARD: *The Strange Life of Charles Waterton*, London ND (1949).
Some Papers of Lord Arundell of Wardour, 12th Baron (preface by Dowager Lady
Arundell), London 1909.
AVELING, HUGH: *Post Reformation Catholicism in East Yorkshire*, E. Yorkshire Local
History Society 1960.

— *The Handle and the Axe*, London 1976.

BEDINGFELD, HENRY: *Oxburgh Hall*, National Trust 1987.

BEDINGFELD, KATHERINE: *The Bedingfelds of Oxburgh*, privately printed 1915.

BENCE-JONES, MARK: *Ancestral Houses*, London 1984.

BENCE-JONES, MARK and MONTGOMERY-MASSINGBERD, HUGH; *The British Aristocracy*, London 1979.

BERKELEY, JOAN: *Lulworth and the Welds*, Gillingham, Dorset ND (1971).

BIGGS-DAVISON, JOHN AND CHOWDHARAY-BEST, GEORGE: *The Cross of St Patrick*, Bourne End, Buckinghamshire 1984.

BLANCH, LESLEY: *The Wilder Shores of Love*, London 1954.

BLUNDELL, DOM F.O., OSB: *Old Catholic Lancashire*, 3 vols, London 1925–1941.

BLUNT, WILFRID SCAWEN: *My Diaries*, London 1919, 1920.

BRENAN, GERALD AND STATHAM, EDWARD PHILLIPS: *The House of Howard*, 2 vols, London 1907.

BUCKLE, RICHARD: *The Prettiest Girl in England*, London ND (1958).

BURTON, JEAN: *Sir Richard Burton's Wife*, London 1942.

BUTLER, J.R.M.: *Lord Lothian, 1882–1940*, London 1960.

Catholic Record Society volumes, 1904 onwards.

CHADWICK, HUBERT, SJ: *St Omers to Stonyhurst*, London 1961.

CLIFFORD, SIR BEDE: *Proconsul*, London 1964.

CLIFFORD, HUGH: *The House of Clifford*, Chichester, Sussex ND (1987).

CLIFFORD, LADY: *Our Days on the Gold Coast*, London 1919.

CONSTABLE MAXWELL, ALICE: *Avenue of Ancestors*, Dumfries 1965.

CREWS, CLYDE F.: *English Catholic Modernism, Maude Petre's Way of Faith*, Notre Dame, Indiana 1984.

Hon Henry Edward Dormer, A Biographical Memoir, 1868.

Hugh Dormer's Diaries, London 1947.

ELWES, LADY WINEFRIDE: *Gervase Elwes*, London 1935.

— *The Feilding Album*, London 1950.

Faber, Poet and Priest: Selected Letters by Frederick William Faber (ed Raleigh Addington), Cowbridge and Bridgend 1974.

GILBERT, MICHAEL: *The Claimant*, London 1957.

GRAHAM, JEANINE: *Frederick Weld*, Auckland NZ ND (1983).

GUNN, PETER: *The Actons*, London ND (1978).

GWYNN, DENIS: *Cardinal Wiseman.* London 1929.

— *The Struggle for Catholic Emancipation 1750–1829*, London 1928.

— *A Hundred Years of Catholic Emancipation 1829–1929*, London 1929.

— *Lord Shrewsbury, Pugin and the Catholic Revival*, London 1946.

HIRST, VERY REV JOSEPH: *Memoir and Letters of Lady Mary Arundell*, Ratcliffe College, Leicester 1894.

HOWARD OF PENRITH, LORD: *Theatre of Life*, 2 vols, London 1935, 1936.

HUNTER BLAIR, RT REV SIR DAVID, BT: *John Patrick, Third Marquis of Bute*, London 1921.

— *A Medley of Memories*, London 1919.

— *More Musings and Memories*, London 1931.

— *A Last Medley of Memories*, London 1936.

— *In Victorian Days*, London ND (1939).

HUSENBETH, F.C.: *The Life of the Rt Rev John Milner, DD*, Dublin 1862.

Jerningham Letters (ed Egerton Castle), 2 vols, London 1896.

LANCASTER, M.E.: *The Tempests of Broughton*, Broughton Hall, near Skipton, North Yorkshire 1987.

LANGDALE, HON CHARLES: *Memoirs of Mrs Fitzherbert*, London 1856.

LESLIE, ANITA: *Mrs Fitzherbert*, London 1960.

LESLIE, SHANE: *Mrs Fitzherbert*, London 1939.

LINDLEY, SIR FRANCIS: *Lord Lovat*, London 1935.

LINES, CHARLES: *Coughton Court and the Throckmorton Story*, Manchester ND.

LITTLE, BRYAN: *Catholic Churches since 1623*, London 1966.

Cecil Marchioness of Lothian (ed Cecil Kerr), London ND (1922).

LOVAT, ALICE LADY: *The Life of Sir Frederick Weld*, London 1914.

LOVAT, LORD, *March Past*, London 1978.

MATHEW, DAVID: *Lord Acton and his Times*, London 1968.

—*Catholicism in England*, Third Edition, London 1955.

MATTHEWS, JOHN HOBSON: *The Vaughans of Courtfield*, London 1912.

MAUGHAM, LORD: *The Tichborne Case*, London 1936.

'A Mill Hill Father', *Remembered in Blessing*, London 1955.

MOWBRAY, SEGRAVE and STOURTON, CHARLES BOTOLPH JOSEPH, LORD: *The History of the Noble House of Stourton*, 2 vols, privately printed 1899.

NORRIS, REV D.: *Baddesley Clinton*, London and Leamington 1897.

PETRE, M.D.: *My Way of Faith*, London 1937.

— *The Ninth Lord Petre*, London 1928.

POLLEN, ANNE: *John Hungerford Pollen 1820–1902*, London 1912.

PURCELL, EDMUND SHERIDAN: *Life and Letters of Ambrose Phillipps de Lisle*, 2 vols, London 1900.

The Recollections of a Northumbrian Lady (ed L.E.O. Charlton), London ND (1949).

Recusant History, Journal of the Catholic Record Society.

ROBINSON, JOHN MARTIN: *A Guide to the Country Houses of the North-West*, London 1991.

— *The Dukes of Norfolk*, Oxford and New York 1982.

ROSKELL, DAME MARY FRANCIS, OSB: *Memoirs of Francis Kerril Amherst*, London 1903.

SMITH, HARRISON: *Lord Strickland, Servant of the Crown.* Amsterdam 1983.

SNEAD-COX, J.G.: *The Life of Cardinal Vaughan*, 2 vols, London 1910.

STONOR, ROBERT JULIAN, OSB: *Stonor*, Newport Mon. 1951.

Mary Elizabeth Towneley, a Memoir. London 1924.

Letters of Herbert Cardinal Vaughan to Lady Herbert of Lea 1867–1903 (ed Shane Leslie), London 1942.

WAUGH, EVELYN: *Ronald Knox*, London 1959.

The Diaries of Evelyn Waugh (ed Michael Davie), London 1976.

WILKINS, W.H.: *Mrs Fitzherbert and George IV*, London 1914.

WISEMAN, CARDINAL: *Recollections of the Last Four Popes*, London 1858.

WOODRUFF, DOUGLAS: *The Tichborne Claimant*, London 1957.

INDEX